Da Capo

BEST

MUSIC

WRITING

2003

Da Capo
BEST
MUSIC
WRITING
2003

The Year's Finest Writing on
Rock, Pop, Jazz, Country, & More

Matt Groening
Guest Editor

Paul Bresnick
Series Editor

DA CAPO PRESS
A Member of the Perseus Books Group

List of credits/permissions for all pieces can be found on page 295.

Copyright © 2003 by Da Capo Press
Introduction © 2003 by Matt Groening

Designed by Jeffrey P. Williams
Set in 10-point Janson Text by the Perseus Books Group

Cataloging-in-Publication data for this book is available from the Library of Congress

First Da Capo Press edition 2003
ISBN 0–306–81236–3

Published by Da Capo Press
A Member of the Perseus Books Group
http://www.dacapopress.com

Da Capo Press books are available at special discounts for bulk purchases in the U.S. by corporations, institutions, and other organizations. For more information, please contact the Special Markets Department at the Perseus Books Group, 11 Cambridge Center, Cambridge, MA 02142, or call (800) 255–1514 or (617) 252–5298, or e-mail j.mccrary@perseusbooks.com.

1 2 3 4 5 6 7 8 9——06 05 04 03

CONTENTS

Contents

Introduction

I've been having confusing, scary dreams about music lately.

I've been having confusing, scary dreams about music all my life.

I've dreamt I'm in the basement of a squalid little nightclub packed with slamdancing punks, getting my head stomped on by some band I've apparently given a bad review to. (In real life, I've only had threats left on my phone machine.) I've dreamt I'm listening to a gigantic brass-heavy orchestra play my own symphony, which in my dream-state sounds like a cross between Stravinsky and the *Jetsons* theme, augmented by Balinese gongs and barnyard animal noises. I've dreamt I've confidently strutted onstage to sing with a rock band, even though in real life I can't sing and have no musical talent whatsoever.

It all started when I was a little kid, and some addled adult had given me an LP called *Burl Ives Sings "Little White Duck" and Other Children's Favorites*. I was only four years old and afraid of robots and loud noises, but even then that record seemed pretty namby-pamby. Because it was basically the only album I owned, however, I played it over and over. The "Little White Duck" song was OK, but it was followed by a song that haunted me for the rest of my childhood.

A song about donuts that I've never been able to get out of my brain. A song about donuts that I've dreamed about for decades.

In that just-a-little-too-friendly geezer-warble that makes kids want to run away and hide, Burl Ives sings: "As you go through life, make this your goal: watch the donut, not the hole."

I played the song again and again, but I couldn't figure out what it meant. Soon I had the song memorized, and could lie awake at night pondering.

If anything, after listening to them so many times, the lyrics became even more unclear in their meaning. I would eventually fall asleep at night, tossing and turning as the nightmare of the donut song returned. In my recurring dream I couldn't escape Burl Ives. I was forced to sing along with him, and the words always began tangling up into meaningless syllables rolling around my mouth . . .

And then I'd wake up, with the song still running through my head, but . . .

Nothing.

No insight, no brainstorm, no nothing.

I remained haunted and perplexed throughout my formative years.

I've moved on. I still wake up on a regular basis singing about donuts, but over the years, I've also dreamed repeatedly about "Mr. Sandman" (a song about dreams by the Chordettes), Alton Ellis's reggae song "I Can't Stand It," and the haunted organ theme from Vic Mizzy's movie score of *The Ghost and Mr. Chicken.* I've also dreamed about musicians I've actually interviewed, including Joe Venuti, Frank Zappa, Yma Sumac, and the Boredoms.

I wrote about music for about five years, stopping in 1986 to move on to other scams. I had the enthusiasm, but I didn't have the discipline. I just liked what I liked. I can fake it if you ask me about the Willem Breuker Kollektief or Shirley Anne Hofmann or Daniel Johnston or Speedy West or Orchestra Baobab or Unknown Hinson or Olivier Messiaen or Milton Brown and His Musical Brownies, but please don't ask me about Springsteen or Dylan or U2 or Radiohead or the White Stripes or 50 Cent or that jerk with the hat or that dead lady. I've never watched the Grammys. I've never filled out the *Village Voice* Pazz & Jop poll. I dig Bing Crosby, accordions, the Tiger Lillies, yodeling, and Melt Banana. I sometimes reviewed bands that I'd made up. The pay was so low that I got kind of delirious.

In picking the pieces in *Da Capo Best Music Writing 2003*, with the expert guidance and handholding of Ben Schafer of Da Capo Press and Paul Bresnick, Series Editor, I didn't try for any kind of overview reflecting the significant trends of the year—I just went for essays jammed with information and conveyed with style, passion, and wit. In what seems to me a fairly dismal time in general for music, when so much dreck is so unbelievably popular, and so much writing seems just as artificially sweetened yet utterly deflavorized, I'm especially impressed and grateful that these writers are able to knock out great, heavily researched pieces. Frankly, I'm a little bugged that in this century I can't seem to tell the difference between a rock anthem and a car-commercial jingle, but I'm hoping maybe this is just another one of those dreams again.

— MATT GROENING

BILL TUOMALA

Best Band in the Land

Prologue

You may not be familiar with them because they were a band that couldn't catch a break. They never sold many albums and they never played anything bigger than a small theater, but damn do they sound better and better over time. They came out in the late seventies with this sound that was catchy and smart and playful; problem was that was the era when the Ramones, the Sex Pistols, and the Clash were dominating the charts. It was tough for any metal band to get airplay, as punk had dominated hard rock charts all decade long. If you were lucky and knew someone in the know or if you hung out in the right record store, you might have gotten turned on to some metal during the seventies. Like there was underground favorites Led Zeppelin, a band that threw so many varied sounds into their mix—funk, folk, blues, reggae—that they were bound to be a bust commercially; they also had this song, "Communication Breakdown," from which the Sex Pistols acquired their sound. And there was Aerosmith, who combined James Brown with the Yardbirds. And of course there was Black Sabbath, who were creators of a gloom-n-doom lude-rock that was as brilliant as it was bleak. But punk had been The Thing since the Stooges' *Fun House* and the MC5's *Back in the USA* albums had taken huge top-selling steps towards molding the hard rock landscape back in 1970. Or as Jon

Landau said: "I've produced the future of rock 'n' roll and its name is the MC5."

In the early seventies, this dude named Lenny Kaye released an album of near-forgotten garage-rock singles from the sixties that was called *Nuggets*. Aspiring garage bands nationwide lapped this up, what with all the proto-metal tunes like "Dirty Water," "Psychotic Reaction," and "Pushin' Too Hard" on it. Soon every town had some weirdo band playing amplified blues riffs and singing horny songs about chicks, pills, and booze. Everyone who saw a metal band and loved it went on to form their own band. A grass roots movement was born, though for most of America through the seventies, metal was this heard-of-but-not-really-heard-much thing.

1978–1979

"Rock critics love Van Halen and hate me because rock critics look like me but want to party with David Lee Roth."

—Elvis Costello, 1979

Punk ruled the charts and when Van Halen (Eddie Van Halen on guitar, Alex Van Halen on drums, Michael Anthony on bass, David Lee Roth on vocals) debuted in 1978, the mainstream ignored 'em. Van Halen flirted with the punk sound, their first album had a doozy of a song called "Atomic Punk" and their second album had this song called "DOA," which sounded uncannily like the Stooges. Unlike many other metal bands, Van Halen's songs were three-point-five minutes long; filled with humor and hooks. But their blues base, aggressive sound, and haircuts got their albums filed in the metal section at the record store. If you were seen with their albums or teeshirts, you'd probably get picked on and called names. In the late seventies to be sporting long hair was an invitation to disaster at school. The prevailing fashion was spiked hair, ripped tee-shirts, and black leather jackets. The popular kids would form gangs where they pretended they had the same last name, and they'd make fun of metalheads, calling 'em names like "stoner" or "burnout." Plus they insulted the music, calling it crap and noise and laughing at the nowhere status of metal bands. Much of the same behavior was repeated by mainstream rock bands when the grassroots metal scene momentarily bubbled to the surface in the late seventies.

Van Halen's first two albums stiffed on the charts and their best hope for a hit song, "Dance The Night Away," also bombed. America's kids just wanted the fast chords and throaty vocals of punk; not the everything-but-the-kitchen-sink eclecticism of Van Halen. It was too messy—youngsters didn't want to deal with all the blues, vaudeville, and covers of Linda Ronstadt hits that they were serving up. The kids dug the Ramones because they were easier to dig; their jokes were simpler, as was their music—you knew what you were getting each and every time. Van Halen was the cool name to drop in certain circles and they got glowing reviews in the rock press, but their sales were lousy.

1980

"The Seventies are over."

—Lester Bangs, writing in 1980 on how *Women and Children First*'s "Romeo Delight" and "Take Your Whiskey Home" were insightful indications of a society that had increasingly learned how not to love.

1980's *Women and Children First* showed the strain of commercial failure. It was a bummer from the start, signified by the distorted electric piano that begins "And the Cradle Will Rock . . ." There were no attempts at even trying to win over the public, mostly the album was a dark exploration of eventual dead-ends. Some of the songs went over the four minute barrier, and most of those tended to not have much form—the band created magnificent noise while Roth improvised over it. It was a noisy, arty album that dared you to like it. As Dave Marsh wrote: ". . . finally: white rock's answer album to *There's A Riot Goin' On*."

1981

It was followed up the next year by the even darker *Fair Warning*. The fall of 1980 had brought the re-election of Jimmy Carter. The previous April, the president had freed the hostages in Iran with a military rescue. It pumped him up in the polls and he easily beat Republican candidate Ronald Reagan in November's election. Being a Democratic president, he continued to make promises out of the left side of his mouth while barking orders out of the right side. Carter started his second term by paying lip service to social causes while increasing military spending and escalating the Cold War by funding covert operations in Soviet-occupied Afghanistan. America was standing tall—yet it was a weird, uncomfortable time if you were paying attention.

With this as a backdrop, into the studio stepped Van Halen. They'd alienated their record company, they'd abandoned their good times sound, and they had something to say. Say it they did. You could tell by the first two tracks that something unique was under way. The album kicks off with "Mean Street," a moody funk-metal look through urban decay. It was followed by "Dirty Movies," where your Prom Queen turns to porn. The sound of the music tended to be liquid bass, spacey drums and Eddie hammering out squawking riffs and powerchords like a possessed Pete Townshend. The lyrics were about Relationships On The Rocks or America In Decline. In a country where the haves were rapidly separating themselves from the have-nots, Van Halen looked at it all from the street.

"Hear About It Later" caught the desperation of the average joe perfectly. It starts with a thoughtful instrumental intro, then Roth sings:

> *Ain't got no money*
> *got no house on the hill*
> *tell me honey*
> *will your lovin' pay my bills?*

later, the chorus:

> *See I've been tried and convicted*
> *it's winner take all*
> *I wanna run for my money*
> *that's all*
> *I don't wanna hear about it later*

In "Unchained," Roth stops to yell: *Hey man—that suit is you!* Seemingly, he's knocking a Mr. Jones-like square, the yuppiefied type that took over America in the coming years. Or maybe it was a shot at the tie-wearing new wave bands who personified the distanced irony that contrasted Van Halen's go-for-broke passion. Even the optimism of the catchy "So This Is Love?" came with a question mark tacked on. The album ends with Roth scrambling to get out of a jealous husband's bedroom, the band was a half-step ahead of him.

Fair Warning was the album where Van Halen, appearing to have given up hopes of stardom, settled for mere greatness. The critical response was overwhelming. Greil Marcus wrote that *Fair Warning* was "where Van Halen stared down these bleak eighties and barely won. Brutally vicious hard rock mixed with funk and fervor." Legend has it that the Clash themselves (who had made a ploy for metal credibility by having Blue Oyster Cult producer Sandy Pearlman produce their second album) stepped down from their multiplatinum thrones, took one listen to *Fair Warning*, and scrapped the work that had been done to date on their next album. Mick Jones himself confessed: "We knew we had to turn it up a couple of notches."

1982

After *Fair Warning*, retreat seemed inevitable. Van Halen became scared of their own shadows. A "fun" record followed, and while *Diver Down* was fun and had some nifty covers, the tapping of

Motown and especially the Kinks seemed like a desperate reach towards a mythical, better past.

1984

"Our albums are all thirty minutes long, we play half of our shows drunk off our asses and everyone says we take our fans for granted. Van Halen's albums are all thirty minutes long, they play half their shows drunk off their asses and they get hailed as some sort of charming throwback to the very essence of real rock 'n' roll."

—Paul Westerberg, 1984, while trying to disavow the similarities between the Replacements' "Take Me to the Hospital" and Van Halen's "Somebody Get Me a Doctor."

Van Halen's *1984* album contained one last gamble for stardom. But "Jump," a Who-influenced synth-pop gem went nowhere on the charts, though it did find its way into dance clubs across the country. It was a giant hit in another universe, I guarantee you. The rest of the album swings mightily, with the rhythm section throwing out a dry-hump groove that Eddie plays over. This is Eddie's album through and through—half the songs seem to exist solely for him to shimmer and shake over, tossing out powerchords, fills, and sheer melodic virtuosity. There was a certain type of genius at work here that blew the likes of Eric Clapton away; the songs avoided jamdom completely and Eddie's playing never ever sacrificed any rhythm, making it all that much stronger—a style unparalleled by most guitar gods.

1984 was the same year that Vice President Walter Mondale was running for president against John Anderson. The Republicans presented Anderson as a moderate alternative to the likes of Ronald Reagan, whose right-wing, trigger-happy, Goldwater-redux image scared most Americans. Anderson starting co-opting traditional Democratic issues like being nice to poor people and minorities. Mondale, because he was a boring putz who made even Anderson look charismatic, was struggling in the polls and was looking for an issue. He had learned red-baiting from a master, Hubert Humphrey.

A big part of red-baiting is lying and distorting the truth about the person(s) you want to crush or maybe just merely scapegoat. The version of red-baiting that Mondale came up with was nastiness in rock 'n' roll lyrics. He didn't accuse Van Halen and other bands of being communists, he just took their jauntier sex-and-booze lyrics and ran with 'em. Soon, Democratic senators and their wives starting howling about "dirty" lyrics, with the wives forming an anti-free-expression association that managed to snag congressional hearings. One of their fave targets was "Hot for Teacher" by Van Halen, which they claimed glorified pedophilia. (It's always been okay for grown men to sing about teenage girls, but once a song is written about an adult female and a teen boy—look out.) Van Halen was targeted by censors and the pressure on stores to not sell their albums was immense.

Mondale had his issue and forced Anderson to stick up for artistic expression and he paid in the polls. The Washington Wives proceeded to badmouth Van Halen so much that eventually David Lee Roth's apartment was invaded by the police. Roth had been the photo subject of a bondage poster that was included in the *Women and Children First* album, and he was jailed on obscenity charges. The band broke up soon after, in part due to the legal hassles that accompanied their harassment.

Epilogue

Eddie Van Halen went on to work with soundtracks. Alex Van Halen and Michael Anthony went to work for producer Lee "Scratch" Perry. A couple of years later, David Lee Roth (free at last) released a version of his first solo album, *Eat 'Em and Smile*, that had the vocals in Spanish. It sold tons in the Hispanic communities of the American Southwest, where metal has a huge following. For his effort in multi-culturalism, he was honored by the NAACP. At the banquet, he dedicated the award to Def Leppard's Joe Elliot.

A shadow of early fun-lovin' Van Halen lived on in the mid-eighties glam-metal trend that passed through on tiny indie labels

such as SST and Twin/Tone. Bands like Poison, Ratt, and Cin-
derella upped the flash quotient of Van Halen by slapping on mas-
cara and squeezing into spandex pants. Though they had their
moments, they lacked the diversity, humor, or verve of Van Halen.

Metal remained underground (though through the eighties it was
sampled or accessed by four out of five rappers worth their salt)
until Nirvana broke big in 1991 (i.e. "The Year Metal Broke.") One
listen to the first three songs on *Nevermind* and you knew those guys
had done their headbanging homework. In a classy move during
their *MTV Unplugged* gig, they brought out Eddie and Dave to run
through "Take Your Whiskey Home" and "Could This Be Magic?"

Last year, Van Halen played a comeback show here in town at
First Avenue. With "Feel Your Love Tonight" being the theme song
of *That Seventies Show* and indie rock bands everywhere namecheck-
ing Van Halen, they now have quite the (still not huge, but dedicated) following. Their eyes have crow-wings and Diamond Dave
can't quite jump like he used to; but the music is timeless. The kids
(grown or not) that filled that room were ecstatic. From the opening
of "And the Cradle Will Rock . . ." to the finale of "Panama," it was
one great song after another. The glee in the smiles that filled that
room almost matched the glee of the smiles on stage. And finally, a
band ignored for so long got its due. Finally.

TERRY McDERMOTT

Parental Advisory:
Explicit Lyrics

The beginning of the end of life as we know it occurred here, on a beaten patch of asphalt out in the vast, flat no man's land of greater Los Angeles.

The beginning of the end came unannounced. There was no salute, no blast of trumpets or heavenly choir. It came in the sunken heat of summer at an abandoned drive-in movie theater called the Roadium.

The Roadium was graced by a grand arched gate that, in its day, promised entry to whatever secret kingdom Hollywood could conjure. By the summer of 1985, though, the drive-in, its dreams and innocent magic are relics of a long-gone past. The dull blur of south county towns the Roadium served—Torrance, Lawndale, Hawthorne, Gardena, Carson and Compton—are staging areas in a decade-long descent into what feels at times like a war zone; and at times is. Street corners are outposts in a new crack economy, boulevards battle lines dividing endless variations of Bloods and Crips, usually from one another, always from themselves.

With the drive-in theater gone, the stuff of dreams has been traded for just plain stuff. The Roadium's arch now frames an open-air bazaar piled high with cheap Chinese toys, one-size-fits-all Sri Lankan socks, used car batteries, secondhand tool chests, last year's

Barbie dolls and canned peas with last week's use-by date. The Roadium is a swap meet.

The first thing you notice are the people. The place is so jammed you wonder how they ever got along without it. At the moment, the biggest crowd surrounds a little stall just inside the old arch. Kids are lined up two, three deep along the perimeter of the stall, whooping and hollering. A lanky Japanese guy, whippet-thin and wired, presides behind a homemade plywood table in the middle of the noise. The table is stacked high with records, LPs and those 12-inch singles that disc jockeys spin. He's got more of the same displayed on a 20-foot-wide pegboard behind him.

He's got so much product that some days, days when the heat is so thick you could lean against it, the table legs sink an inch into the melting asphalt.

The whole place isn't much bigger than a walk-in closet, and it's hot in every way imaginable. The air's an oven, the kids fired by the desire for the new.

"Yo, Steve. Whatcha got?"

"Stevie, Stevie, whatcha got new, man?"

Steve Yano is the man of the moment, an East L.A. guy who has somehow swapped a career as a high school guidance counselor to become the uncrowned king of a swap meet music underground. He has turned his table into the hippest, hottest record store on the West Coast. He's got everything—all the new East Coast hip-hop, the best old-school R&B, all the L.A. dance jams, that locking-and-popping stuff you see on "Soul Train." He has stuff nobody else has, stuff nobody else has ever heard of. He has stuff so new it doesn't even exist yet (not officially), stuff with no labels, no packaging, just the stamp of the new.

It is the new that tugs at the ears of the man who will deliver the beginning of the end of life as we know it. He's a little guy, 5–5, 5–6, tops, with the slow swagger of a hustler fat on house money. Steve Yano remembers him showing up that first day at the Roadium, going through piles of 12-inch singles. Big piles.

"He looks 'em over, stacks 'em up. Then says, 'I'll take these.'"

The guy has maybe 20 records in front of him. Yano is used to kids buying one, maybe two at a time. These are not rich kids. They wouldn't be at the swap meet if they were. Yano thinks this guy is scamming.

"All those?" he asks.

"Yeah," the kid says. He's got a high, squeaky voice that makes him sound even younger than he looks. And he looks about 13. He picks up one of the 12-inchers, a cut from some local DJs called the World Class Wreckin' Cru.

"Where you get that from?" he asks.

The question doesn't even register with Yano, who still can't believe the kid has money to buy all the records he has in front of him.

"All of them?" he asks.

"Sure," the kid says and reaches down in his sock. He comes back up with a roll of cash. He peels the bills off. Bam. Just like that.

Then he says: "Tell Dre, Eric says, 'Whassup?'"

With that, Eric Wright turns and walks off with a stack of records half as big as he is. Yano, of course, tells Dre nothing. Dre, Andre Young, a member of the Wreckin' Cru, is one of the hottest young DJs in L.A. He doesn't need to be bothered, man. Not with this kid anyhow.

Wright comes back the next weekend, asks about Dre again, wants his numbers. He's polite but persistent and comes back every week. Yano finally asks Dre if he knows a homeboy named Eric Wright. And damned if Dre doesn't.

"Next thing I know," Yano says, "those guys are on a three-way call with me at two in the morning. Eric wants to open a record store. I tell him, 'Don't do it. It's a bad business. I can show you how, but don't do it.'"

Eric has money—street money, dope money—and wants to go straight. Dre, meanwhile, bugs Yano, who knows every low-level somebody in the record business in all of Los Angeles, to start a record label. Dre wants a place to put out his own music.

In time, these dreams merged and came true. Eric went into the record business, all right, not with a corner store but with his own label and Dre was on it. Soon that label, Ruthless Records, sent out into the world some of the weirdest, funniest, saddest, maddest music anybody every heard. Out of that little swap meet stall came the partnership that rocked, then overran the record business.

The partnership took full form in the hip-hop group Niggaz With Attitude, which in 1988 released a record called "Straight Outta Compton." This was the group's first national release. N.W.A was largely unknown. The record contained no hit singles. In most of the country, nothing from the record was played even once on the radio. It was too crude, too misogynistic, too violent. MTV, which had by then established itself as the primary gatekeeper of popular culture, refused to play N.W.A videos.

No radio, no television and no publicity.

"Straight Outta Compton" sold 3 million records.

The music it contained was so perverse, so nihilistic, so forbidden, politicians—then and still—elbowed each other out of the way to condemn it. Highbrow critics couldn't find language strong enough to critique it; they went further, questioning whether it was even music at all. It's barbaric, they said. Hide the women and children; bar the doors. Too late.

Gangsta rap was in the house.

Locking and Popping

The content of youth culture today is, to a significant extent, hip-hop: hip-hop records, hip-hop fashion, hip-hop film, hip-hop attitude. It is the only genre of popular entertainment that cuts consistently across class, ethnicity, gender and age. Just as rock music was a vehicle for the countercultural attitudes that provoked social upheaval among the middle classes in the 1960s, hip-hop in general and gangsta rap in particular have carried urban underclass snesibilities to the wider society—which has reacted with equal parts enchantment, imitation and outrage.

But in the first half of the 1980s, people in the Los Angeles-based record industry saw hip-hop as an East Coast fad. Hip-hop's few national hits were dismissed as novelties. Southern California was in the grip of a dance epidemic, a local disco fever. A DJ collective called Uncle Jamm's Army played Culver City east to Pomona; the Dream Team owned South-Central. A forceful young man named Lonzo Williams worked the clubs and parties from Gardena to Long Beach.

Lonzo had been an ardent dancer who started DJing to make money. While still at Compton High School, he booked house and block parties, graduating to 1,000-plus-seat venues such as Alpine Village in Torrance and even the Queen Mary.

Lonzo landed a regular gig at Eve After Dark, a new Compton nightclub. On Fridays he would spin records from 9 at night until 5 the next morning, turning the crowd over three or four times. To share the load, Lonzo, in the early 1980s, built a team of DJs called Disco Construction; then, as disco died, the World Class Wreckin' Cru. The Cru played the usual: Donna Summer, Average White Band, George Clinton, Parliament and Prince.

Eve was a high-class club—dresses for the ladies and ties and slacks for the gentlemen. Lonzo dressed his Jheri-curled DJs in matching lavender outfits and devised Temptations-style choreography. The club became a fixture on the dance map of Los Angeles. "People came out in droves," Lonzo recalls. "It was a constant party."

A young Compton kid started hanging around outside Eve, which didn't serve alcohol but had an age limit. His name was Andre Young. He was 17, still a student at Centennial High, and already a three-year DJ veteran.

Young pestered Lonzo for a spot on the Cru. On a night when one of the regulars didn't show, Lonzo gave the new kid a shot.

Lonzo says the key to DJing in such a competitive scene was to "find the most obscure record you could and play it." Dre was young, but he had tremendous musical knowledge. He'd been listening forever to his mother's extensive rhythm-and-blues and jazz record collection. When she came home after work at night, he once said, the stereo went on before the lights. He DJed for her and her friends when he was barely school age.

That first night at Eve, Young mixed the old Motown song "Please Mr. Postman" over Afrika Bambaataa's seminal hip-hop recording, "Planet Rock"—two songs with completely different tempos and moods. For whatever reason, it worked.

The crowd went crazy and Lonzo went, "Hmm, what do we have here?"

One of the most popular acts in town at the time was Uncle Jamm's Army, in which the DJs built identifiable characters—essentially roles they played onstage. One, a heartthrob named Egyptian Lover, did several numbers exploring the racier dimensions of his love life. Lonzo admired Young's musical talent, but even more he saw the good-looking young ladies' man as a draw, his answer to Egyptian Lover. Young joined the Wreckin' Cru under the stage name Dr. Dre in honor of Julius Erving, the basketball player known as Doctor J. Lonzo booked other acts into Eve, including the first L.A.-area appearances of New York rappers Kurtis Blow and Run-DMC. When the Wreckin' Cru saw Run-DMC for the first time, they looked at one another in amazement, recalls Antoine Carraby, a DJ known as Yella.

Run-DMC was a Eureka moment.

"'This is it? It's not even a 10-minute show. We can do this.' That's exactly how it started," says Yella. "We can do this."

They began writing their own material. It didn't seem to matter that none of them were musicians. Yella could program a drum machine. Otherwise, they were lost.

"We were DJs. What we knew was partying," Lonzo says. "I can't play dead. I can't play the radio."

No matter. Dre was naturally musical in a way that most DJs only dreamed about. Dre and Yella hung out during the day at Eve After Dark, listening to records, figuring out how to replicate instrumental tracks on an old four-track recording deck in the back room. It was, Dre says, how he learned record production.

In 1984, they went into Audio Achievements studio in Torrance, where for $100 they recorded two tracks—one called Slice, the other Kru Groove. The music—a fast-beat techno sound influenced by the German band Kraftwerk—consisted mainly of drum tracks programmed by Yella and Dre's turntable scratching, the distinctive wicky, wicky sound made by manipulating a turntable by hand.

Another member of the group, Marquette Hawkins, known as DJ Cli-N-Tel, rapped lyrics that mostly said how clever Yella was to have written them. They took the tracks to Macola Records, a small, independent label in Hollywood where you could have records pressed in lots as small as 500. For virtual pocket change, they were now proud owners of a two-sided, 12-inch dance single. They began selling it out of the trunk of Lonzo's car to independent record stores throughout Los Angeles.

"We sold 5,000 of them," Lonzo says. "Five thousand! That's like ghetto gold."

The New Mall

Steve Yano was a grad student in educational psychology at Cal State L.A. when he saw an ad on campus for a part-time job delivering records to stores in the area. Within a year, he found himself part of a record store with the man who had hired him. The store did well enough but couldn't support them both, so Yano sold his half of the business to his partner. Yano took payment in merchandise.

"At about this time, the West Coast swap meet scene just blew up," Yano says. "I spent the week, Monday through Friday, searching for product. Hitting all the spots in town, going through used record bins. Weekends, I'd sell at the meet. I went to every single pawnshop in L.A. You could buy 10 records for a dollar. I knew I could sell three of them for two bucks each."

At the peak of disco fever, Yano got a stall at one of the busiest swap meets in California—the Roadium on Redondo Beach Boulevard in Torrance. Customers at the Roadium were mainly African American, and Yano began to tailor his product to fit the customers. "Then there started to be this new type of talk—R&B, Grandmaster Flash, Kurtis Blow, Run-DMC," Yano says. "These guys are popping. Kids are talking about it. Do you have any 12-inch? Nobody has it. They've never heard of it. Finally, I found out places you can get some."

Among those sources was Lonzo Williams. Yano called him.

"Oh yeah, sure," Lonzo said. "How many you need?"

"Three or four," Yano answered.

"Pretty soon it was, 'I'll take 10 of these. Then 50,'" Yano says. "Pretty soon Lonzo is coming to me with stuff and I'm carrying 100 titles. I'm selling 100 a week of some of them. The DJ craze hits. Now everybody and their mother is a DJ and they all want the latest [music]. So they all come to me. I was selling a lot of 12-inch vinyl. I mean, a lot. Pretty soon other dealers are coming to me. I'm meeting these guys outside bowling alleys in parking lots at midnight. It was like we were dealing drugs.

"I become for a while a very important guy. I'm buying 500 copies of a title. The first place anybody called in L.A. was me. 'Play this. Whattya think?' All these label guys are starting to bring me their new records. I could tell the first weekend if something is going to sell just by how the kids react. If it was good, kids would start to break dance right there in the stall."

One day, when Yano went to Eve After Dark to meet Lonzo, he heard Dre and Yella in one of their practice sessions.

KDAY, a local radio station, had converted to an all hip-hop format, the first station in the country to do so. The station had a daily feature called Traffic Jam, and it solicited local DJs to make mixes. Dre and Yella did mixes several times a week—Yella on the drum machine, Dre scratching on the turntable.

Yano listened, rapt. "Is that how you do it?" he asked.

"You want us to make you a tape?" Yella answered. Yano took the tape to the swap meet the next weekend.

"I'm playing it," Yano says, "and people go, 'Who did that tape? Can I get that?'"

Calling Dr. Dre

By the mid–1980s, much of the record business had evolved into large integrated companies that did everything from signing artists, assigning them producers and songs, then promoting and selling their records through sales staffs. More and more, the records were marketed through giant retail chains.

Low profit margins made store rack space too valuable to waste on unknown artists. This was less true in black communities, where small, locally-owned retailers hung on and where there was an enduring demand not just for what was popular but for what was novel. These stores provided an outlet for the new music that the big chains wouldn't risk stocking. This helped make hip-hop possible in the first place.

While Lonzo worked the local market, Don MacMillan, the owner of Macola Records, distributed Wreckin' Cru recordings to an informal network of independent distributors around the country. MacMillan had several hip-hop acts on Macola. The artists were drawn to him by the easy terms. He would press records in small quantities and send them out. He didn't care who was making the records or what was on them.

MacMillan let the artists put their own labels on the recordings and control their own publishing. Lonzo called his label Kru-Cut Records.

After modest success with its first 12-inch single, the Cru had a hit with "Surgery," a 1984 number written and produced by Dre that sold 50,000 records—a huge amount for an independently made and distributed record. "Surgery" was typical of the Wreckin' Cru's music: basic electronic funk, a fast drum machine beat, lots of turntable scratching and silly lyrics ("Calling Dr. Dre to surgery").

The Wreckin' Cru started making the transition from dance hall DJs to recording artists. They followed "Surgery" with "Juice" in 1985 and put out an album called "World Class" that same year. CBS Records called. Larkin Arnold, an executive, wanted a meeting. "Larkin was like the black godfather of music. If he said there was a meeting, there was a meeting," Lonzo says.

The meeting went well. Arnold said he'd get back to them, and the Wreckin' Cru went on tour as an opening act for Rick James. The Cru measured its success night to night by how many girls they could coax to their hotel rooms. Most nights, they earned high marks. "We had showmanship," Lonzo says.

They did their dance steps, wore lace gloves, makeup and rhinestone satin costumes. These were, in their way, almost quaint reminders of Lonzo's old-school roots. On the road, Lonzo got a call from his lawyer. CBS was offering a contract with a $100,000 advance.

Are you interested, the lawyer wanted to know.

"Interested? Sign the damned contract!" Lonzo screamed. "You got power of attorney. Sign it before they change their minds."

Lonzo pauses at this point in the story. He now owns a small club on Manchester Boulevard in Inglewood. It's empty in the way that only a nightclub at noon can be. He looks around and shakes his head.

"It was the worst thing that ever happened," he says. "From that point on, we had nothing but dissension over money."

Dre complained that Lonzo wasn't paying him enough. He was the musical foundation of the Wreckin' Cru but was being paid as one of the guys. That category—one of the guys—meant everybody except Lonzo, who, in his own defense, says that no one understood how much it cost him to keep the Wreckin' Cru operating. It was his group; he paid for everything—advertising, recording costs, travel, equipment. It was only fair that he be paid more money. The irony was that the more successful the group became, the worse things got. This had been Lonzo's one big chance. It left without him. He shakes his head again. "One day you're cool, the next day you're not. By the time we came off the road, we were on the down slide," Lonzo says. "Something happened with those guys."

Boys Become Boyz

The Wreckin' Cru was Lonzo's group. He decided what music they did. As much as Dre complained about money, he told friends that he was equally frustrated with the Wreckin' Cru's musical direction.

"I'm inviting Dre and Yella out to the stall. They're cutting records right there at the Roadium," Yano says. "Somebody plays it at a party. Everybody goes, 'What's that?' But you can't get it. You can't buy it anywhere. It was unbelievable. Dre says, 'Why don't you make a label?' I said, 'No way.'"

Dre kept asking. Yano kept saying no.

"Then one day," Yano says, "along comes Eazy."

There was no reason to think Eazy-E (Eric Wright) knew anything about any business but selling dope.

But being a dope man imposed certain career limitations. When he wandered by Yano's swap meet stall in 1985, at 22, he had resolved to get a new occupation. He told one friend if all else failed he would do what his father had done: go to work at the post office.

First, though, he wanted to give the music business a try. And it was clear to everyone that it was the money more than the music that interested him.

"Even as a kid, he was a businessman," Yano says.

This was something Dre notably was not. He was a terrible manager of his own affairs, forever broke. He made matters worse by ignoring money matters when he could. He racked up parking tickets and traffic citations, then didn't pay them until the fines doubled or tripled or he was jailed for not paying at all.

"What you gonna do? Couldn't leave him in jail, you might have a gig that weekend," Lonzo says.

So Lonzo bailed Dre out repeatedly. Finally, it happened one time too many. The call came, Dre asked and Lonzo said: "You know what? I'm gonna let your butt sit in jail for a while. Maybe you'll learn something."

"So he calls Eazy," Lonzo says.

Eazy and Dre cut a deal: Eazy would bail Dre out of jail; Dre would produce records for Eazy's new record company. Of course, Eazy's record company existed only in Eazy's mind. The idea of a minor-league dope dealer starting a record company from scratch was not as preposterous as it might seem. It was possible to create a virtual record company, although nobody called it that at the time. The existence of Macola Records, basically a fee-for-service pressing plant, lowered the bar to enter the record business to next to nothing.

Macola provided all of the infrastructure to manufacture and distribute records. Studios could be rented. And the music itself could be made quickly and cheaply. All Eazy really needed was ambition, which he had, and Dre.

"They come by the stall one day," Yano says. "I got a guy there doing T-shirts, spraying them. Eazy says, 'Whattya think of Ruthless? Ruthless Records?'" "That's cool," Yano said.

And the T-shirt guy painted what would become the logo for Ruthless Records.

Eazy Duz It

Eazy now had a name but still no artists, no material, no plan. Dre gave him a tape from a New York rap duo called HBO. Eazy agreed to record them as the debut artists for Ruthless. He booked time at Audio Achievements, where the Wreckin' Cru records were made. He asked Dre for a song.

Dre had been writing with O'Shea Jackson, a young Compton MC who lived who lived four doors down from one of Dre's cousins. Jackson had been writing rhymes since grade school in L.A.'s Crenshaw district. Dre became a mentor. He'd pick Jackson up after school and take him along to clubs and to Lonzo's garage, which they had converted into a ramshackle recording studio.

Dre produced an album by Jackson, Dre's cousin Jinx and a third friend, Kid Disaster. They called their group CIA (Criminals In Action). Jackson adopted the stage name Ice Cube. Like a lot of kids, Cube was a huge fan of the comedian Richard Pryor. Cube's parents had Pryor's records, which in addition to being hilarious were exceptionally profane. Cube listened to the albums when his parents left the house. He started writing similarly obscene rap parodies of popular songs.

"We knew the value of language, especially profanity. We weren't that sophisticated, but we knew the power it had," Cube says.

He and Dre started DJing together at clubs and the Compton Skateland roller rink. Dre would play the instrumental tracks of popular hip-hop songs and Cube would rap obscene versions of the original lyrics. One of the highlights was a version of the Run-DMC hit "My Adidas" that Cube transformed into "My Penis." The Skateland kids loved it. Cube wrote constantly. "I never stopped," he says. "I had notebooks full of raps." Among them was one called

"Boyz N Tha Hood" that Cube wrote during English class at Taft High School in Woodland Hills, where he was bused from South-Central. Cube showed the rhyme to Dre, who made an instrumental track for it. When HBO showed up in Torrance to record, Dre gave them "Boyz." HBO balked. Too West Coast, they said, and walked out. Eazy was stuck with the bill for an empty recording studio. Since Dre, Cube and the others were already in various groups, Dre urged Eazy to rap the song. Eazy resisted. He was a businessman. He knew nothing about rapping. Dre persisted, and with no other option, Eazy did the song.

He had no rap experience or skills, and it showed. It took two days to make the track. "We all laughed 'cuz it was so bad," Lonzo says.

"Boyz N Tha Hood" is the story of a young man's misadventures with friends, cars, girls and guns on a single afternoon. It opens with him "cruisin' down tha street in my '64." He sees a friend driving a stolen car. He catches another friend trying to steal his car stereo and shoots him. He has a couple of drinks, gets in a fight with his girlfriend, then with her father. He wrecks the car and, finally, walking home, sees the guy with the stolen car from the first verse fight with police. A busy day. "I can sell that," Yano said.

Eazy took it to Macola, had a pressing done, and Yano started selling the 12-inch singles at the swap meet.

"Kids are just loving it," Yano says. "We had the best promotion you could ever get, promotion at the grass-roots street level."

Eazy would drive up to Hollywood, ostensibly to talk to Don MacMillan. "He'd go to Macola, go into the back room and steal his own records," says Lorenzo Patterson, a young rapper whom Eazy recruited to join his label. "We'd take 'em out through the back door and throw them into his Jeep."

Eazy hired "snipers"—friends, gangbangers, ordinary guys who wanted to make a couple bucks—to take the records around the neighborhood stores. They gave away cassette copies to kids in the projects who were leaders in their own little cliques.

Against all odds, "Boyz N Tha Hood" became a hit.

"The response told us we'd found our niche, to be ourselves," says Cube. Eazy persuaded Dre, Cube, Yella and another local rapper named Mik Lezan, known as the Arabian Prince, to form an all-star group. Dre and Yella would make the beats; Cube would write the lyrics; Arabian Prince, Cube and Eazy would rap them. They could all continue to do their own things and get together on the side to make wild records for Ruthless.

It was an informal collective. People came and went in the studio. Cube, just out of high school, surprised everybody by leaving town to take a course in architectural drafting in Arizona. "If this record thing didn't work out, I didn't want to be out there digging ditches," Cube says. The Arabian Prince left too—for a solo career. As replacements Eazy brought in Patterson, who went by the name M.C. Ren, and Tray Curry, a Texas rapper who performed as The D.O.C. Eazy auditioned Ren in his mother's Compton garage, where he had recording gear set up. Ren had been writing rhymes since junior high. He rhymed equations in algebra class.

"He told me to start rapping about anything," Ren says. "So I started rapping about [stuff] in the garage. He liked it, took the tape to Dre. Dre signed me on the spot. Took me to a notary public he knew in Lakewood, signed me to a contract. There was no money or nothing. I didn't care. I was like, 'Fine.'"

Ren says Eazy's pitch was straightforward: at Ruthless, you could make records you couldn't make at other labels; it would be a place where nobody would tell you what you couldn't do. The records would all be like "Boyz N Tha Hood"—full of sex and guns, drinking and drugging. It would be stuff their friends would buy. At 24, Yella was the oldest of the crew. Eazy was 23; Dre, 21; Ren, 20; Cube, 18.

One day, hanging out at the Arabian Prince's house in Inglewood, they arrived at a name for the new group. They wanted something everybody would identify with the West Coast. Somebody suggested From Compton With Love.

"Hell, no!" everyone shouted.

"Then," Ren recalls, "Eazy says, 'How 'bout N.W.A, Niggaz With Attitude?' Everybody's like, 'Hell, yeah. N.W.A it is.'"

The Permanent Business

As the label took shape, Eazy bugged Lonzo for an introduction to Jerry Heller, a vetaran talent manager. Lonzo had met Heller at Macola, which was a kind of social club for the emerging local hip-hop scene.

"We all heard of Jerry. He was always there at Don's," Lonzo says. "At one time he had almost everybody on the West Coast signed up. Throw it against the wall and see what sticks. That's what he was doing."

Lonzo and Heller had become friendly. Lonzo was older than many of the other guys, and he and Heller had an easy rapport. Lonzo didn't much like Eazy. For one thing, he thought Eazy was prying Dre away from him.

"The original plan was for Dre to produce Eazy and stay in the Cru," Lonzo says. "Dre was enticed by Eazy's lifestyle. He got tired of the flashy costumes, got tired of practicing the choreography. He wanted to be a rapper.

"I'm fighting for the Wreckin' Cru and I can't compete. There's a musical divide. I thought their music was good, but I wasn't into it. I loved ballads."

In the end, Lonzo agreed to introduce Eazy to Heller, but he made it clear he wasn't doing it as a friend. He charged Eazy $750. The introduction took place in March 1987 in the Macola lobby. "Eazy took the money out of his sock right there and paid Lonzo," Heller says.

Heller was an old pro, a part of what music people call "the permanent business." Denizens of the permanent business have a genius mainly for endurance. They hang around, surfing the erratic waves of popularity that define pop culture. Heller had made and lost at least one fortune already. A middle-class, middle-aged, middle-of-the-road white guy with no musical ability, he had been managing musicians dating back to Creedence Clearwater Revival in the 1960s. By the 1980s, Heller's fortunes had declined. He was, he says, "burned out on the industry."

"Then I heard about this scene at Macola, this pressing plant on Santa Monica Boulevard," Heller says. "For a thousand dollars, he'd press 500 records."

Eazy told Heller about the kind of record company he wanted. Then he played "Boyz N Tha Hood" and a new N.W.A song, "Straight Outta Compton."

"It blew me away," Heller says. "I thought it was the most important music I had ever heard."

They agreed to form a partnership and sealed the deal with a drink at Martini's, a Hollywood hangout. Heller decided that what N.W.A needed most was better promotion and distribution. That fall, Heller sent the band on tour and went shopping for a partner. The tour was far from glamorous. For much of it, N.W.A shared the bill with Salt-N-Pepa, a group of three women with national hits. Salt-N-Pepa flew between dates while N.W.A drove in a van.

Salt-N-Pepa found it greatly amusing that the hard-core Compton "gangsters" had to drive themselves. "Used to laugh at us: 'When y'all's plane leaving?'" Ren says.

Heller wasn't having a great deal more fun trying to sell the group. He says Columbia Records executive Joe Smith's reaction, upon hearing a demo tape, was typical. Smith offered to purchase the name Ruthless, which he thought had possibilities, but wanted nothing to do with the records.

"Are you crazy?" Heller remembers Smith asking. "What the hell would make you believe somebody is going to buy this crap?"

Some evidence was beginning to accumulate that Smith was wrong. Heller took Eazy to New York to introduce him at an industry gathering. They were in an elevator at the Park Lane Hotel. The elevator stopped and let on Joseph Simmons and Darryl McDaniels, the front men for Run-DMC. Heller and Eazy immediately recognized Simmons and McDaniels, who in turn gave Heller and, especially, Eazy the once over. Then, recognition having dawned, Simmons and McDaniels started softly rapping the lyrics to "Boyz N Tha Hood."

"They knew every word," Heller says. "The record had never been played on radio anywhere. It's a 12-inch single distributed locally. And they knew the whole thing." Seizing on the under-ground success of "Boyz," Macola's Don MacMillan compiled that song, a bunch of demos and rough recordings various people had done under the Ruthless banner and issued it as an album under the name "N.W.A and the Posse." Only three of the songs on the album were performed by what would become N.W.A. The record didn't sell in huge numbers, but it started building N.W.A's reputation.

Johnny Phillips, a record distributor in Memphis, remembers a call around this time from one of his accounts, an independent record store in Cincinnati, asking about a record by a group called N.W.A that was being played in local clubs.

"I called Macola, bought a couple hundred of them. By the next month we were reordering five, six, seven thousand a week. As soon as we got 'em, we sold 'em."

Phillips, the nephew of Sam Phillips, the man who discovered Elvis Presley, was a key distributor for Priority Records, a fledgling company in Los Angeles. He sent Priority a copy of the Macola album. Priority was the creation of Bryan Turner and Mark Cerami, former K-Tel Records executives. They had started the label just two years before and made some money issuing a line of rap compilation albums. Then they hit it big with an unlikely novelty hit, the California raisins.

Television commercials for the California raisin industry had featured a musical quartet of animated raisins singing the soul classic "I Heard It Through the Grapevine." Priority licensed the rights to the singing raisins and put out an album of soul oldies. They sold 2 million copies. As a result, Priority was flush with cash and looking for new talent.

Coincidentally, Priority's offices were on the same floor of a Hollywood building as Jerry Heller's office. Turner, Cerami and Heller knew one another casually, and Heller had just been in to pitch N.W.A.

Cerami went to see the group perform. It was like the Beatles, he said. That sealed it. N.W.A was set to follow in the footsteps of the California raisins.

Paint Ball Politics

In the record business, money is spent on two things: recording music and promoting it. By the time N.W.A went into the studio to make its first real album, "Straight Outta Compton," a typical studio album cost well more than $100,000 to produce. Some cost 10 times that much.

The more money that was spent and made, the greater the size of the record company that would manage it.

One of the great gifts hip-hop gave to the music community was liberation from these corporate bureaucracies. Most hip-hop records were being made by small companies on low budgets—"on machines you could buy for $200 at Toys R Us," Heller says.

The other half of up-front costs—promotion and marketing—is spent mainly trying to get radio stations to play records. With N.W.A, there was no chance radio stations were going to touch the stuff, so there was no sense throwing money at them.

"You couldn't spend money on radio, so basically you couldn't spend money," Turner says. This, coupled with low production costs, made the economics of an N.W.A record utterly different.

"I could sell fifty, sixty, seventy thousand of these records and make money," Turner says.

With those numbers and with almost no investment, Priority could afford to both sign N.W.A and leave the group alone. After its brief tour, N.W.A, with Cube back home from Arizona, went into the studio with complete freedom to make whatever record they wanted to make. And they did.

"Straight Outta Compton" has been described variously as a work of revolutionary genius, a painful scream from the bleak streets of black America and, more commonly, as reprehensible trash with no redeeming value. It is all of that, and remains startling because of it.

"It's just an image," says Ren. "We got to do something that would distinguish ourselves. We was just trying to be different."

The fifth word on the first song on "Straigh Outta Compton" is unprintable in *The Times*. The same word and many variations of it recur with regularity thereafter.

The record is laced with language you don't hear on the radio or in polite society. That was the beauty of it and, from the group's point of view, the joy of it. "We were going to write about the street. Cussing and hollering," Ren says. They didn't give a damn about polite society, or anything beyond the narrow world of the low-level street hooligans they wrote about.

What is most shocking about the album is not the language but the gleeful, celebratory hedonism of it, the misogyny and violence and dark-as-midnight nihilism. As a listener, you get the sense you're learning more about something than you really want to know, something you might at some point be called to testify about.

When people talk about the album's political and social power, they're referring mainly to the first three of 13 songs: "Straight Outta Compton," "F— Tha Police" and "Gangsta, Gangsta."

The other 10 tracks are party songs, some of them great dance tracks but lyrically silly and forgettable. Several songs had been recorded previously and were redone for the album. It is a measure of the power of the first three songs that they have been able to drown out memory of the other 10. Dre has at times seemed embarrassed at the rawness of the whole affair, saying the record was crudely made. Others see this as a virtue, part of the album's immediacy. The record was made in just six weeks. It cost about $8,000 and has the loose sense of a bunch of guys having one hell of a good time—except Ice Cube, who is ferociously angry throughout.

"Think about how you felt at that age," Cube says. "I was mad at everything. When I went to the schools in the Valley, going through those neighborhoods, seeing how different they were from mine, that angered me. The injustice of it, that's what always got me—the injustice."

The group was not political in any way other than the most elementary sense. Cube's lyrics were more socially aware than he was. "F— Tha Police" was at least as dismissive of the police as it was an attack on them. The group wasn't even going to record it initially. When Cube first showed the lyrics to Dre, he passed. "What else you got?" Dre asked.

It was only after Dre and Eazy were caught shooting paint balls at people at Torrance bus stops that Dre changed his mind about the song.

Cube was the main lyricist for the album. Dre and Yella shared the producer's credit. They were almost always the first ones in the Torrance studio and the last to leave. Others came and went as need or whim dictated. It was clear who was in charge.

"Dre was like the main ear," Ren says. "He'd tell you, 'Try to make it like this.' You'd do it. He'd be like, 'Cool.' Or, 'That's terrible.' Dre'd look at you like, you dumb mother. . . . "

The results do not match Dre's later musical sophistication; few things do. It was, as Priority's Bryan Turner points out, his first real album. Even so, the sound of the album is as powerful as the lyrics—and more varied. The fast-beat Wreckin' Cru techno is absent, replaced by slower, deeper, funkier rhythm tracks set in a scrap heap soundscape of sirens, gunshots, shouts, curses and cars. The overall effect can be ominous.

Hip-hop from its beginnings has been intensely place-based. Rappers have told us about their neighborhoods and towns, praising them and criticizing others. Regional chauvinism became a defining characteristic; geographic feuds a part of the drama. N.W.A made a virtue of necessity in celebrating Compton, a place few people had ever heard of outside Southern California. To this day, all that many people know of it is what N.W.A told them. In a way, people read both too much and too little into "Straight Outta Compton." Too much was made of supposed political motivations and probably not enough of the fact that these were kids making records for other kids.

Few people placed the record inside a broader regional tradition to which it clearly belongs. California pop music in the last 40 years has had four periods of peak popularity: mid-'60s surf and hot-rod music; late-'60s psychedelia; '70s laid-back country rock; and gangsta rap of the late '80s through the '90s.

As distinct as these genres are, they share a notably self-indulgent worldview. No matter who's singing—Beach Boys, Jefferson Airplane, the Eagles or Niggaz With Attitudes—or about what, California hedonism prevails. As Cube put it in "Gangsta, Gangsta," life is just girls and money, or words to that effect.

In almost any other medium, the same content would have been received more calmly. It would have been analyzed as an artistic stance, not a lifestyle. (These weren't, after all, real gangsters.) Dre would have been exalted as a postmodern master, Frank Gehry at the mixing board, cobbling scraps of James Brown funk to cool Euro techno in a way that made both seem more alive. Cube would have been doing political commentary on CNN and Eazy's autobiography would have been a business school staple.

People forgot that these were songs, fictions. Almost inevitably, establishment forces denounced "Straight Outta Compton." It set off a long-running, unresolved debate about the content of pop culture.

The ubiquity of pop music encourages overreation; it's the only art form that blasts out of a 200-watt amp in the Toyota next to you at the stoplight on Slauson, the artillery thump of the bass vibrating shop windows a block away. Or, more to the point, the stoplight might be on Magic Mountain Parkway in Valencia; or any intersection in Bethesda, Md., Waukegan, Ill., or Redmond, Ore. Or, for that matter, in Tokyo, Paris or Rio.

From nearly the beginning, as soon as N.W.A broke out of the swap meet scene, the group sold most of its records far beyond the boundaries of black neighborhoods. Eventually, Priority calculated, 80% of the sales of "Straight Outta Compton" were in the suburbs, mainly to teenage boys who wouldn't know real niggaz if one woofed in their ears.

The FBI Helps Out

The record came out in late 1988. Radio wanted nothing to do with it. When the group taped a music video, MTV refused to play it. Still, sales climbed into the hundreds of thousands.

"How did it happen? I was there from the beginning and experienced pretty much every part of it from up close, and it's still inexplicable," says David King, a Priority salesman. "Other labels would

ask me how we did it. I couldn't answer. Basically, we just manufactured and shipped records. And people kept asking for more."

In other words, "Straight Outta Compton" sold itself.

Johnny Phillips, the Memphis record distributor, cites the
unusual relationship between small, black-owned record stores and
their customers. "Black consumers in particular will buy where they
can trust the store. Doesn't matter what it is. We've sold to combination record store/barber shops, even a pet store/record store."

Turner says the knowledge of distributors such as Phillips was
crucial in getting the record introduced nationally. "Those were the
really critical relationships, with the mom-and-pop stores, because
there was a whole list of them that could actually get your record
promoted, get your record sold because kids would come buy it.
There was such a demand for rap and such a lack of supply."

At first the album received little national attention; sales built
region by region. When it broke within an area, it crossed over to
white markets almost immediately, King says. The hardest part was
getting stores to stock it. "Once you got it in, that's all it took," King
says. "It sold fast with junior high kids. It was illicit, forbidden
fruit."

By the middle of 1989, six months after its release, "Straight
Outta Compton" was a stealth phenomenon. Then N.W.A got
lucky—perversely so. Milt Ahlerich, an assistant director of the
FBI, sent a letter to Priority, accusing the label of selling a record
("F— Tha Police") that encouraged "violence against and disre-
spect for the law-enforcement officer." Ahlerich didn't propose to
do anything. There was nothing he could do. He said merely that
"we in the law enforcement community take exception to such
action."

The bureau's interpretation of the song was so literal it's a wonder it
didn't form a task force to dig up the bodies that Eazy, Ren and Cube
bragged about dispatching. Bryan Turner didn't know how to react.

"I was scared. You kidding? It was the FBI. I'm just a kid from
Canada, what do I know?" Turner says. "I showed it to some
lawyers. They said they [the FBI] couldn't do anything. That made
me feel better. Then we circulated the letter. The thing was like a

nuclear explosion. Once we circulated that, everybody wanted to hear the record the FBI wanted to suppress."

N.W.A went back on tour. Sure enough, they were banned from performing in some cities, touching off small riots. Every time it happened, there was a spate of publicity followed by a spurt in sales. "It was free publicity as far as I was concerned," Yella says. Bill Adler, a former rap label executive, says it's simple to identify elements of a hit record. "Pop music is teen music. The stuff that's going to explode are the things that appeal to teens. Girls want somebody cute. Boys want somebody tough."

What could possibly be tougher than to have the FBI after you?

"The FBI helped out," Heller says. "MTV banned the 'Straight Outta Compton' video and we sold 100,000 copies. A whole cultural phenomenon. Several months into it, *Elle* did a 10-page spread on gangster chic in the foreign edition. We did a *Newsweek* cover." N.W.A woke the music industry to the huge commercial possibilities of hard-core hip-hop.

Eventually people quit asking if hip-hop was a fad. Rap music worked its way on to the radio, dominated it to some extent, ending what had been a decade of de facto radio racial segregation. Hip-hop, now dominated by gangsta rap descendants, is the best-selling music in the world.

"The economics of it were staggering. Just staggering," Heller says. If you were with Warner Bros., for example, and you sold 500,000 records, they might drop you from the label. The way we were doing it, if you sold 200,000 records you made a quarter million dollars. And you made it right there. We'd take the check to the bank, cash it and split it up on the corner."

Whether all of the checks were for the right amount would later become a subject of much debate and litigation, but for the time being N.W.A was riding down Main Street in the biggest parade any of them had ever imagined.

Consider the things that had to happen for "Straight Outta Compton" to become a hit record.

It required an economic catastrophe to overwhelm metropolitan Los Angeles, leaving African American neighborhoods in shambles, their residents in despair. It required a crack epidemic to then sweep through those same streets, offering more misery but also complicated opportunities that enriched people such as Eric Wright.

It required the invention of the VCR and the sudden, unforeseen decline of drive-in movie theaters, creating the space where new American bazaars—the swap meets—would rise. It required the existence of Macola Records, an old-school oddity hanging on in a new-school world, and the persistence of inner-city, word-of-mouth recommendations in an age of mass-media dominance. It apparently even required the existence of animated raisins lip-synching Marvin Gaye records.

This history is a crooked street, crowded with more happy accidents than are comfortable to contemplate. It begins to seem like fate. It begins to seem as if Puffy Combs might have underestimated Dr. Dre when he said, "Dre is to rap what God is to the church."

I Shot a Man in Reno

Here are sample lyrics from yet another song without redeeming social value:

> *Early one morning while makin' the rounds,*
> *I took a shot of cocaine and I shot my baby down*
> *I shot her down then I sent to bed,*
> *I stuck that lovin' forty-four beneath my head.*

The song continues with the protagonist chased and caught by police, then sent to prison. In the last verse, unrepentant to the end, he laments that he "can't forget the day I shot that bad bitch down." He regrets only getting caught.

Rap critics would be right in finding very little social uplift in this song, "Cocaine Blues," recorded by Roy Hogshead. Hogshead, however, was not a rap star. He didn't even have a nickname.

He recorded this song in 1947, and at least five versions of it have been made since. Johnny Cash sang it on his best-selling *Live at Folsom Prison* album in 1968. Nobody protested or even noticed.

Alan Light, founding editor of *Vibe* magazine, an influential hip-hop publication, says he asked Cash about the potential harmful effects of rap lyrics. Cash referred back to the Folsom Prison record, specifically to the title song, which includes the line, "I shot a man in Reno just to watch him die." "You know," Cash said, "I don't recall ever hearing about anyone listening to that song, then going to Reno and shooting somebody."

Neither, as far as anyone knows, has anybody killed a police officer after hearing N.W.A's "F— Tha Police." So why did the FBI send a letter to N.W.A? Alan Light contrasts the reception of rap music with that of other popular arts that sometimes celebrate violence. Some of the best movies ever made—the "Godfather" series, for example—are exceptionally violent, and no one attempts to ban them. Dre points this out when he compares "Straight Outta Compton" to "Pulp Fiction." His songs are dark comedies, he says; he wonders why people don't see that.

"The difference is the level of respect accorded not to the artists but to the audience," Light says. The audience for movies is presumed to know better, to distinguish fact from fiction. The hip-hop audience, presumably, cannot.

Maybe that's the key to understanding the feelings "Straight Outta Compton" aroused, the success it enjoyed and the effects it continues to have. Maybe it disguises its fictional base too well. It's too real. When N.W.A shouted at you, you were compelled to shout back. N.W.A was together in its most potent lineup for less than two years.

Cube, financially frustrated, left before the end of 1989 for a highly successful solo career. He has since become a screenwriter, actor and movie producer, a virtual corporation unto himself. The other four members put out two more N.W.A records, but to considerably less effect.

Dre split acrimoniously from Ruthless in 1992 to help form Death Row Records, where he recorded the second most influential hip-hop album ever, *The Chronic*, which defined the sound of rap for a decade. He has discovered and produced two of the biggest individual stars in hip-hop history—Snoop Dogg and Eminem.

Ren and Yella have had more limited solo careers. Ren is still recording, while Yella has a pornographic movie production business. Eazy continued to run Ruthless and to record until his death from AIDS in 1995. There continues to be talk of a reunion, with Snoop taking Eazy's spot.

Whatever comes of that, N.W.A had more of an effect in less time than probably any figures in pop music history. It's as if Sinatra had become Sinatra by cutting a single record, as if Dylan quit before going electric. N.W.A incited a revolution that redefined hip-hop just as hip-hop was poised to overrun popular culture. As pop has increasingly become the culture that matters, hip-hop has reached deep into mainstream America.

It really was the beginning of the end of life as we knew it. The beginning of the end, it turned out, was accompanied not by heavenly choirs but a rhythm section.

This is not an idle point. Rhythm is a drug. Maybe, like medicine, it should never be consumed in combination with other dangerous substances.

Maybe that's what happened with "Straight Outta Compton." Maybe by combining deadly rhythm with taboo subjects—violence and sex and drugs—it gathered unprecedented strength. Maybe it was unstoppable; just too powerful, too forceful.

Maybe, in other words, it was just too damn good.

LYNN HIRSCHBERG

Who's That Girl?

Amanda Latona has a voice, but she needs a sound. It is January, and she is standing in a small, closetlike recording booth in Midtown Manhattan, where she is recording part of her first album for J Records. Her handlers are still trying to decide what kind of platinum-selling pop sensation she should be. Originally, the idea was that Latona, who is 23, should be Britney Spears. Latona admires Spears, and they almost performed together in Innosense, a girl group from the home of teen pop, Orlando, Fla. Innosense was designed to be an American version of the Spice Girls, but Britney left to pursue her solo career. Lately, Spears's star has fallen; her last record sold disappointingly, and her HBO special revealed that she can't sing live. With 'N Sync and the Backstreet Boys dismantling and Christina Aguilera still recording the follow-up to her 1999 debut, the teen-pop phenomenon seems to have fizzled.

And yet Latona was signed to J Records in February 2001, with the idea that she would be that label's Britney. Of course, she couldn't be an exact replica; the executives at J know that it takes at least a year to record a debut album and that the public's taste—especially that of 12-year-old girls—shifts easily. Latona wasn't signed because she was an original artist. Like Britney, she was an attractive package: poised and pretty, Latona could be poured into various molds and carefully shaped to fit the marketplace. "If her material is right," says Clive Davis, the C.E.O. of J Records, "Amanda could do anything."

Latona is dressed this afternoon, as she usually is, in hip-hugger jeans and high-heeled boots. She steps away from the microphone. "Britney's career was my direction for so long," she says. "I've been waiting *forever* for this." She has long, black hair that is blown straight; her heavy eye makeup, coupled with the fact that she's wearing a lacy fringed shawl tied around her hips and a low-cut top revealing several of her nine tattoos, gives Latona a witchy, "gypsies, tramps and thieves" look. She's the best-looking biker chick you've ever seen.

"In the record business, today is over," says James Diener, Latona's artists-and-repertoire director at J. "We have to figure out what they want to hear tomorrow." Diener, who is sitting on a worn couch in the studio, is the arbiter of all things Amanda. Latona is not a songwriter and doesn't play any instruments, which means that Diener's job is to create a persona for her through the vision of others who do write songs and play instruments. Latona's voice is powerful but not particularly distinctive. Though she can belt out a song, she does not have, say, the gospel shadings of Whitney Houston or the five-octave range of Mariah Carey. Latona's voice is notable, however, in its ability to accommodate different genres. She could perform in a Broadway musical, make a Pepsi jingle work or shout-sing like a rock star. "With some artists, only one style fits them," says Diener, who is wearing a leather porkpie hat and is never far from his cellphone. "Fortunately, Amanda has the looks and the attitude to carry off many different ideas." His phone rings. "Some artists are resistant to ideas," Diener adds, checking the number of the incoming call. "Amanda is not resistant."

Grooming careers is a specialty of J Records' founder, Clive Davis, who has turned artists as diverse as Whitney Houston, Patti Smith and Barry Manilow into stars. (His last protégée, Alicia Keys, won five Grammys last year for her soul album *Songs in A Minor*.) Taking his cues from Davis, Diener is searching for "the right spot for Amanda." It won't be easy; with Britney losing appeal, Diener has to predict what sound will be popular seven months from now— and these days, that seems harder than ever. In Latona, he has a singer who wants to be a star. The question is, which star?

"I'm thinking there might be room now for a cool, young, beautiful girl in the spirit of Shania Twain," Diener says, as Latona leaves the studio to get some water. "Or even more rock, like Pat Benatar from the 80's. Will it help that Amanda's stunning? Absolutely. So will the right marketing campaign. But what's going to capture the audience is her first song. That defines everything. And it *has* to be a hit." Diener pauses. "If she misses," he continues, "with a singer like Amanda, who is not a self-contained artist who writes her own material, it's hard to get another opportunity."

The hit-single formula has worked well at J Records and its parent company, BMG, but has not fueled sales of records industrywide. According to SoundScan, single sales are down 64 percent this year, and album sales have declined 9.8 percent, continuing a downturn that began in 2001. What's more, pop artists no longer inspire loyalty. Alanis Morissette, whose 1995 debut album sold 16 million copies, has stumbled with subsequent efforts. No longer able to rely even on superstars like Mariah Carey or Michael Jackson for a guaranteed hit, record companies are scrambling to engineer fresh talent.

The woes of the record industry are routinely attributed to the consolidation of radio, which makes it hard to break new acts; the growing power of Wal-Mart, which stocks fewer titles than traditional music outlets; and the Internet, which allows consumers to acquire music free. These are big problems considering the industry's thin profit margins. To break even on Latona's record, J must sell 500,000 copies; last year, of the 6,455 albums distributed by major labels, only 112 sold that many.

J is confident, however, that it can succeed with Latona. "We've never had an artist sell less than 150,000," says Tom Corson, J's head of marketing. "To do that, we have to create a place for Amanda to shine. And it comes down to one song."

This afternoon's potential hit single is "Can't Take It Back." After Latona was signed to J, Clive Davis set up a showcase for a group of top songwriters to hear her sing. This event took place the day after the Grammys, in a suite at the Beverly Hills Hotel. These songwriters were not just searching for inspiration; they were trying to define Latona as an artist. If they wrote crossover country, she'd be the new Shania. If they wrote teen pop, Latona would mutate in that direction.

Perhaps it was her dark, good looks and her sexy-rough clothes, but most of the songwriters seemed to imagine Latona as an independent woman who was fed up—an update of Helen Reddy's "I Am Woman" attitude. Latona has never heard of Helen Reddy, nor is she a student of any of the great female vocalists like Aretha Franklin and Tina Turner. But if Latona heard any of them sing, she could approximate their phrasing, just as she can ape Mariah Carey's roller-coaster melismas. Schooled by karaoke and "Star Search," Latona is all about selling the song. And if girl empowerment is what people are buying, Latona will gladly sing the part.

The tough-chick thing is not actually her personality. Latona doesn't smoke, doesn't drink or do drugs and has the peppy cheeriness of a beauty-pageant contestant. (She was, in fact, Miss Junior Florida.) But looks, in her case, dictated the mood of J's songwriters. Meredith Brooks, who had a hit a few years ago with the female-power anthem "Bitch," teamed up with the Nashville songwriter Taylor Rhodes and the L.A.-based Shelly Peikin to write "Can't Take It Back" for Latona. The song's lyrics—"You're crying this time, wish you could rewind/But that's the price that you pay, and that's that/You can't take it back"—wrap around a catchy guitar line and a sing-along chorus of "No-no-no-no-no-NO!" The song is a successful mishmash: there's a short rap in the center, a touch of Shania twang and a few rock growls scattered among the pop hooks. On the first listen, "Can't Take It Back" sounds like a song you already know by heart, one best heard in a car with the windows rolled down.

So far, the plan is for Latona to record 11 songs out of the 75 submitted to J. The rivals for the first single are "I Quit," another female-empowerment anthem ("Loving you's a job I don't need!") and "Better to Be Lonely," which is more teen-oriented but still pushes the independence theme (I don't mind hanging out with me/I like the company"). Another option, "Do You Still," is darker, more narrative in feel. "Do you still find it hard to sleep?" Latona almost whispers. "Do you have everything you need?/I gotta know, baby/Do you still love me?" Each song conjures a slightly different image. "Better to Be Lonely" could be sung by Britney; "Do You Still" is a more mature ballad. "I Quit" and "Can't Take It Back" are savvy mixes of young and old; each is a melange of pop, rock and a touch of country.

Latona returns to the studio. "I'm so excited," she says. She is working with Shep and Kenny, a production team known for fashioning radio-friendly singles. Today they are tweaking the sound of "Can't Take It Back." Their small studio, located on the 24th floor of a nondescript Eighth Avenue office building, is dark, illuminated only by scented candles and computer screens. Those computers contain both a slick instrumental "backing track" and a "demo vocal" that interprets the song the way her producers prefer. "She's pretty open-minded," Shep says. "She'll try anything."

As Latona rhythmically bangs her water bottle against her leg like a tambourine, she listens to a playback of the rap in the center of "Can't Take It Back." She talks-sings along with the demo: "And did you really believe it wouldn't come back to me/That you wouldn't regret it?"

"Omigod, I love that," she says, looking for Kenny's reaction.

"You were pushing the vocal," he says.

Latona nods. She goes back into the tiny booth to rerecord the rap. Shep and Kenny replay their demo, phrase by phrase, and she copies it exactly. "One-take Amanda," Diener says with admiration. "The lyric to the song is *so* Amanda, don't you think? It's very uncompromising." He pauses. "Some artists walk in and they won't budge. Amanda is open to direction."

As Diener listens to Latona, he talks about fine-tuning her image. At J, they are impressed with Shania Twain, who sold 30 million records with a mix of pop, country and soft rock. Latona can look and sound like Twain, so it's easy to link them up, but then again, Twain hit it big five years ago. "She's something like Shania," Clive Davis says, "but not country. Amanda should be rock and pop, but her looks and her eyes and her manner are compelling like a young Shania Twain."

Diener says: "We have to listen to the rest of the music. But from what I'm hearing, 'Can't Take It Back' is a strong contender for the first single."

Coming out of the booth, Latona hears what Diener is saying and kicks her leg high like a Rockette. "Yay!" she exclaims.

A few days later, Latona is having lunch at Beacon, a restaurant picked by Diener for its location near J's offices. "I've eaten here already," she says, staring at the menu. "I'd never seen fish with skin on it before. I was thinking, fish with skin? What do I do with this?" She laughs. "McDonald's is good for me," Latona says, deciding on a steak sandwich. "I'm not a diva—not yet, anyway."

Latona laughs again. She likes tossing around show-biz lingo. She has wanted to be in this world from the age of 10, when she sang "Over the Rainbow" at a karaoke club. "I had vibrato and every-thing," she says. Latona, who was born in 1979, is a TV baby; she grew up not listening to music but watching it. Her mind is geared to the marriage of sound and pictures. As a child in Pittsburgh, she studied the moves of the dancing kids on the *New Mickey Mouse Club* and imitated the Mariah Carey songs she saw on MTV. She has always been focused on being the girl in the video and has never really thought about writing a song. Latona had talent, she was pretty and she was driven, not necessarily in that order.

"I've always wanted to work in entertainment," Latona says. "My family moved to Orlando when I was 15 so I could make it. I would do anything, as long as it was related to show business. I was Snow White, Mary Poppins and Esmeralda at Disney World. I learned four-part a cappella singing to perform with the Hollywood High Tones at Universal Studios. I am *so* not a pageant girl, but I signed up for the Miss Junior Florida contest because I thought it would be good experience. I was so nervous at the contest; I went to the car and said to my mother: 'I'm not going to do this. Are you going to be upset?' She said, 'No, but I'm always going to wonder.' I said, 'Me, too!' So I went back in. I was the only brunette, but I won." Latona pauses. "It was all experience. And that's taken me to now."

Latona picks at her sandwich. She is wearing jeans and a white peasant blouse that sets off her Florida tan. She is an unusual combi-

nation of malleable and confident: she is willing to be coached, but
never seems to doubt that her stardom is a certainty. Perhaps this is
because she has had so much proximity to pop fame in Orlando. She
is friends with the members of 'N Sync and dated A. J. McLean of the
Backstreet Boys for two years. She went to awards events with him,
and she saw the screaming throngs at close range. "Everyone's like,
'Gosh, it's Backstreet!'" she says. "I've known those guys so long. 'N
Sync had a house in Orlando, and I'd just go over there." She laughs.
"I should've taken something. People would pay for that."

When Latona left her girl group, Innosense, she knew she wanted
to be a solo artist. "I didn't know exactly what style, although Britney was really big," she recalls. "But I try not to think about what
other people do, because it's either intimidating or it makes me
competitive or jealous. I think of my career almost like a research
project. I try things and look at what works and what doesn't work."
She pauses. "You never know in this business," she says, sounding a
little weary. "But I've been waiting for this a long time. I want this
album to be right, and if that means six different looks that look
nothing like me, I'll still give it a shot."

She pauses. She likes "Can't Take It Back" and the other three
songs that are in contention for the first single, but she isn't sure
about the Shania makeover. J took test photos a few weeks ago, and
Latona was posed wearing a fluted jacket that was frillier than anything she'd ever pick for herself. The pictures were taken in a bar
with a country-western-honky-tonk ambience, and Latona agreed
to J's plan, although she didn't feel the photos matched her idea of
herself. But since she wasn't certain what alternative to suggest, she
went along. "Maybe they'll work," she says hopefully.

It's a wintry day in mid-March, and Latona and her manager,
Larry Mazer, are walking through Times Square on their way to the
W Hotel, where Latona is staying for the week. Mazer, who is in his
late 40's, wears aviator glasses and is overgrown in an appealing big-
dog sort of way. He has managed musicians from Pat Benatar to
Kiss to Peter Frampton, but always on the downward slopes of their
careers. "I've worked with legendary artists," he says, "but I've been
trying to resuscitate their careers. I always wanted to find that one

artist who could encompass movies, TV and music. When I met Amanda, I thought, Here's the one I waited my whole life for. I hadn't seen her sing or dance, but when you saw her, you just got it."

"Yay!" says Latona, beaming at Mazer. Her looks often have this effect. Mazer, Diener and Davis all circle back to the power of her appearance. It is probable that men in their 30's (and up) will find Latona's almost chiseled features more compelling than teenage girls will, but her looks were a big part of her appeal to J Records. "Amanda is stunning," Davis says. "Her looks create a presence. And her star power comes from that presence."

Today, Latona is bundled into a down parka, and she mostly looks like a tourist. "Look at that," Mazer says, pointing at a billboard of Britney Spears posing for Pepsi. "That'll be your billboard." Latona smiles. Mazer turns her around and points at a bus stuck in traffic. "See that ad on the side of the bus?" he says. "That will be you." He gestures toward the crowds waiting to be on camera for MTV's *Total Request Live*. The studio is visible from the street, and Mazer looks up. "That will be you on 'T.R.L.,'" he says. "They'll be playing your No. 1 song from your platinum album."

"Yay!" Latona says, loving his vision.

They arrive at the hotel and take the elevator to a lounge on the seventh floor. Mazer perches on a tiny stool, while Latona, who takes off her parka to reveal a flowered chiffon blouse, sits on an equally low sofa. They met in October 1998, when Mazer was trying to sign the Backstreet Boys. The group went with another management company instead, but Mazer was fascinated by the Orlando scene. As Seattle was to grunge and Manchester was to house music, Orlando was to teen pop. Justin Timberlake of 'N Sync, Britney Spears and Christina Aguilera all got their starts on *The New Mickey Mouse Club*, which was taped there.

"I auditioned for *The New Mickey Mouse Club* when I was 11," Latona recalls. "I lost out to Christina Aguilera." That was back in Pittsburgh. Latona's parents—her dad is a retired truck driver, her mother currently works the graveyard shift as head of security at Planet Hollywood in Orlando—eventually decided to home-school their two kids and moved the family to Florida so that Amanda and her older brother could pursue entertainment careers. "In Orlando, my brother and I got annual passes to Universal Studios," says Latona, who still lives with her parents. "Everyday we'd watch *Beetlejuice's Graveyard Revue*. It was go great. One day, we're leaving the auditorium after seeing it for the millionth time, and Joey Fatone was standing there. This was before he was in 'N Sync, and he started flirting with me. He said: 'I do this show. I'm Wolfman.' I said, 'Where do you go to do this?'"

Fatone directed Latona to Dr. Phillips High School, which specialized in the performing arts; by age 16, she was the Bride of Frankenstein, in fish nets and a sparkly green bustier, belting out "(You Make Me Feel Like) A Natural Woman." Offstage, she made extra money posing as an Elizabeth Hurley look-alike. Through Fatone, she met Lynn Harless, Justin Timberlake's mother. Fatone suggested that Latona audition for a new girl band, Innosense, which Harless was managing.

"Groups were happening then," Latona recalls. By now dating Backstreet's A. J. McLean ("I love bad boys"), Latona started rehearsing with Innosense. The group went through several stylistic incarnations, which may have prepared Latona for J's persona shopping. First, Innosense was conceived as a Spice Girls clone. ("I was Sexy Spice," Latona sighs. "I'm always the sexy one.") When that seemed redundant, the group went hip-hop. ("I was wearing huge jeans with boxers sticking out the top.") Finally, Innosense opted for elegance. ("They cut our hair, and each girl wore one color," Latona says. "I was blue.")

The group never took off. Latona left the band before an album was recorded. "It's so awesome to be by myself," she says now. "Five girls with their period is not good. We were all like, Give me chocolate."

Mazer laughs. He knows the teen-pop world is fading, but he still views Britney Spears's early career as a template for Latona. "Her single '. . . Baby One More Time' came out in November 1998," he recites from memory. "The single was No. 1 when Jive Records released the album. They shipped 600,000, and it debuted at No. 1. That's how to do it."

Latona nods, as she usually does when Mazer or Diener dream aloud about her possibilities. She believes what they believe: that she will be a star on the order of Mariah Carey or even Madonna. Even though she has never recorded an album, Latona has an online fan base that has followed her for years, primarily because she was the girlfriend of a Backstreet Boy. She claims to have 40 Web sites devoted to her. There is something suspicious, however, about how often the specifically Amanda word "Yay!" appears on these sites; moreover, the "fans" report information that only Latona, J or Mazer would know. "Oh, no," Latona says, when asked if a firm like ElectricArtists controls her sites, as they have with artists like Aguilera. "I can't even go on the sites or the fans go crazy. They can't wait for my record."

This week, Mazer is leaning away from "Can't Take It Back" and toward "Better to Be Lonely" as the first single. Not convinced the teen thing is over, he thinks this song has a broader pop appeal. And he's shying away from the Shania idea. He and Latona have seen the photos, and they don't present her well. Diener, who keeps one of the Shania-style shots on his desk, realizes they make Latona look too old. But he is still enthralled with "Can't Take It Back." As for Latona, she doesn't care which single they pick.

Making the decision is complicated, because the pop audience is shifting before J's eyes. The reigning sound has gone from flirty and soft (Britney) to rebellious and loud, as personified by the 22-year-old singer Pink, whose current hit, "Just Like a Pill," has an angry-girl rock chorus: "Instead of makin' me better, you keep makin' me ill!" (Pink's second album, *Missundaztood*, has gone triple platinum.) J, Mazer and Latona want to pick a song and image that will fit this new pop mood. Latona may have been signed to be J's answer to Britney, but she can just as easily be J's answer to Pink.

Mazer and Latona discuss her first video. "All I know," Latona says, "is that I don't want to show my stomach like everyone else does. I want to relate to the girls as being a cool girl, not someone they are intimidated by."

Mazer agrees. "Look how much more successful Mariah was when she didn't take off her clothes," he says. "Now, it's, like, Just get naked already! Same with Britney. After you start stripping, there's nowhere to go but naked."

Latona pauses. "But Pink has a hot record now, and she shows her stomach," she says. "So does Gwen Stefani." Latona has an idea that she could be a rock singer, something like Stefani, who fronts the group No Doubt.

"Maybe we could be tasteful about it," Mazer allows. Latona is quiet. No one has encouraged her Gwen Stefani idea, although Diener does want her to have a harder edge, especially image-wise. "Mariah is a great artist," Mazer continues, "but she's not managed properly. I'd do it in a second."

Latona punches him softly in the arm. "You have to focus on me!"

"That's right," Mazer says, tossing his arm around Latona's shoulder. "You're going to be the next superstar. Or I'm going to die trying."

In March 2001, J Records holds a meeting at the Equitable Center in Manhattan to introduce new product to executives of its parent company, BMG, which also owns the labels Arista and RCA. In the last decade, the music business has been consolidated into five supercompanies. "The consolidation has made the record business more about business," says J's Tom Corson. "Before, it was more about records."

Today it is announced that EMI, one of the big five, has fired 1,800 employees and canceled the contracts of a quarter of its 1,600 artists in an attempt to save $140 million. This news comes in the wake of the announcement that Mariah Carey—who had signed a reported $100 million contract with EMI label Virgin—has been bought out of the deal for $28 million. Carey's last record, "Glitter," tanked, and she was acting strangely—she had an emotional breakdown. EMI did not want to wait it out; instead of viewing her as an artist, they saw her as a shaky business venture.

Clive Davis takes the stage at the BMG meeting around 9 a.m. He plays the new additions to the J family: a classic Davis mix of old-style rock (Rod Stewart's new record), R&B (Mario, a 15-year-old phenom) and hard rock (Silvertide, which sounds something like Guns N' Roses). For his pop entry, Davis plays all four of Amanda Latona's single contenders.

Unfortunately, Davis doesn't have a photo for Latona. Davis, a stickler for the right pitch, felt the images of her were still wrong. The first shoot, taken when she was just signed to J, has her wearing a torn T-shirt that is spray-painted AMANDA, and her tummy tattoo is fully exposed. The second shoot was the Shania experiment. In those photos, her hair is styled in big country curls. She looks like Loretta Lynn's not-much-younger-sister. Youth is a key factor in the Latona presentation. She has to appeal to the Top 40 demographic, which is 12 to 24. "Clive felt that seeing Amanda in the flesh would be much more effective," Diener says diplomatically.

At 69, Davis is one of the last great music impresarios. At Columbia Records from the 60's until 1973 and then at Arista until 2000, Davis showed his gift for seeing the potential in an artist and brilliantly constructing a career. Worried about Davis's age, BMG forced him out of Arista three years ago, but he persuaded BMG to back him in what he called "an instant major." Davis had just given Arista its biggest hit ever—Carlos Santana's comeback record, "Supernatural," which grossed $350 million— and BMG was embarrassed by the bad press it received for ousting him. BMG handed $160 million to Davis to start J (named after his middle initial) and allowed him to take five artists from Arista with him. One of those artists was Alicia Keys, whom Davis nurtured. "Her album was almost *too* original," Davis says. "But she had it." On the strength of one great single, "Fallin,'" Keys sold five million albums.

Last year, Davis introduced Keys by asking her to perform at his annual Grammy party. He didn't ask Latona this time around. In fact, the two have had little contact. He conveys his thoughts about the singles through Diener, which might suggest he has reservations about Latona. He says, however, that he has expectations of greatness for her. "I don't sign someone," Davis says, "unless I believe they can headline Madison Square Garden. Amanda is an entertainer with range. She's beautiful and lighthearted, yet she has drive and determination." He pauses. "Look, there's *Playhouse 90*, then there's that comedy that will entertain you. You know when you're making one or the other. Both are valid."

It's notable that Davis is more concerned with finding the best songs for Latona than with trying to predict the next musical fashion, like Diener. When Latona auditioned for Davis ("I wore dark Diesel ripped jeans, a black top with 68 spelled out in gold rhinestones and black pointy boots"), his only comment was that her material was subpar. "When you're singing," Latona recalls, "he has his eyes closed, and you can't read him."

Davis signed her on a Thursday, the day after her audition. By Monday, Latona had received her advance. J will not say what the terms were, but going by industry standards, Latona probably received between $50,000 and $100,000. In addition, the label pays for the cost of recording and promoting the album, and when Latona's presence is required for an event, J pays for her airfare and hotel room. But "incidentals," which include food, gym fees, dry cleaning and cabs, are paid by Latona. A standard new-artist contract entitles the record company to six albums with payments (and possible renegotiation) dependent on sales. If an album sells over 500,000, the record usually becomes profitable, and royalties kick in. But after her manager and the producers take their cuts, a 15-percent royalty payment would leave Latona with around $1 a record.

With a singer like Latona, who does not write or play her own songs, a hit single becomes even more crucial than it is with a singer-songwriter. Generally, critics do not embrace pop singers; they are kinder to artists who write (or co-write) their own songs, like Sheryl Crow, Avril Lavigne, Vanessa Carlton and Pink. A pop vocalist's fan base, therefore, evolves entirely from radio play.

Perhaps that's why Davis has been less concerned with Latona's, image and more interested in her songs. As the demos came in, Davis would play them and make suggestions to Latona. "Let the listener into your boudoir," he told her after hearing the demo for "Do You Still," then adding, "You're *angry* and still in love." And with his very experienced ear, Davis would tell Latona that the fourth measure of the second verse needed to be sung faster.

Latona and Mazer have welcomed Davis's suggestions. "Clive builds artists," Mazer says. "And J has the feel of an independent label with the clout of a major. J is new. If you have a hit, you own the place. Unfortunately for us, Alicia Keys got there first. But we'll be next."

Because of Davis, and because Keys was such a phenomenon, J also has clout throughout the world of radio. "People listen to us," says Richard Palmese, head of promotions at J. "Local stations tell me, 'We look forward to records from J.' There's nothing like success to fuel success."

The BMG presentation is followed by lunch at the Judson Grill. Latona introduces herself to reps who will promote her album worldwide. She loves this game: flirting with a promoter from England; chatting about Orlando with BMG's German rep. Latona is good at selling herself. Mazer has told her than an international profile is important, and Latona does what she is told. Besides, she knows that her looks are one of her assets, and there was no visual presented today. "I want you to remember me," she says to a French J executive. "When you hear the song, I don't want you to forget."

Mazer is having fun, too, but he's worried that Davis doesn't see Latona as his next Whitney. He's encouraged, however, that Davis played all four songs today, and that Latona seems to be wowing the foreign reps. Latona is either oblivious or completely unconcerned about whether she's the label favorite. She doesn't mind that Davis is heavily promoting Mario, the 15-year-old R&B singer. Mostly, she is impatient; she wants her single, whichever one it is, to be released. "It seems like I'm always *waiting*," she says. "The longer we wait, the more things change in music. On the radio, the rock thing is the new style. And that's good. That's setting it up for me."

Songs for Latona are still coming in, but the focus is now on songs with "edge." Three tunes by the prolific songwriter Diane Warren have been rejected as too Celine Dion. Pure teen pop is no longer Latona-esque, either. The Shania idea is dead, and Pink is the new standard—Latona's image has to be redesigned along that harsher silhouette. So J is pushing Latona in a rock direction, which means "Better to Be Lonely" is definitely out—and "Can't Take It Back," which mixes pop with rock, is the likely single again. "It has the right mix," Diener says. "But we're still getting music in. Clive wants to hear everything, and then he'll decide."

The J Records offices on Fifth Avenue look as if they were designed by NASA. Sliding glass doors open onto a raised granite-floored reception area where a large, silent television plays a loop of videos from J recording artists like the rapper Busta Rhymes and the boy band O-Town. Tom Corson, the marketing director, has a small corner office decorated with the essentials (computer, phone, piles of CD's). "My job," Corson says on a May afternoon, "is to differentiate our artists. Many acts have a close demographic: what makes one boy band different from another? Why is Busta Rhymes different from Jay-Z? My job is to clarify those subtle distinctions for the consumer." Corson smiles. "But nothing differentiates an artist like a hit track. That's what Amanda needs."

To help land Amanda a hit, Corson and J have certain strategies. When J picks a single, it will turn the record over to its promotion department, headed by Palmese, who is a veteran of the music business. "Getting on the radio is like mounting a military campaign," he says. "The first thing I do, a month or so before the record comes out, is get it in the hands of radio program directors across the country. We try to identify who our 'heroes' are, the program directors who like the song enough to step out and add it to their rotation."

Palmese's strategy with Latona is to start pitching her record to "Top 40-Adult" stations with a demographic of 25–54. "Amanda's true audience is probably younger," Palmese says, "and we'll go there next. But Vanessa Carlton, Avril Lavigne—they are on Top 40-Adult, and it's broadened their audience. Radio wants the 18–24 audience. That's where the money is. If a record just appeals to teens, you'll only hear the song between 7 and 11 at night, not when there's prime advertising. When you're played on both teen Top 40 and Top 40-Adult, you get the daughters and the moms."

Radio is tricky. Clear Channel Communications, which owns 1,200 stations, carefully tests songs before adding them to its nationwide playlist. Once Clear Channel samples a song on the air 150–200 times ("You have to make sure they don't play it late at night when no one can hear it," Palmese warns), they conduct "call out" research. A "call out" consists of phoning listeners at random and playing them 10 seconds of a song; if enough callers recognize it and express enthusiasm, the song is added to the playlist. "Call-out has become dominant," Palmese says. "Very few program directors rotate records by gut. The hardest part of promotion is getting a record played."

The looming presence of Clive Davis will help Palmese sell Latona. J is also sending Latona on the road to meet program directors. "Radio is so competitive," Palmese says. "And Amanda is so charming. She has a passion for her music. It gives the program directors a visual on her, and it sends a message that the company is serious about this artist." Recently, the singer Nelly Furtado had great success with this strategy. After visiting radio stations coast to coast, she landed a top 10 hit, "I'm Like a Bird."

Palmese has a staff of 10 at J, and he also employs at least 10 independent promoters who work the entire country. "I know that's controversial," he says. Recent reports claim that independent promoters pay radio stations to add new songs to their playlists. These "indie" promoters are paid by record companies with an upfront fee reportedly between $100,000 and $400,000; the promoter then sends the record company a weekly bill for every song added to a playlist. It can cost anywhere from $250,000 to $1 million to get a single on Top 40 radio.

Radio stations say that they are paid not for playing the song but for "notifying" the promoter that a song has been added to the playlist. The government may soon crack down on "pay for play," but for now the practice, although it smacks of payola, is standard throughout the industry. "For a hit song to find its way," Palmese says, "you have to have a great machine in place."

This week, James Diener got the final mix of "Can't Take It Back." Mike Shipley, who has mixed hit records for Aerosmith and Shania Twain, "sweetened" the sound of the original recording. The music is brighter now, and Latona's voice sounds sultry and accessible. It's got a hook that sticks in your head. And unlike the other Latona contenders, it bridges a lot of musical genres.

"Clive likes 'Can't Take It Back,'" Diener says, sitting in his even smaller office down the hall from Corson's. Diener's cell is dominated by *Jaws* paraphernalia ("It's the perfect movie") and his own pile of CD's.

"I want to play you this," he says. He puts on the new mix of "I Quit," which sounds more like a rock song. Latona's voice has been amped and seems to have more sass. "I *love* this," Diener says, "but I'm feeling 'Can't Take It Back' is it."

Latona likes both tracks. She's still fine with any of the top four candidates. She has only three more songs to record. She trusts J to make the right choice, although she's clearer now on not looking or sounding too soft. The success of Pink and Avril Lavigne has made clear the need for an image that's less bubblegum.

"I like 'Can't Take It Back,'" she says on the phone from Los Angeles. "But I love this new song." Latona is about to record the Joan Jett classic "I Hate Myself for Loving You." It's something of a departure—a straight-ahead rocker. "At first," Latona says, "I didn't want to be rock. When I think of rock, I think of heavy metal. I said, what about pop with a lot of guitars? But my clothes have always been rock. And I love this song." She pauses. "I think it could be the single!"

For the first time in the year since she has been signed to J, Latona seems to be shaping her own image. Suddenly, she's no longer a would-be teen dream—she's a rock chick. Until recently, Latona only knew the teen-pop world. When she works out at the gym, she listens to 'N Sync (or to herself). Latona doesn't know music—she had no idea, for instance, that "(You Make Me Feel Like) A Natural Woman" was recorded by Aretha Franklin when she sang it every night in *Beetlejuice's Graveyard Revue*. She also didn't know that Aretha Franklin famously worked with Clive Davis. "I was surprised Amanda chose that song for her audition," Davis recalls. "But she didn't know the history. That doesn't mean she can't sing. We know the history. The important thing is that Amanda Latona has a voice."

Latona may not be a strategic thinker, but she is keenly aware of the power of media. She scrutinizes the images she sees in teen

magazines and on MTV—not to mention her own. "That first picture of me with 'Amanda' in spray paint *really* doesn't work," she
says now, even though she styled herself in that picture, bare stomach and all. "The second shoot didn't work, either. That just wasn't
my look. The next shoot will be better. I'm like, YAY! I finally get to
look like myself!" Of course, Latona remains willing to adopt virtually any persona that would lead to stardom. "I want to be a household word in every household," she says, rather sweetly.

Now that Pink and Avril Lavigne have proved that a tougher (but
sensitive) look and sound is the way, Latona knows how to proceed.
Even if she didn't like their music, success makes sense to her.

"People are fickle," Latona says. "And everyone changes their
mind. That's the hard part." She pauses. "I do think the rock thing is
the new style, though," she says again. "Which is good."

"Listen to this!" Latona is saying. It's early June, and she has just
run up to her room at the W Hotel in Midtown to get her CD
Walkman and the final version of "I Hate Myself for Loving You."
She looks different. She has cut her hair in a layered 70's-style shag,
and although she's wearing her trademark jeans and boots, Latona
has streamlined her look. She still has a gray cloud of makeup above
each eye, but her style today is less Orlando and more bohemian
chic.

"Dude, listen to this!" Latona repeats, sitting on a low, armless
chair. She puts the CD in the machine. "I was playing this in the
room, singing to myself," Latona says, "and they knocked on my
door and said, 'Could you turn your music down?'" She laughs.
"Clive loves this song. We're thinking of making it the first single."

She presses play, putting her head next to mine as we both listen
through the tiny headphones. It's a classic heavy-guitar rock song
with a sing-along chorus: "I wanna walk but I run back to you, that's
why/I hate myself for loving you!"

Basic, but kind of great. Keith Naftaly, another executive at J,
suggested the song for Latona. She's singing along now, kicking her
heel into the chair to mark the beat. "YEAH!" she shouts with herself, "I HATE MYSELF FOR LOVING YOU!"

The song ends, and Latona sort of swoons. "Dude, I am so into it," she says. This "dude" thing is also new—I've never heard her say it before. "This is the most rock of any of the songs I've done," she continues. "Larry says it's a Grammy winner for best pop-rock vocal. We have to get the song out so we can win the Grammy."

She laughs, but you know she has that awards-show visual in her brain. "Dude, I can perfectly see the video for this song. All of my ex-boyfriends line up, and it says ex, ex, ex. It would be cool to duplicate what my ex-boyfriends look like. There'd be a blond and one with a goatee to look like A. J. In the video, I see myself as mad but horny."

"I Hate Myself for Loving You" seems to have crystallized something for Latona. She's suddenly livelier, more self-assured and direct in her opinions. She now *loves* this rock idea. Pink has fully replaced Britney as the one to watch. That direction is music with bite. And Latona isn't going to miss her moment.

"I recorded a Richard Marx song in Nashville," she says. "And it didn't work. I didn't feel it. The lyric was, 'I'm falling in love from my head to my heels.' Dude, I would never say that. The word 'heels' cannot be used in a song. It's just not cool."

Yesterday Latona went shopping with a stylist from 10 a.m. to 8 p.m. to buy clothes for her album-cover shoot, the photo that will set her new image. They worked their way from SoHo to Barneys; Latona had sent ahead photos clipped from magazines that had the look she wanted to capture. "I was very open," she says, "but dude, the first two shoots didn't work. I want to be able to look at the pictures we take this weekend and say: 'Oh, I get it. *She sings rock.*'"

They picked out jeans at Diesel, a floaty pink silk dress by Ann Demeulemeester at Barneys, a pair of suede boots and 30 or so other pieces. Latona is meeting with hair and makeup people today, and she's going to show them Polaroids that she took of herself. She wants them to see how she looks when she goes out to a club. "Girls always come up to me and say, 'Dude, I love your style,'" she says. The first two photo shoots now considered failures, this weekend's shoot will be crucial. It's hoped that Latona will be revealed to be a genetic hybrid of Chrissie Hynde and Elizabeth Hurley. "I think

I've finally come up with the style I'm looking for," she says. "Do you want to hear the song again?" Latona slaps the side of her chair and starts to sing.

"You can't start a career with a remake," says James Diener the very next day. "A new artist should have original material." Latona didn't really protest. She did tell Diener that she hadn't heard the Joan Jett song before and that nobody else her age (or younger) would recall it, but Diener dismissed this argument. Clive Davis said he loved "I Hate Myself for Loving You" but felt they should stick with "Can't Take It Back" as the first single. "It's decided," Diener says. "'Can't Take It Back' will hit Top 40 radio on Aug. 5."

Latona was a little disappointed, but her belief in the wisdom of J is firm. "Can't Take It Back" still fits the tough-girl, Pink-manqué strategy, and it also appeals to a wider musical base than a straight-ahead rock song like "I Hate Myself for Loving You," which may be a little too hard for a first single. Latona preferred the full-out rock-chick approach, but "Can't Take It Back" also sounds like a hit to her.

It doesn't hurt that even before the song hits the airwaves, Karen Lamberton, who looks for TV and film opportunities for J artists, has sold "Can't Take It Back" to the movies. *Slap Her, She's French* is a teen comedy starring Piper Perabo, and Latona's song will close the film. J has also booked Latona on the YM Fashion and Music Explosion Tour. Starting in late July, she'll be performing at five malls from Texas to Minnesota. Then there's the radio-station tour. "That'll be fun," Latona says. "I'll say, 'C'mon dude, play my song!'"

Five days before Latona's album-cover shoot in June, the original incarnation of *Beetlejuice's Graveyard Revue* ended its 10-year run at Universal Studios. "They had a party," Latona says, sounding uncharacteristically forlorn. "Joey Fatone was there and all the casts from the last decade. It was the end of an era, the end of a particular time in Orlando."

Even the young can feel old, and Latona suddenly turns philo-sophical. "I want to create something like that show," she says. "I want my album to be a classic." She pauses. "That's why these new pictures are so important."

The third shoot is a success. They layered her hair and added some highlights; they toned down her makeup and let her freckles shine. "There was a lot of pressure," says Alli Truch, the art director of J. "For a month I heard, *This has to be fantastic.* I knew from when we signed Amanda it was going to take a lot of time to make her who she will be. These photos had to be timeless—not Britney or Christina. We didn't want the image to say Orlando or teen pop. That's over."

The photos are beautiful—Latona looks fresh and sophisticated, which is far from where she began. The main publicity photo that J chose is not the most glamorous, however. Latona looks tomboyish, like a prettier Patti Smith. Her look is almost insolent, but somehow wounded. It's a moody pose, far from the sunny Shania shoot and the mall-girl Orlando photos. Some at J fear that she may not look young enough in the photos and that the leather bra she wears in some is a little revealing, but overall, the pictures set the right tone. "Dude, I look like a star," Latona says, with mock grandeur. "I think I'm getting the hang of this thing."

J doesn't yet have a release date for Latona's album, however. The number of albums shipped will be dependent on the single's radio success. If "Can't Take It Back" fails, J will release the album with considerably less fanfare. "They're going to wait until the single goes Top 10," Latona says matter-of-factly. "If you want to ship a high volume of albums, you have to wait until the single is Top 10. So that's the plan."

"She said that?" Diener exclaims when told this. "Well, I'm glad she's optimistic." He laughs softly. "That Amanda," he says. "She's a quick study. Children grow up so quickly these days."

PAUL TOUGH

City Still Breathing: Listening to the Weakerthans

The bar downstairs at Wellington's on Albert Street in Winnipeg wears its history on the walls. It has a sunken dance floor surrounded by glowing purple neon tubes from the club's disco days. The fake spiderwebs draped over the wrought-iron chandelier near the bar are from when it was a goth place. Before that, twenty years ago, Wellington's was where local punk bands played; there are probably still some holes in the walls from back then.

On the February night I visited, Winnipeg was in the middle of a mild spell, only a few degrees below zero outside; T-shirt weather for Winnipeg. I was sitting at a square black table with a square black ashtray on top of it, watching a band go through their sound check. Behind me the bartenders were setting up, unloading cases of beer and jamming quick-pour nozzles into bottles of whisky and rum.

There were four people on stage, four white men in their late twenties and early thirties playing electric guitar and bass and drums. The shortest and skinniest one was standing in the middle, in front of a microphone, a guitar strapped around his neck. He was wearing a black T-shirt and jeans rolled up at the bottom in a single wide fold, like a farmer. His hair was dyed blond, or at least part of it was, and he had a smile on his face that sometimes seemed confident and sometimes seemed nervous. His name, I knew from reading the back of the cd, was John K. Samson, and the band was called the Weakerthans.

At the back of the room the sound guy adjusted some knobs and the band launched into a song called "Left and leaving." It starts with a finger-picked guitar and a single voice singing:

> *My city's still breathing*
> *(but barely, it's true)*
> *through buildings*
> *gone missing like teeth.*

Back in my tiny apartment in New York City, those lyrics are written in ballpoint pen on a scrap of yellow lined paper and stuck to the side of my refrigerator with a souvenir magnet of the World Trade Center. When I wrote them down and magneted them up last fall, it was because they felt to me as though they were about New York during its season of loss, though even then I knew that they were not; they were about Winnipeg. Every Weakerthans song is about Winnipeg.

Winnipeg matters to me because my sister lives there. As I have moved from city to city and job to job over the last decade, she has stayed put, a minister and a homeowner, drilling roots down into the permafrost. Listening to the Weakerthans in my apartment last winter, I found myself wanting to visit. Now I wasn't certain, sitting at my table watching the band warm up, whether I was in Winnipeg because of the Weakerthans, or whether I cared about the Weakerthans because I care about Winnipeg. But I knew I was trying to figure something out about home: what it means to love or hate where you live, how to write about a place, how to claim a home with words.

Toward the end of my Winnipeg trip, I came across this passage in a book by Joan Didion:

Certain places seem to exist mainly because someone has written about them. Kilimanjaro belongs to Ernest Hemingway.

Oxford, Mississippi, belongs to William Faulkner, and one hot July week in Oxford I was moved to spend an afternoon walking the graveyard looking for his stone, a kind of courtesy call on the owner of the property. A place belongs forever to whoever claims it hardest, remembers it most obsessively, wrenches it from itself, shapes it, renders it, loves it so radically that he remakes it in his own image.

Reading that, I wondered if my visit to Wellington's was a courtesy call, too, though the owner of this property is still alive: in fact, John Samson is only twenty-nine. When the sound check was over, I introduced myself and asked if he had a moment to talk about Winnipeg and the Weakerthans and he said, all right, let me just get a light. We found a table in a back room that looked as though it dated from yet another Wellington's incarnation: it had mirrors and purple neon lights just like the dance floor, but all along the walls, up high near the ceiling, there were vaguely erotic drawings of cartoon cats with large breasts, wearing space suits.

I first heard the Weakerthans in the fall of 1999, when Dave Bidini, the Toronto author and musician, gave me a copy of *Fallow*, their first cd. But I didn't get excited about them until last year, after my friend Craig put "Left and leaving" on a cd he burned and sent me. I think the song meant something similar to Craig, a Canadian living in London, and to me, a Canadian living then in San Francisco and now in New York: it's about the pull of home, and its equivalent push: about leaving and coming back and deciding to stay away. I listened to it over and over.

My enthusiasm quickly snowballed, the type of immersive musical attachment that had happened to me a dozen times before—with Prince, Bob Dylan, Jane's Addiction, Lyle Lovett—but not for several long, vacant years: the kind of attachment where you play someone's records into the ground, hunt record stores for obscure eps, search lyric sheets for hidden clues. So it felt familiar, falling in love with the Weakerthans, although they are a band that almost no one I know has ever heard of, a band that measures its record sales in tens of thousands, not millions, a band from Winnipeg.

The word Winnipeg never appears anywhere in the songs on the Weakerthans' two albums, but the idea and the fact of the place infects them. The lyrics for *Fallow* are printed over a faint, close-up map of the city (you can make out the corner where my sister used to live, at Wolseley and Evanson, under "Diagnosis"); there's the "all night restaurant, North Kildonan" where "lukewarm coffee tastes like soap"; there are "clocks stopped at the corner of Albert St.,"; there's the Disraeli Bridge, which takes you over the Red River to East Kildonan and which also ends up, in the song "Fallow," right here:

> *Out under the Disraeli,*
> *with rusty train track ties,*
> *we'll carve new streets and sidewalks,*
> *a city for small lives,*
> *and say that we'll stay for one more year.*

Images of revision and reconstruction—of tearing up streets and pulling down buildings and planting a bomb at city hall and spray-painting construction sites—are all over John Samson's lyrics. It's as if he's saying that the only way to stay sane and stay put in a frozen, isolated, broken-down city like Winnipeg is to re-imagine it, to rip it up and put it back together in your head.

Two nights before the Wellington's show I had gone with my friend Miriam Toews to another Weakerthans concert. That week, at the end of February, was the band's fifth anniversary, and they were celebrating by playing four concerts on four consecutive nights at four different clubs. Miriam and I went to the first concert, at the Royal Albert Arms Hotel—which Dave Bidini in his book calls "the grotty, cursed Royal Albert Arms"—just a few doors down Albert Street from Wellington's, past a tattoo parlour and a Chinese restaurant. It was the night that the women's hockey team won the gold medal in Salt Lake City and Miriam and I waited for the concert to start in a coffee shop around the corner and talked about that idea of remaking and re-imagining a city. The lyric that was buzzing in my head that night was from a song called "This is a fire door never leave open," a song, like so many

Weakerthans songs, about memory and leaving and childhood and silence (it talks about "forty years of failing to describe a feeling," which Miriam says is a very Winnipeg kind of experience). It's a loud, fast, guitar-heavy song, and this is how it ends:

> *And I love this place;*
> *The enormous sky,*
> *And the faces, hand*
> *That I'm haunted by,*
> *So why*
> *Can't I forgive these buildings,*
> *These frameworks labeled "Home"?*

Miriam and I had talked about the enormous Manitoba sky, its epic flatness, and how you can love a city and resent its buildings, but I still didn't get what those lyrics meant, exactly. So after Samson found a match and started smoking his cigarette and we sat down under the pornographic cartoon characters in the black light of the Wellington's back room, that's what I asked him about.

"That's one of those lines that I thought I understood when I first wrote it," he said. "But I keep changing my understanding of it."

He sat and thought for a few long seconds and then he started telling me a story about writing another song, "Left and leaving," the one with the buildings that have gone missing like teeth.

"I used to live two doors down from here, on Albert Street," he said. "I had been away on tour and I came home and went up to my apartment, which at the time was just a big room with a bed in it. I was getting back after six weeks of travelling around and I was feeling really disconnected to what my place was here, and therefore what my place was anywhere in the world.

"And I went out for a walk. It was a summer evening. I walked down Albert Street and across Exchange Park. And as I reached the far side of the park—the site of a huge amount of history, the place where the General Strike gathered in 1919—there was a hotel that was burning to the ground. People were just standing around watching. I kept trying to picture what the building had looked like.

I couldn't. It suddenly struck me that I had never paid any attention to this building, but that I was profoundly sad that it was burning down.

"And I think that that relates a lot to this place. It's quite a meta—"

He stopped himself, uncertain whether he really wanted to use the word "metaphor" in the back room of Wellington's. After a second he decided to press on.

"It is a metaphor for this place. Maybe a crude one. But it's that idea that there are stories and there are people in my life here that are like that building. I think it's the point of what we do: to try to express those stories and to make the lives of those people relevant if we can. That ties directly into the idea of loving this place and not being able to forgive the buildings. Because they are imbued with such history."

One of my favourite Weakerthans songs is about politics, or maybe about the limitations of politics. It's called "Pamphleteer" and it's written from the point of view of a weary, discontented activist standing on a street corner at rush hour, handing out leaflets. The song borrows nicely from the literature of the left; it ends with the line "A spectre's haunting Albert Street," echoing the first line of the Communist Manifesto: "A spectre is haunting Europe." And it quotes from the protest hymn "Solidary Forever," like this:

> Sing "Oh what force on earth could be
> Weaker than the feeble strength Of one"
> like me remembering The way it could have
> been.

The quote is from "Solidary Forever"—there's a footnote in the lyric sheet that says so—but what I love about it is the way that the lyrics subvert the anthem, so that it's no longer about political struggle but about lost love.

I had to resist the urge to ask him for explanations of any more songs. When you've been listening to Weakerthans songs as much as I have, all you want John Samson to do, if you're sitting down with him, is decode his lyrics, which tend to be allusive and elusive and elliptical, full of unexplained images of dead men's neckties and snow fences and a puke-green sofa—but presumably he's written them elliptically for a reason.

I had just read an article, in fact, about Neil Young at a taping of the VH–1 show *Storytellers*, with Crosby, Stills and Nash. The idea of the show is that songwriters tell the stories behind their best-known songs. In the article, Neil Young is pacing the halls of VH–1 like a caged animal, and he says, "I thought the song was supposed to tell the story."

Neil Young is from Winnipeg, too. There's something muted in the songs of both men, though maybe it's more implicit in Neil Young's songs and more explicit in John Samson's: the ache of silence and miscommunication, of leaving things unsaid and then regretting it later. It's that "forty years of failing to describe a feeling" that Miriam likes; in another song, relying "a bit too heavily on alcohol and irony"; in others, references to letters that aren't sent and lists of things you meant to say.

An unmistakable feeling of deep-seated civic regret flowed through my conversations with both Miriam and John: a sense that when you live in Winnipeg, the city's entire twentieth-century history is present in every moment, from its golden age of promise and prosperity as the railway-and-wheat hub of a growing nation, to its current status as a misplaced and impoverished city, off the radar, what Miriam calls "the coldest nowhere nothing mosquito-ridden barren bleak and desolate city in the world—the punchline of every joke about hellholes."

There's something magical about a city in decline. Especially in moneyed times like these on a moneyed continent like this one, cities like Edmonton and Buffalo and Pittsburgh and Winnipeg feel protected from a certain type of urban degradation: the erasure that goes along with giant malls and theme restaurants and off-ramps and luxury boxes at baseball stadiums, even as those crumbling cities embody an apparently harsher, more tangible decline.

What is hopeful about those cities is that new and original art and ideas often grow in them in unexpected ways. "There is a lot of

potential in places that are removed from the centre of power,"
Samson said. "I have this feeling that that's where a lot of interesting
things are going to emerge—things that have the potential not to be
sullied or defeated as soon as they're created. They can be ignored
for a while. They can hover in between." In between success and
failure, I guess he meant; fame and oblivion.

At the same time, there is a small-town resentment that often gets
expressed as a complicated kind of self-loathing. When I got to Winnipeg the day before the first Weakerthans show, I had picked up a
few local newspapers to see if I could read anything about the concerts or the band, since I really didn't know the first thing about
them except for what was on the CD. There were a few articles—a
photo of the band appeared on the cover of the local weekly, and
there was an interview on the arts page of the *Winnipeg Free Press*—
and even though the articles were generally enthusiastic, there was
an odd backhandedness to some of the compliments, a subtle accusation that maybe the band was getting a bit too big for its britches,
doing four straight days' worth of shows. "I can't help wondering if
this February carnival of sorts is really just grandstanding—a way of
demonstrating a measure of greatness by seeing how much the band
can take on, and get away with," the rock music columnist, James
Turner, wrote in *Uptown*. In every interview I read, the band down-
played the importance of this four-concert home stand: In the *Winnipeg Sun*, Samson described the shows as "some little project,
something fun to do in February"; in *Uptown*, he said they were "not
a big deal" and insisted, "We're just doing this for kicks, man."

When I asked Samson about those interviews, he laughed right
away and nodded his head. Of course it was shtick, he said. "That's
playing the Winnipeg press game. There's a self-deprecation inher-
ent in anything you do here. You can't just go out and say, 'We're
fucking awesome.' That's one of the things that I find beautiful about
art and music in bigger cities. You're allowed to have a persona there.
I would never be able to have a persona here. I'm a hayseed."

I asked him if he ever thought about leaving Winnipeg, and he
answered, "Of course. I've always had the urge to leave. I still have
it. In fact, it's become more a part of me than an urge. It's a fact of

who I am now, living here, that I don't want to be here all the time, because sometimes it's not a great place to live. It is a small town and it has the mentality of a small town, but with all the social and economic problems of a bigger city."

It's the deepest relationship you can have with a place, I think: hating it and staying. It's the flip side of officially sanctioned civic pride—something I'd seen plenty of, living in Toronto—which always feels lightweight, defensive, insubstantial: a cheap substitute for a real relationship with a place. Samson may think about leaving, but that only makes him more at home here: everyone in Winnipeg thinks about leaving, all the time.

A few hours later, the Weakerthans took the stage again. Wellington's was sold out and pretty packed, but even packed it only held three hundred people, tops. The band started off by playing every song on *Fallow*, in order, which was an interesting idea, but which had the effect of subduing the crowd a bit; we wanted to hear the band's more recent songs.

After *Fallow* they left the stage for a while, and then came back for an encore. They passed around a bottle of fifth-anniversary champagne to the fans up front and they handed out curling trophies to various people who had helped the band—the director of their video, the two young girls who do all their postering—and then they started to play some new songs. I was thinking about Winnipeg as I listened, of course, because of the band but also because I was leaving the next day to go back to New York. I was thinking of something Neil Young says at the beginning of "Journey Through the Past," his song about leaving Winnipeg and moving to the United States: "This is a song about a home." And I was thinking about a quotation by Alden Nowlan, the New Brunswick poet, that the Weakerthans use as an epigraph in the "Left and leaving" lyric booklet:

for those who belong nowhere and for those who belong to one place too much to belong anywhere else.

From the stage, John Samson said he wanted to play something brand new, a song called "One Great City!" after the slogan adopted by Winnipeg a couple of years ago, which still appears on highway signs as you approach, always with exclamation point included. The song was arranged for a single guitar, a single voice, and handclaps, and it started out with an image of a dollar store where

The clerk is closing up and counting loonies. She's trying not to say I hate Winnipeg.

Weakerthans songs don't usually have a chorus, but this one did: "I hate Winnipeg." The song alternated between the chorus and these little vignettes—the golden statue that sits on top of the provincial legislature looking out over the city, "watching the north end die"; a car stalled in the turning lane in front of you—and each time the chorus recurred, more of the audience would join in, and we'd sing it louder and louder each time. By the time we got to

The Guess Who sucked The Jets are lousy anyway.

"I hate Winnipeg" was practically a shout.

After a few more new songs the band left the stage and I thought they were gone for good, but then they came out one last time and made my day by playing "Pamphleteer" and then ending with "This is a fire door never leave open," and when they sang about loving this place and the enormous sky I knew what they meant, and when they got to wondering why they couldn't forgive these buildings, these frameworks labeled "Home," I thought I might know what they meant by that, too.

After the concert I said goodbye to John, who apologized for playing so long, and then Miriam and her husband Cassady drove me home in their minivan, and they apologized for owning a minivan. A few hours later, at the airport, I felt the wind and realized that it had finally turned cold, seriously cold, Winnipeg cold, the kind of cold I couldn't take for more than a few days, let alone months. It was 6 a.m. and pitch black. I hugged my sister in the wind and waved as she drove away, back into the frozen night of her hometown, and then I walked into the terminal and flew south to mine.

CHUCK KLOSTERMAN

Viva Morrissey!

Some people feel nervous around Cruz Rubio. That's unfair, but it's true. He's a badass: The dude is 20 years old, he's from East Los Angeles, the sleeves are ripped off his flannel shirt, and he looks like an extra from the movie *Colors*. I have no doubt whatsoever that he could kick the shit out of me. But I am not nervous around Cruz Rubio. I am not nervous, because he is telling me how Morrissey makes him weep.

"Some nights I lay in my bedroom and I listen to 'There Is a Light That Never Goes Out,' and I cry," he tells me. "I cry and cry and cry. I cry like a little bitch, man."

Perhaps you are wondering what a cut-like-marble Latino could possibly see in a quintessentially British, marvelously effeminate white guy best known for reading Oscar Wilde and wearing his espoused asexuality on his sweater sleeve. Frankly, there's no concrete answer to that question. But Cruz Rubio is definitely seeing *something*, because he is not the exception; within the walls of the sixth annual Smiths/Morrissey convention in Hollywood's Palace theater, he is the rule.

For two days in April, fans of a disbanded Mancunian pop group and its forgotten frontman smoked clove cigarettes, picked over U.K. bootlegs, and danced to "Hairdresser on Fire" like dehydrated Helen Kellers, which is how people at Smiths conventions are supposed to behave. Yet these fans are not the glowering white semi-goths you'd except to encounter; this scene looks like a 1958 sock hop in Mexico City. To argue that Morrissey's contemporary audience skews Hispanic would be inaccurate; Morrissey's contemporary audience *is* Hispanic, at least in L.A. Of the 1,400 people at this year's convention, at least 75 percent of the ticket buyers—and virtually all under 20—were Latino. For reasons that may never be completely understood, teenage Hispanics tend to be the only people who still care about Manchester's saddest sack. And they care a lot.

"He speaks to us, man. As Latinos. He addresses us personally," Rubio explains. "His music fits our lifestyle. I mean, where was the one place Morrissey always said he was dying to tour? It was Mexico, man. That's where his heart is."

Moments later, 23-year-old construction worker Albert Velazquez expresses a nearly identical sentiment. "The last time I saw him live, he looked into the audience and said, 'I wish I had been born Mexican, but it's too late now.' Those were his exact words. And the crowd just exploded. He loves the Mexican culture, and he understands what we go through."

Velazquez is 235 pounds and 6'5" (6'8" if you include his pompadour). He plans to celebrate Morrissey's birthday on May 22; everybody at this convention knows that date. Velazquez also tells me he's going to drink a few Coronas that afternoon, because that's Morrissey's favorite beer. Everyone seems to know that, too. Morrissey once sang that we must look to Los Angeles for the language we use, because London is dead. And so it is: The question is no longer "How soon is now?"; the question is "*¿Es realmente tan extraño?*"

The fact that the Smiths have sustained a cult following 15 years after their demise is understandable. They were a band built for the darkly obsessive: In a decade categorized by excess, the Smiths—and especially their sexually baffling frontman—were introspective, iconoclastic, and alienated. There weren't "casual" Smiths fans in the America of 1986; it was an all-or-nothing equation. Though superstars in the U.K., the Smiths were fringe interlopers in the U.S.—the well-read rock gods for the fey underground. That being the case, it isn't surprising to discover there's been a Smiths/"Moz" convention in Los Angeles every year since 1997. It's easy to imagine 30-year-old ex-wallflowers digging out their black turtlenecks and reminiscing about how *The Queen is Dead* convinced them not to hang themselves while everyone else was at the prom. Generally, that's who rock conventions appeal to—aging superfans embracing nostalgia.

That's why *this* Smiths convention is so startling. Those predictably pasty people don't show up (at least not in significant numbers). For the kids who live between the 5 and 10 highways in East L.A., this is a contemporary event, even though Morrissey hasn't released a solo album in five years. These new Morrissey fans— these Latino "neo-Mozzers"—see him as a completely relevant artist. Moreover, their interest goes against the grain of traditional Caucasian Moz fans; these kids like Morrissey's solo material as much as his work with the Smiths, and almost nobody here gives a damn about Johnny Marr (the guitarist originally perceived as the Smiths' true genius). Nobody even seems to care about Britpop in general. The focus is almost singularly on the 43-year-old Steven P. Morrissey and his infinite sadness.

"Morrissey's family emigrated to England from Ireland, and they were kind of socially segregated from the rest of the country," says Gloria Antunez, a 23-year-old junior high teacher who uses Morrissey lyrics as a teaching tool in her English class, notably "Reader Meet Author" from 1995's *Southpaw Grammar.* "That's very similar to the Latino experience here in Los Angeles. We see things within his songs that we can particularly relate to. He sings about loneliness. He sings about solitude. Those are things any minority group can relate to."

The impact of Morrissey's immigration experience is the most widespread hypothesis for why he's been embraced by Mexican-Americans, but that theory has flaws. He's never mentioned or implied it in any of his songs, and it seems the majority of Latino neo-Mozzers have never even considered the significance of that connection. "I don't think it has anything to do with immigration," says Kristin Kaiser, a 22-year-old who looks like a bookish Penélope

Cruz. "The greasers are into him because they completely associate Morrissey with rockabilly, which pisses off some of the original Smiths fans," explains Kaiser's friend Michelle Perez. "But what pisses me off more is when people try to say the 'pomp' evolved from Morrissey. I don't think so, man."

Perez is referring to the second most common explanation for the Hispanic Moz revival—that Morrissey's flirtation with rockabilly invokes Latino "greaser" culture, à la the 1950s of James Dean and Ritchie Valens, Morrissey hired rockabilly musicians for 1992's *Your Arsenal*; though it's impossible to quantify, one suspects this movement started in earnest sometime after the release of that album.

It's also possible that Morrissey's L.A. address amplifies his local profile, although he's infamously reclusive and never attends these conventions. (Despite repeated attempts on *Spin*'s part, Morrissey couldn't be reached for this piece.) But maybe it's much simpler than that. Maybe it's just that Latino kids still hear what conflicted bookworms heard during the Reagan administration: the soul of a man who's tirelessly romantic yet perpetually unloved. Assembly-line stars such as Ricky Martin and Enrique Iglesias simply can't touch the authenticity of Morrissey's quiet desperation.

"We're passionate people. He's passionate like us," says Martha Barreras, standing outside the Palace doors with her well-coiffed, tattooed boyfriend. "The music our parents played when we were growing up was always about love and emotion, and it's the same thing with Morrissey."

It's possible this whole "Why do Latinos love Morrissey?" question will haunt us forever. Fortunately, Canadian academics are on the case.

Colin Snowsell is a 31-year-old Ph.D. candidate at Montreal's prestigious McGill University. He couldn't make it to the Smiths convention because he was busy working on his dissertation, an extension of his master's thesis, "Monty, Morrissey, and Mediatized Utopia." Frankly, Snowsell doesn't know why all this happened, either—but he's certainly thought about this paradox more than most.

"It really seems like Morrissey wouldn't have any career whatso-ever if it wasn't for these Latino fans," Snowsell says. "The rest of the world sees him as a has-been, by and large, and it's rare to see Morrissey covered by the media in any way that isn't negative. But maybe Latino kids don't read the Anglo media."

There's no question that Morrissey's persona has been universally hammered over the past decade, especially in the U.K. Though the British weekly *New Musical Express* recently classified the Smiths as the most influential act of the last 50 years, it often paints Morrissey as a self-absorbed caricature, fascinated by skinhead culture and bent on alienating his adoring minions.

Meanwhile, there are signs that he's aware of—and enthused by—his new fan base. He dubbed a recent tour ¡Oye Esteban! and has performed while wearing a MEXICO belt buckle. Perhaps more significantly, rumors persist that Morrissey wants to serve as the opening act for a Mexican rock group called Jaguares at the Holly-wood Bowl, a venue he sold out as a headliner ten years ago.

"If he's trying to get back his old Smiths fans, I don't think open-ing for a Mexican rock band would be the way to do it," Snowsell says. "I think he relishes being seen as a messianic figure among these young Latino fans, and I think he feels it validates his rele-vance. Morrissey has really done everything in his power to reject his old fans. I suspect he'd love it if the only people who cared about him were these Hispanic kids. I think he hates the fact that he tried to change the world, but most of those original Smiths fans now see him as no different than Echo and the Bunnymen."

Snowsell's use of the word *messianic* is telling, particularly when applied to someone like 19-year-old Carlos Torres, who tells me "Morrissey is like God" and is "immortal." However, when Torres talks about the time he met Morrissey at an in-store record-signing, he illustrates the most confusing aspect of neo-Moz culture: Just about everybody who's ever seen or heard Morrissey assumes he is gay—except for these Latino kids.

"I kissed Morrissey once," Torres says. "I kissed his hand. I wish I would have kissed him, but his hand was good enough. But I'm not gay or anything. It's just that he's Morrissey, you know? There is sort of a homophobic vibe among some Latinos, and they seem to think, 'Well, we like him so he can't be gay.' But that's stupid."

Torres' take is pretty liberal; a few Latinos at the convention concede that Morrissey might be bisexual, but none would classify him as gay. "People are always asking me if I'm gay because I have a photo of Morrissey hugging Johnny Marr," says Alex Diaz, a 16-year-old Smiths fanatic who plans on joining the marines when he's old enough. "My friends always ask me, 'Why do you like these queers?' But, you know, he's probably just bisexual. His songs aren't all about guys. Look at 'Girlfriend in a Coma'—that's about a girl. I think there probably would be some people who'd hate it if Morrissey ever came out and said he was gay, but, personally, I don't really care. And like I said, he's probably bisexual."

Though it's understandable how a culture that invented the term *machismo* might be uncomfortable lionizing a gay icon, it's ironic that Morrissey has now been adopted by two diametrically opposed subcultures. Fifteen years ago, closeted gay teens loved Morrissey because they thought he shared their secret; today, future marines try to ignore the fact that their hero might find them foxy.

Young Latinos worship an aging Brit who aspires to live at the YWCA and get hit by a double-decker bus, and that's pretty crazy. But imagine how crazy it seems to the guys in These Charming Men, the tribute band that performed both nights of the convention (Saturday night was mostly Smiths songs; Sunday was mostly solo Moz). These Charming Men are from Dublin, and this is the second year they've made the trip to Hollywood. When they arrived in 2001, they expected to see the same faces that populate the pubs they play in the U.K. What they didn't anticipate was an audience of East L.A. homeboys who mosh when they hear the opening chords of the gingerly raucous "You're Gonna Need Someone on Your Side."

"It was quite shocking when we first came here," recalls vocalist Richard Cullen, his accent thicker than his hair. "My theory is that they picked up on the fashion sense and the visual elements of rockabilly music. And you know, Morrissey is something of an exile, just like a lot of them. I think perhaps they feel like they're living in the present tense with this mysterious character who's just down the road in his mansion."

The performances by These Charming Men were clearly the linchpin of the 2002 convention, and Cullen's attention to detail is remarkable; he's a good singer and a great actor. His band played for two hours each night, expending more energy than Morrissey himself has offered in years. Fans were expected to rush on stage and hug Cullen while he pretended to ignore them, a simulation of every Morrissey concert since the dawn of time. It's very postmodern: The audience becomes a "tribute audience," earnestly simulating hyperkinetic adoration while the band earnestly simulates *Meat Is Murder.*

But not everyone gets what they want.

Mark Hensley Jr. and Flore Barbu refuse to watch These Charming Men, a seemingly odd decision when you consider they each paid $30 to attend a convention where that band was playing *twice.* These are the prototypical "weird white kids": Hensley appears to be auditioning for Bud Cort's role in a remake of *Harold and Maude,* and Barbu seems like the kind of woman who thinks Sylvia Plath was an underrated humorist. Both are wearing neckties for no apparent reason. These are the people you remember as being Smiths fans. And heaven knows they're miserable now.

"I don't think a true Morrissey fan would want to see a Morrissey cover band," Barbu says without a hint of inflection. "Morrissey would be depressed if he showed up here. He'd cry for a week. Have you seen those people around here wearing T-shirts that say GOT MORRISSEY? instead of GOT MILK? It's ridiculous. Morrissey would *hate* this."

It's obvious that Barbu and Hensley are smart, and they're endlessly, hopelessly sarcastic. There was a time when they would have embodied everything Morrissey seemed to represent. But Moz didn't hang on to his friends. He found new ones who like him more. It's not that Barbu and Hensley feel their subculture has wound up in the wrong hands; it's just that these neo-Mozzers are too enthusiastic to be properly dour.

"People have actually said to me, 'You like Morrissey? That's weird for a white guy.' And I find that completely bizarre," Hensley tells me, momentarily dropping his veil of irony for a grain of semi-sincere annoyance. "Most of the other people here wouldn't even know who Jarvis Cocker is. They *only* like Morrissey. We just came here to make fun of people."

But perhaps that joke isn't funny anymore.

LAWRENCE JOSEPH

The Music Is: The Deep Roots of Detroit R&B

"Our attachment to it"—Amiri Baraka says in *The Autobiography of LeRoi Jones*—"one deep definition of who we are and where we think we are going."

Deeply defining. The shape of a world. The complex connections within that world.

"But you really"—Gertrude Stein writes in "To Americans," the conclusion to *Brewsie and Willie*—"have to learn to express complication." You have to learn how to express complication and go easy, "and if you can't go easy go as easy as you can."

"And they'll lay you down low in the easy": the opening of "Glad Tidings," the final song on Van Morrison's *Moondance*.

So now, you go and you be easy, just go easy, be easy, down into the easy now, be easy, be as easy as you can.

In *P.M. Magazine*, March 11, 1945, Richard Wright reviewed Stein's *Wars I Have Seen*. "But, you might ask, why do I, a Negro, read the allegedly unreadable books of Gertrude Stein? It's all very simple, innocent even." He stumbled on Stein's work, Wright said, "without the guidance of those critics who hint darkly of 'the shock of recognition.'" Prompted by random curiosity while browsing one day in a Chicago public library, he took a tiny volume called *Three Lives* from the shelves and looked at a story in it entitled "Melanctha." "The style was so insistent and original and sang so quaintly that I took the book home." As he read it, his ears were "opened for the first time to the magic of the spoken word. I began to hear the speech of my grandmother, who spoke a deep, pure, Negro dialect and with whom I had lived for many years." Told that Stein's tortured verbalisms were throttling the revolution, Wright gathered a group of semiliterate black stockyard workers—"'basic proletarians with the instinct for revolution' (am I quoting right?)"—into a basement and read "Melanctha" out loud to them. They understood, said Wright, every word. "Enthralled, they slapped their thighs, howled, laughed, stomped, and interrupted me constantly to comment on the characters."

Baraka: "We know people by what moves them, what they use as background sounds for their lives, whatever they seem to be. We are talking about feeling and thought, emotion, aesthetics, and philosophy (and science)."

Feeling. Thought. Emotion. Aesthetics. Philosophy. Science. The instinct for form and technique. The instinct for a formal and a technical revolution.

"By the 1960s Middle Eastern and Indian rhythms, scales, instruments, and time signatures were making wide inroads in modern jazz, but in 1957 Lateef was clearly a pioneer in this regard," Lars Bjorn and Jim Gallert note in *Before Motown: A History of Jazz in Detroit, 1920–60* (certain to be a classic). Born Bill Evans in 1920, changing his name after he became a follower of the Ahmadiyya Islamic movement, Yusef Lateef first became interested in Middle Eastern music while he was working in a factory. "I realized I had to widen my canvas of expression," Lateef told Jim Gallert in an interview, "Meet the Artist," at the Montreux-Detroit Jazz Festival on September 6, 1999. "I spent many hours in the library on Woodward studying the music of other cultures. At this time I was also working at Chrysler's. I met a man from Syria and he asked me if I knew about the rabat. He made me a rabat and Ernie Farrow played it on the recording. I was looking to widen my expression and made bamboo flutes on my own."

Nat Hentoff, in *Downbeat*, January 9, 1957: Detroit had become "a spawning ground . . . for modern jazz. Their blowing here is primarily of a low flame, conversational kind. They fuse and pulse well together with the rhythm section, a finely knit, flowing texture of full-sounding but not overbearing momentum." The Detroit style, according to Roland Hanna, "tells a story. You hear other pianists running notes and changes. But a musician from Detroit makes an effort to arrive at his own story and tell it in his music."

"Woodward Avenue. Big parades. The library, the museum"— Saeeda Lateef writes on the jacket of Yusef Lateef's *Detroit: Latitude 42 30—Longitude 83*—"the Toddle House—BEST pecan waffles; cheap . . . Paradise Theatre . . . The old Mirror Ballroom . . . World Stage . . . New Music Society . . . Detroit Symphony . . . Latitude." "Woodward Avenue," one of my favorite tunes on that recording— "Woodward Avenue," and "Belle Isle," and a version of "That Lucky Old Sun"—and oh yes, I almost forgot: "Eastern Market."

When I was ten years old, I used to go to that Toddle House on Woodward and Palmer. My father and my uncle owned a store on John R., a one-way street that ran downtown, one block east of Woodward. If, from the Toddle House, you walked one block east on Palmer to John R., then one block up, there, on the southeast corner of John R. and Hendrie, was Joseph's Market. "The latter half of the 1940s," note Bjorn and Gallert, "saw the development of the 'Street of Music' in two blocks of John R., between Forest and Canfield" (nine to ten blocks south of Hendie). There's a photograph of the store from that time. Above it, a billboard, "CHEVROLET," with a two-tone-silver-and-white, '57 Chevrolet, "filled with spirit and splendor!" "JOSEPH'S MARKET. MON. TUE. WED. THUR. 9 TO 9. FRI. SAT. 9 TO 11." "YOUR NEIGHBORHOOD GROCER SINCE 1935 FREE PARKING AROUND THE CORNER." "5770 JOHN R." "BEER. WINE." "DETROIT PACKAGE LIQUOR DEALER." "BAR B. Q. TO TAKE OUT. RIBS. CHICKEN. PEPSI COLA." I'd walk to the Toddle House for lunch. For less than a dollar you could buy a hamburger, BEST fried potatoes, a Coke.

On the corner of the "Street of Music" and Canfield was a "show bar," the Flame. "Detroit's premier venue in the 1940s for black musical entertainment had been the Paradise Theatre"—Bjorn and Gallert relate—"but with the opening of the Flame in 1949 and the closing of the Paradise in November 1951, the action moved over to the Flame." The Flame was a solid testing ground for black entertainers who wanted to cross over to an adult mass audience. It was similar to the Paradise in presenting top natioal acts, but it also gave some room for local talent. "Berry Gordy's sister Gwen"—Bjorn and Gallert continue—"had the photo concession at the Flame with camera assistance from her sister Anna and two other brothers in the darkroom." Among the top national acts: Ella Fitzgerald, Count Basie, Billie Holiday, Dinah Washington, Billy Eckstine ("Jelly, Jelly, Star"), Sara Vaughan, Erroll Garner. Local talent: Della Reese, Jackie Wilson, Little Willie John, Hank Ballard.

Della Reese, quoted in Arnold Shaw's *The Rockin' 50s*: "The Flame was the place to be. In Detroit, in an area of five to six blocks, there wasn't one without spots of live entertainment. Friday and Saturday nights were get-up-and-go nights, get dressed and go out. But every night was nightclub night. The Flame was the hottest spot in town. The Flame was letting your hair down."

"The Flame was a continuous show, right through the night," Johnny Ray told Shaw. Ray was "the only white guy" who appeared there, but, as far as the club was concerned, the scene was black and tan. The Flame's house band, led by Maurice King, backed Ray on his first two records. Ray's next tune, "Cry," was a number-one hit on both the pop and R&B charts. Many listeners, hearing "Cry" on the radio, assumed that Ray was black. During live performances of the song, Ray, in the middle of singing, would break down in sobs. A band member would come to his aid, helping him back onto his feet.

"I always wanted to be a guitar player and a singer," Bob Dylan, born Robert Zimmerman in Duluth in 1941, says in the notes to his Biograph collection. "Since I was ten, eleven, or twelve, it was all that interested me. That was the only thing that I did that meant anything, really." "Henrietta" was the first rock and roll record he remembers hearing. Before that he listened a lot to Hank Williams and, before that, Johnny Ray. "He was the first singer whose voice and style, I guess, I totally fell in love with. There was just something about the way he sang [the opening to 'Cry'] 'When your sweetheart sends a letter' that just knocked me out. I loved his style, and wanted to dress like him, too."

On November 22, 1980, at the Fox Warfield Theater in San Francisco, Dylan told the audience that across the lake from Duluth is a town called Detroit. When he was around twelve, he happened to go to Detroit with a friend of his who had relatives there. Though he couldn't remember how, he found himself in a bingo parlor, where, he said, people came to eat and to dance to a dance band. Where he was from, said Dylan, he'd heard mostly country music—Hank Williams, Hank Snow, "all the Hanks"—but the first time that he was face to face with rhythm and blues was in Detroit. He then broke into a wailing gospel rendition of Little Willie John's "Fever."

Baraka: "Flame itself has different colors. The old blues, spirituals, quartets, and rhythm and blues, the jazz and bebop plus the multicolored pop, the identifiable American flying object."

My father, I remember, pulled the car over to the curb on Woodward Avenue in Highland Park—in the background Henry Ford's original assembly plant, used already as a warehouse—a July Sunday afternoon, the sky absorbed by a solid red sun, and told me to listen, to listen closely—he played with the radio dial to get the sound as clear as he could—listen to how beautiful the voice was in the song that was playing: Dinah Washington's rendition of "Harbor Lights."

"I've been writing songs since I was six years old," William "Smokey" Robinson told Bill Dahl for a December 10, 1993, article, "Going to a Go-Go with Smokey Robinson and the Miracles," in *Goldmine*. "My mom and my two sisters played a lot of Sarah Vaughan. I heard all kinds of music in my house. Mostly Sarah Vaughan, Billy Eckstine, Ella Fitzgerald, Count Basie, people like that." Sarah Vaughan, Robinson said, was "probably my favorite vocalist out of all of them. She used to cry her songs. She was like an instrument to me. She just did things with her voice that only she and Ella could do." (Robinson's playmates included the Motor City's first family of gospel, the Franklin's—sisters Aretha, Carolyn and Erma among them. . . . By the time he was in fifth grade, Robinson was writing songs and singing songs regularly, forming a vocal quartet in junior high school that included Aretha's brother, Cecil Franklin.) When he was eleven or twelve, Robinson became interested more, he said, "in what they termed then as the R&B music and rock and roll kind of sound." He had five idols: Clyde McPhatter, Nolan Strong, Frankie Lymon, Sam Cooke, and Jackie Wilson. (Prime examples of the R&B rock and roll kind of sound at the time were Nolan Strong and the Diablos' local hit "Mind Over Matter" and Hank Ballard and the Midnighters' top-of-the-charts "Work with Me, Annie." Ballard also wrote, and with the Midnighters recorded, "Finger Poppin' Time," and, later, "The Twist," covered by Chubby Checker.) The "greatest idol" he ever had "as far as an entertainer," Robinson told Dahl, was Jackie Wilson. "The other guys could sing, but Jackie could sing *and* dance *and* entertain."

Replacing Clyde McPhatter, who had followed Billy Ward as lead vocalist of the Dominoes, Wilson (who credited gospel singers as the main influences on his style) helped shape the doo-wop vocal group tradition in which McPhatter had been a pioneer. Wilson's first record, "Reet Petite," was written by Berry Gordy, Gordy's sister Gwen, and Tyran Carlo. "Reet Petite" never showed on the R&B charts, but went pop, selling a quarter of a million 45s. In *To Be Loved* (the title of Jackie Wilson's first number-one hit, which Gordy also wrote), Gordy tells how, in 1953, he opened, in the Gordy family's building on Farnsworth and St. Antoine (eight or so blocks from Joseph's Market), the 3-D Record Mart. At first, Gordy said, he sold only jazz recordings, but, as time went on, more and more blues. "I finally had to admit to myself blues was in my soul," he said. This probably stemmed from his early exposure to gospel. "There was an honesty about it. It was just as pure and real as jazz. In fact, jazz had its roots in the blues." Ironically, he said, the simplicity that he'd rejected in the blues was the very thing that people related to. Bjorn and Gallert: "Wilson's recordings of 'Reet Petite' and 'To Be Loved' gave Gordy a name, and singers started coming to him for material. One of them was singer/songwriter Smokey Robinson, who was the seventeen-year-old leader of the Matadors (later the Miracles)."

In his liner notes to *Detroit Blues—The Early 1950s* (which includes John Lee Hooker's "House Rent Boogie"), Paul Oliver defines the Detroit blues style. "Often [the Detroit blues musicians] play with strong piano blues and boogie players who—from the days of Will Ezell and Charlie Spand, through to Big Maceo and Floyd Taylor, to Boogie Woogie Red or Bob Thurman—have been a strong feature in Detroit blues." Drums also feature prominently in Detroit—"socking, hard-hitting, played by a Tom Whitehead, or in primitive imitation by a Washboard Willie." A number of guitarists, like Eddie Kirkland and Eddie Burns, double on harmonica, and can play the organ too, "weaving in with the sax players, who play a bigger part in Detroit blues than in that of Chicago." This complexity of instrumentation, played against steady-beat rhythms, gave birth to "a smoother, more sophisticated music where the instrumental lines were carried by vocal groups against similar rhythm backgrounds, and which borrowed freely from the gospel idioms which also form an important part of the Detroit musical scene."

Bjorn and Gallert: "Gordy decided to form his own record company, and with an eight-hundred-dollar loan from his family, Tamla was born in January 1959." In his November 7, 1959, column in the *Michigan Chronicle,* Bill Lane observed that Gordy was "the first Negro in the city to open a recording studio of any noticeable consequence" when he purchased the former Gene LeVett photo building on West Grand Boulevard. Bjorn and Gallert: "Gordy christened the new headquarters Hitsville USA and his increased control over the production, distribution, and marketing of music led to a steady flow of hits. Motown's first number-one R&B hit was the Miracles' 'Shop Around' in 1960, and the first number-one pop hit was the Marvelettes' 'Please Mr. Postman' in 1961. The Motown organization grew rapidly and eventually became the largest black-owned enterprise in the nation."

Berry Gordy: "The 'feel' was usually the first thing I'd go for. After locking in the drumbeat, I'd hum a line for each musician to start. Once we got going, we'd usually ad lib all over the place until we got the groove I wanted. Many of these guys came from a jazz background. I understood their instincts to turn things around to their liking, but I also knew what I wanted to hear—commercially. So when they went too far, I'd stop them and stress, 'We gotta get back to the funk—stay in that groove.'" Gordy would make it, he said, as plain as possible. "I would extend my arms a certain distance apart, saying, 'I want to stay between here and there. Do whatever you want but stay in that range—in the pocket.' But between 'here and there' they did all kinds of stuff—always pushing me to the limit and beyond."

William James (with whom both W. E. B. Du Bois and Gertrude Stein studied philosophy at Harvard): "When I say 'Soul,' you need not take me in the ontological sense unless you prefer to." Soul? "Only a succession of fields of consciousness: yet there is found in each field a part, or subfield, which figures as focal and contains the excitement, and from which, as from a center, the aim seems to be taken. Talking of this part"—James continues—"we involuntarily apply words of perspective to distinguish it from the rest, words like 'here,' 'this,' 'now,' 'mine' or 'me.'" To the other parts are ascribed "the positions 'there,' 'then,' 'that,' 'her,' 'his,' 'it,' 'not me.'" But, says James, "a 'here' can change to a 'there,' and 'there' become a 'here,' and what was 'mine' and what was 'not mine' change their places." What brings such changes about? The way in which the emotional excitement alters.

There: the funk, the groove. Here: in the pocket.

Are you ready?

"When the beat gets the feel, it's hard to get parted"—"you got yours and I got mine": "Monkey Time," written by Chicago's Curtis Mayfield, sung by Major Lance.

"Mickey's Monkey," written by Eddie Holland, Lamont Dozier, and Brian Holland, sung by the Miracles. "When the people see the dancing they begin to sing—lum di lum di lie." Lum di lum di lie—Detroit's Masonic Auditorium, May 1980. Smokey stops and smiles. "We don't know how to spell it, but we sure know how to say it."

Is everybody ready?

In a small yellow circle on the original purple Gordy label: "It's what's in the groove that counts."

John Lee Hooker, "Boogie Chillen'": "You know it's in 'em and it's just got to come out."

Thursday, December 16, 1965. The Fox Theatre, downtown Detroit. The *Motor Town Review*. Junior Walker and the All Stars,

Martha and the Vandellas, Stevie Wonder, the Temptations, Marvin
Gaye. In *Smokey: Inside My Life,* Robinson recollects: "Junior was
such a big-sound, stomp-down saxist, once at the Fox he was dancing so hard, he tripped and fell into the orchestra pit. The pit was
deep, but Junior was a showman, and he kept playing, his wail growing more distant the farther he fell, until he landed on his feet, his
'Shotgun' still firing." That was the night. We arrived early. Sat in
the tenth or eleventh row near the aisle, as close to the stage as we
could. "Shotgun"—you know—"shoot 'em before they run." Dig
potatoes. Pick tomatoes. Stevie Wonder, fifteen years old, Clarence
Paul beside him scatting gospel on Bob Dylan's "Blowin' in the
Wind," followed by a long, pure, frenzied expression on the mouth
harp. Music. Sweet music. Music everywhere. Swinging, swaying,
records playing: "Do you love me / now that I can dance?—The
Contours"—the epigraph to Al Young's first book of poems, *Dancing.* "The field open / the whole circle of life / is ours for the jumping into, / we ourselves the way we feel / right now": from Young's
poem "Dancing in the Street." Eddie Kendrick's falsetto, a Whit-
field-and-Holland song, "The Girl's All Right with Me." "Ain't that
peculiar—peculiarity": written and produced by Smokey, on the
Tamla label, sung by Marvin Gaye. Later, on the radio, Sam Cooke's
"Having a Party," so we stopped the car, opened the doors, and
danced slowly on the street.

  In his unauthorized biography *Van Morrison: Inarticulate Speech of
the Heart,* John Collis reports on Morrison's appearance at the
King's Hotel, Newport, South Wales, on October 6, 1993. Morrison began to lecture the audience. "This is not rock, this is not
pop," he said. "This is called soul music. So instead of all themoth-
erfucking bastards who say something different, this is what it is."
After several attempts to start singing—never getting beyond "I'm a
trans-Euro train"—Morrison continued. "I'm talking about soul.
I'm a soul singer. I'm more a motherfucking soul singer than some
motherfucking motherfucker. I'm a soul singer. I sing soul songs.
Blues."

  George Clinton, in an interview, "Brother from Another Planet,"
with Vernon Reid in *Vibe:* "We came from Motown. I always knew

that I had been trained as a producer and a writer and there was
nothing else like the discipline they had at Motown. Having done
that, then we saw Cream and Vanilla Fudge and all of them take the
music my mother liked, flip it around and make it loud, and it
became cool. We realized that blues was the key to that music. We
just speeded blues up and called it 'funk' 'cause we knew it was a bad
word to a lot of people."

Van Morrison's *Saint Dominic's Preview*, the first cut: "Jackie Wil-
son said (I'm in Heaven When You Smile)." The opening lines:
"Jackie Wilson said it was reet petite, kind of lovin' she gives knocks
me off my feet . . ." On *The Healing Game*, the song "Sometimes We
Cry," Morrison sings, "Gonna put me in a jacket and take me away,
I'm not gonna fake it like Johnny Ray." On *Enlightenment*, in "In the
Days before Rock 'n' Roll": "Come in, come in, come in Ray
Charles, come in the high priest." "I'm down on my knees at those
wireless knobs." Telefunken. Searching for Budapest. AFM. Fats
and Elvis, Sonny, Lightnin', Muddy, John Lee, did not come in, no
they did not come in, did not come in without those wireless knobs.
Soul. Radio. This is the sound of my wavelength and your wavelength
—ya radio. You turn me on when you get me on your wavelength—
ya radio, ya radio.

"Pulsars, blue receding / quasars—their vibrant / radio waves.
Cosmic Ouija, / what is the / mathematics of your message?": the
fourth of five parts of Robert Hayden's poem "Stars."

Released in early 1962, Ray Charles's *Modern Sounds in Country
and Western Music* remained on *Billboard*'s pop album chart for
nearly two years, fourteen weeks in the number-one position. "Not
only did it gain him millions of new fans," writes Todd Everett, "the
album firmly booted the thirty-one-year-old Charles from the 'R&B'
category and let general (let's face it) white audiences know what
connoisseurs had taken for granted for several years, that Ray
Charles had something to say to virtually everybody and that there's
nobody else who can tell it like Brother Ray." The LP's second-to-
last cut is "That Lucky Old Sun," according to Everett "a 1949
smash hit by Frankie Laine, written by the Tin Pan Alley tune-
smiths Haven Gillespie and Fred Coots."

In a three-day recording session at Blue Rock Studios in New York City in March 1971, Bob Dylan, after recording "When I Paint My Masterpiece," did covers of "That Lucky Old Sun," Ben E. King's "Spanish Harlem," and the gospel classic "Rock of Ages."

There are those who maintain that Aretha Franklin's version of "Spanish Harlem" ("a rose in *black* and Spanish Harlem") is one of her finest tunes. The June 28, 1968, cover of *Time*: "Singer Aretha Franklin. The Sound of Soul." She was around nine, Franklin recalled, when she decided to sing. Her father was the prominent Detroit clergyman, the Reverend C. L. Franklin. "The best, the greatest, gospel singers came through our home in Detroit. Sometimes they stayed with us. James Cleveland lived with us for a time and it was James who taught me how to play piano by ear." Most of what she learned vocally she learned from her father. "He gave me a sense of timing in music and timing is important in everything." The opening to Bob Dylan's 1966 book *Tarantula*: "aretha / jukebox queen of hymn & him diffused in drunk transfusion wound would heed sweet soundwave crippled & cry salute to oh great particular el dorado reel." Say what? Sweet soundwave cry salute hymn diffused great particular C-a-d-i-l-l-a-c El Dorado real. Yes, Aretha told *Newsweek* in August '67, she learned a lot from Sam Cooke. "He did so many things with his voice. So gentle one minute, swinging the next, then electrifying. Always doing something else." When he was still with the Soul Stirrers, Cooke brought his dub recording of "You Send Me" over to the Franklins' house for the family to hear. "The song became a hit, and Sam went pop." When Cooke made the change, Aretha said to herself, "I'd sure like to sing like that, too."

Soulin' Sam Cooke. "Cherie LP 1001." "Two Record Soul Pack." Written in a small box on the front cover: "BONUS 45 RPM RECORD INSIDE! Never-Before-Heard 25-Minute Rap Session by SAM COOKE 'What is Soul.'" On the back cover: "Dedicated to J. W. Alexander, who knew the true meaning of Gospel Soul Music and became the first to convert it into Rhythm and Blues." Recorded on it, a two-part rendition of Gershwin's "Summertime," each part exactly two minutes, seventeen seconds long.

The desire of truth bursting from within.

Rapping and mapping every generation's survival.

Igniting a brighter and dedicated flame.

The recently released "Deluxe Edition" of Marvin Gaye's *What's Going On.* Two discs. On disc One: "Original LP Release (May 21, 1971)"; "Original Detroit Mix (April 5, 1971)" (previously unreleased); "The Foundation" ("'What's Going On' rhythm & strings mix") (previously unreleased). On disc Two: "Live at the Kennedy Center (May 1, 1972)"; "Original Single Versions"; "In the Meantime" ("Head Title aka 'Distant Lover'"). The live performance at the Kennedy Center was Gaye's first in four years. He opened with a medley, the first three songs, "That's the Way Love Is," "You," and "I Heard It Through the Grapevine," originally produced by Norman Whitfield. When he recorded for Whitfield, Gaye told David Ritz, "he had me singing so high and hard the veins in my neck nearly popped." After the medley, songs from *What's Going On.* Almost two minutes into "Inner City Blues (Make Me Wanna Holler)," Marvin stops singing and begins conversing, while the band continues to play. "Now Maurice, Maurice King—Maurice King here is my arranger, here, on the piano, and, and, because I want this to be a groovy tune, what I want to do is start all over again from the top, because I want to do it, because we're in the groove now"—the band was still playing—"it's a bit more groovy now, and I want to keep it where it is, from the top, we gonna take it from the *top*, take it from the *top* now . . .

"One, two, three, four, all right, all right, yeah, I got to have it groovy . . .

"Dah dah dah, dah dah dah dah dah dah . . .

"Rockets, moon shots, spend it all on have-nots . . .

"Money we make it, 'fore we see it, you take it . . .

"Make you wanna holler, the way they do my life, make you wanna holler, the way they do my life, this ain't livin', no, no, ain't livin', no, no, no . . . "

Nelson George, in his beautiful elegy "The Power and the Glory," in the *Village Voice,* May 8, 1984: Marvin said he had "three different voices, a falsetto, a gritty gospel shout, and a smooth midrange close to his speaking voice. Depending on the tune's key,

tone, and intention, he was able to accommodate it, becoming a creative slave to the music's will."

Marvin's "Trouble Man": "I know some places and I see some
faces, got some connections, they dig my directions, what people
say, that's okay, they don't bother me—I'm ready to make it, don't
care about the weather, don't care about no trouble, I got myself
together, I see the protection that's all around me."

Smokey's "A Love She Can Count On": "I know that you know
how precious to care is, and you know, my darling, that I know that
there is . . . "

Like sunshine. I got sunshine. You are my sunshine. I feel like this
is the beginning, though I've loved you for a million years, and if I
thought our love was ending, I'd find myself drowning in my own
tears. You are the sunshine. You are the sunshine of my life. That's
why I'll always be around.

Phil Spector, on the radio commenting on the Four Tops' "Reach
Out": "If you *feeeeel* that you can't *gooooooooooonnn* . . . ": it's black
Dylan.

From *The Changing Same (R&B and New Black Music)*, Baraka:
"But it is interpretation. The Miracles are spiritual. They sing (and
sing about) feeling. Their content is about feeling . . . the form is to
make feeling, etc. . . . 'Walk On By,' 'Where Did Our Love Go?'
'What Becomes of the Brokenhearted?' 'The Tracks of My Tears,'
high poetry in the final character of their delivery . . . A blues which
bees older than Ray Charles or Lightnin' Hopkins, for that matter.
'I got to laugh to keep from cryin',' which the Miracles make, 'I got
to dance to keep from cryin',' is not only a song but the culture itself.
It is finally the same cry, the same people. You really got a hold on
me. As old as our breath here . . . James Brown's screams, etc., are
more 'radical' than most jazz musicians sound, etc. Certainly his
sound is 'further out' than Ornette's."

As old as our breath. The ancient streets. The back streets. Back
on the street. The street only knew your name. Back on the street
again.

George Clinton answering Vernon Reid's question "How did
funk come into being?": "Our show was basically R&B and we got

happy and we became, you know, like churchy. And once we experienced what you could do to people just jumping around from the soul to the blues parts of our songs, we realized that nobody could even be our competition, and we didn't have to worry about doing it fast—everybody in the band would tell you that I said it's gonna take fifteen years for this to work."

Space? Marvin: "Funky space. Peaceful space. It's every place" ("A Funky Space Incarnation"). "Time for countdown, please. Give me the countdown, Zack. Here we go, here we go—you ready?"

"One, fun. Two, you. Three, me. Four, more. Five, no jive. Six, no tricks. Seven, we in heaven, eight, everything is straight. Nine, fine. Ten, next week we'll do it again."

From the top. All over again. Back on the top again. from the *top*.

Stevie Wonder's second LP—he was thirteen years old—*Tribute to Uncle Ray*.

John Rockwell's December 26, 1986, review, "Pop: Smokey Robinson in Six-Night Engagement," in the *New York Times*: "But Mr. Robinson has hardly abandoned his falsetto. Instead, he has integrated it ever more seamlessly into his total method of vocal production, so that most of the time, one can't say for sure exactly what the proportion of 'chest tone,' 'head tone,' and falsetto really is. The now-moribund French operatic style of singing that flourished in the nineteenth century called this blending of registers a 'voix mixte,' and Mr. Robinson mixes his registers as well as any singer alive, operatic or otherwise."

Aretha Franklin's first album in seven years, the CD *A Rose Is Still a Rose*. In an interview with Christopher John Farley from "her hometown of Detroit" in *Time*, March 2, 1998: "I'm a very versatile vocalist. That's what I think a singer should be. Whatever it is, I can sing it. I'm not a rock artist. But I've done some rocking. I love the Puffy song ("Never Leave You Again") on my album. It's very jazzy, very cool, very easy."

Van Morrison, "Queen of the Slipstream": "There's a dream where the contents are visible. Where the poetic champions compose. Will you breathe not a word of this secrecy and will you still be my special rose?"

Thought. Feeling. Form. Emotion.

A rose in . . .

A bit more groovy, now, right?

A rose is . . .

Two.

Me. You.

Need a shot of rhythm, need a shot of blues. On the side? A little rock and roll just for good measure. Like, you know, when the chill-bumps come up on you. When the hands start to clapping and the fingers start to popping, and your feet want to move around. When the feeling finally gets you . . .

Hey. Hey now. Hey now, go easy now, keep on keep on pushin' easy now, in the easy now, and, if you can't go easy, then just go as easy as you can.

Bob Dylan: Almost Went to See Elvis. Cool Daddy Productions. Made in Egypt. The second cut: Sam Cooke's "Cupid." Recorded at the Columbia Studios, Nashville, May 1969.

St. Andrew's Hall, Detroit, July 6, 1999. Between versions of "Silvio" and "Man in the Long Black Coat," Dylan pauses and says: "This afternoon I went over to the Motown Museum. I went over the Motown Museum and went in, and I asked the man there, 'Where's the Smokey Robinson stuff?' And he says to me, 'I don't know where the Smokey Robinson stuff is,' I say, 'Say what? You don't know where the Smokey Robinson stuff is?' 'No,' he says. 'I don't know where the Smokey Robinson stuff is.' 'Well,' I say, 'that's why I'm here. That is what I am looking for, the Smokey Robinson stuff. That's what I am here looking for. I am here looking for the Smokey Robinson stuff.'

ELIZABETH GILBERT

Play It Like
Your Hair's on Fire

He never looked quite right as a child. He was small, thin, pale. He stood funny. He had a trick knee, psoriasis, postnasal drip. There was no comb, lotion or prayer in this world that would get his hair to lie down flat. He read too many books. He was unduly fascinated by carnivals, buried treasure and mariachi music.

When he grew nervous, he rocked back and forth like a rabbi deep in prayer. He was often nervous.

Moreover, there was something kind of wrong with him (maybe, he thinks now, some minor brush with autism) that made him almost painfully obsessed with sound. He heard noises the way van Gogh saw colors—exaggerated, beautiful, shimmering, scary. There were sounds all around him that made his hair stand on end, sounds nobody else seemed to hear. Cars driving by under his bedroom window roared louder than trains. If he waved his arm near his head, he heard a sharp whistle in his ear like the whipping of a fishing line. If he ran his hand across his bedsheets, he heard a harsh scrape, rougher than sandpaper. Engulfed by these noises, he'd be compelled to clear his head by reciting rhythmic nonsense syllables aloud (*shack-a-bone, shack-a-bone, shack-a-bone, shack-a-bone...*) until he could think straight again.

When he was 11 years old, his father—a Spanish teacher who used to drive his boy out of San Diego and over the Mexican border for haircuts—left the family. So now the child didn't have a dad around anymore. He became fixated on dads as a result. He would visit the houses of his friends and neighbors, not to hang out with his buddies but to hang out with his buddies' dads.

While the other kids were outside playing kickball in the sun, he would slip into the darkened den and sit there with somebody's father for the entire afternoon, listening to Sinatra records and talking about home insurance. He'd pretend to be a much older man, maybe even a father himself. Kicked back in some grown man's Barcalounger, this skinny little kid would clear his throat, lean forward and say. "So. How long you been with Aetna, Bob?"

He wanted to be old so bad it drove him nuts. He couldn't wait to shave. At 11, he wore his grandfather's hat and dreamed of walking with a cane. And he loved the music that old men loved. Music with some grizzled hair on its chest. Music whose day was long over. Dead music. *Dad* music.

"How 'bout that brass section, Bob?" he'd say to somebody's father while listening to the hi-fi on a quiet afternoon. "Can't find players like that anymore, can you, Bob? That minor-seventh chord kind of ties the whole song together, doesn't it? After Nelson Riddle, there wasn't really anything left, don't you think, Bob?"

This was back when he was in, like, sixth grade.

So, yes, in case you were wondering—Tom Waits was *always* different.

I'm waiting for Tom Waits on the porch of the Washoe House— one of California's oldest inns. It's in the middle of the grassy countryside of Sonoma County, across the street from a vineyard, next to a dairy farm and somewhat near the mysterious, secret rural location where Tom Waits lives. It was his decision to meet here. No mystery why he likes this place. The sloping wooden floors, the sticky-keyed piano in the bar, the yellowing dollar bills thumbtacked to the ceiling, the weary waitresses who look like they've been on the business end of some real hard love their whole lives— every story in the house is a true one.

So I'm waiting for Tom Waits when a homeless man wanders up to me. Thin as a knife, weathered skin, clean and faded clothes. Eyes so pale, he might be blind. He's dragging behind him a wagon, decorated with balloons and feathers and signs announcing that the world is coming to an end. This man is, I learn, walking all the way to Roswell, New Mexico. For the apocalypse. Which will be happening later this spring. I ask his name. He tells me that he was christened Roger but that God calls him by another name. ("For years I heard God talkin' to me, but he kept calling me Peter, so I thought he had the wrong guy. Then I realized Peter must be my real name. So now I listen.")

With no special alarm. Roger-Peter informs me that this whole planet will be destroyed within a few short months. Pandemonium unleashed. Madness and death everywhere. Everybody burned to cinders. He points to the passing cars and says calmly, "These people like their comfortable lives now. But they won't like it one bit when the animals get loose."

Appropriately enough, this is the exact moment when Tom Waits shows up. He wanders over to the porch. Thin as a knife, weathered skin, clean and faded clothes.

"Tom Waits," I say, "meet Roger-Peter."

They shake hands. They look alike, in a way. You wouldn't know at first, necessarily, which one was the eccentric musical genius and which one was the derelict wandering doomsayer. There are some differences, of course. Roger-Peter has crazier eyes. But Tom Waits has a crazier voice.

Waits, immediately comfortable with Roger-Peter, says, "You know, I saw you around here just the other night, walking down the middle of the highway."

"God redirects the traffic around me so I don't get hit." replies Roger-Peter.

"I don't doubt that. I like your wagon. Tell me about all these signs you wrote. What are they all about?"

"I'm finished talking now." Roger-Peter says, not impolitely but firmly.

He stands up, gives us a Bible as a parting gift, takes hold of his wagon and heads east to meet the total destruction of the universe.

Waits watches him go, and as we head inside, he tells me that he recently saw another hobo with apocalyptic signs walking down the same road. "He offered to sell me a donkey. A pregnant donkey. I had to go home and ask everyone if we could invest in a pregnant donkey. But they decided, no, that would be too much trouble."

For the past thirty years, Tom Waits has had a musical career in this country unlike anybody else's. His was not a meteoric rise to fame. He just appeared—a rough, tender, melancholic, thoroughly experimental, lounge singing, piano-playing, reclusive hobo in a $7 suit and an old man's hat—and that is what he has remained. Although he tinkers endlessly with his music (since his first album, 1973's *Closing Time*, he has given us tragic blues, narcotic jazz, sinister Germanic operas and delirious, drunken carnival mambos, to name just a few styles), he has never once tinkered with his image, and that's how you know it isn't an "image."

You don't see much of Tom Waits in public, although he's not a total hermit. He does go on tour every now and again, he has performed on *The Tonight Show*, and he shows up in the occasional movie (*The Cotton Club*, Francis Ford Coppola's *Dracula*, Robert Altman's *Short Cuts*) as a brilliant, scene-stealing character actor. Still, he prefers his privacy. He agreed to meet me today only because he has a new album coming out and he guesses he should probably promote it. Actually, he has two new albums. (One is called *Alice*, the other is called *Blood Money*, and their singular complexity and dark beauty shall be discussed at a later point in this article, so please hold right.)

Tom Waits is, famously, not the easiest interview out there. Reporters often get frustrated with him because he speaks inaudibly or "won't give straight answers." (When, asked once why he had allowed six long years to pass between albums. Waits replied stonily. "I was stuck in traffic.") He's notorious for telling make-believe stories about himself. Not out of malice, mind you. Mostly just to pass the time. He quite enjoys the lies that have been printed about him over the years. ("My father was a knife-thrower," he has said. "And my mother was a trapeze artist. So we were a show-business family.")

He's not the most marketable guy out there, either. He doesn't have conventional good looks or a very nice voice. He has been called "gravelly voiced" so many times over the decades, you'd think music journalists were required by law to describe him this way. Tom Waits has grown a bit weary of this description. He prefers other metaphors. A little midwestern girl once wrote him a letter saying that his voice reminded her of the combination of a cherry bomb and a clown, to which he replied. "You got it, babe. Thanks for listening."

As a songwriter, he has an unerring instinct for melancholy and melody. His wife says that all his songs can be divided into two major categories—Grim Reapers and Grand Weepers. The latter will knock you to the very floor with sadness. (A devastating little number called "Christmas Card from a Hooker in Minneapolis" comes to mind.) He has never had a hit, though Rod Stewart did take Waits's "Downtown Train" to the top of the charts. But other Tom Waits songs aren't so radio-friendly. (How 'bout this for a catchy pop lyric: *Uncle Bill will never leave a will / And the tumor's as big as an egg / He has a mistress, she's Puerto Rican / And I heard she has a wooden leg.*)

It's this darkness and eccentricity that have kept him from being a megastar. Still, he has never vanished into obscurity. For thirty years, as bigger and more conventional rock stars have shimmered and melted away in hot spotlights all around him, Tom Waits has stayed on his dimly lit side stage, sitting at his piano (or guitar or sousaphone or cowbell or fifty-gallon oil drum) creating extraordinary sounds for a loyal audience.

As for the devotion he inspires and how he claimed his unique position in American music, the artist has only this to say:

"There's an aspect of going into show business that's like joining the circus. You come to learn that there's certain people in show business who do the equivalent of biting the heads off chickens. But, then of course, there's the aerialists. . . and sideshow curiosities. You work with what you came in with. Well, maybe I came in with no legs. But I can walk on my hands and play the guitar. So that's just me using my imagination to work within the system."

His is not the voice of the common workingman. It's more like the voice of the common working circus freak. But his voice is heartfelt, epic and honest, and he represents his peculiar constituency with true honor. Which means this: If only there were as many circus freaks in this country as there are workingmen. Tom Waits would be Bruce Springsteen.

Tom Waits is full of facts.

He leans in close to me and says, "The male spider. After he strings four strands of his web, he steps off to the side, lifts one leg and strums them. The chord that this makes? This attracts the female spider. I'm curious about that chord. . . ."

Waits keeps these facts jotted down in a small notebook, which also is filled with driving directions and unfinished songs and hangman games he has been playing with his young son. His handwriting is a crazy wobbling of huge, scrawly capital letters. You'd swear it was the penmanship of a crippled man who has been forced to hold his pencil in his mouth.

He thumbs through this notebook like he's thumbing through his own scattered memory. This provides me excellent opportunity to stare at his face. He looks good for a man of 50-however-many-years-old-he-is. He's been clean and sober for almost a decade, and it shows. Doesn't even smoke anymore. No puffiness along the jaw. Clear eyes. Four deep parallel lines are grooved into his forehead, as evenly spaced as if they'd been dug there with a kitchen fork. He's far better looking (handsome, even) in real life than he is on stage and screen, where—lost in the struggle of performance—he often employs such puzzled facial contortions and shambling postures and spastically waving arms that he looks (and I'm sorry to say this about my hero) something like an oversize organ-grinder's monkey But here, in this dark old restaurant, he's nothing but dignified He even looks like he's in shape. Which leads me to try to picture Tom Waits jogging on a tread-mill At a gym. Wearing *what*?

"Ah, here's another interesting fact," he says. "Heinz 57."

He picks up the bottle of Heinz 57 from the table to illustrate his story.

"Between 1938 and 1945." he says, "Heinz released a soup only in Germany It was an alphabet soup. But in addition to every letter of the alphabet, they included swastikas in every can."

"You're kidding me."

He puts the bottle down. "I imagine it would be called pastika."

It's a great story. Too bad further investigation proves it to be an urban myth. Not that that matters. What matters is that it gets Tom Waits to thinking. Gets him thinking about a lot of things. Pigs, for instance. He's concerned because scientists are splicing human genes into pigs these days. Apparently, this is to ensure that the animals' internal organs are more accessible for transplant into human bodies. Ethically, Waits thinks this is a horrific notion. It's also having an unsettling effect on the appearance of the pigs.

"I saw pictures of these pigs." he muses. "You look at 'em and you say. 'Geez! That's Uncle *Frank*! Looks just like him!'"

Which brings us to his wife.

Chances are, it was Tom Waits's wife who showed him the photograph of the experimental pig-humans, because she reads four local newspapers a day and cuts out all the weird stories. You can also bet she's the person who dug up the story about the swastika-noodle soup. And if there's anyone around who has ever heard the mating chord of the male spider, it's probably Kathleen Brennan.

But who *is* Kathleen Brennan? Hard to know, exactly. She's the most mysterious figure in the whole Tom Waits mythology. Newspaper articles and press releases always describe her the same way, as "the wife and longtime collaborator of the gravelly-voiced singer." You will see her name on all his albums after 1985. ("All songs written by Tom Waits and Kathleen Brennan.") She's everywhere, but invisible. She's private as a banker, rare as a unicorn, never talks to reporters. But she is the very center of Tom Waits—his muse, his partner and the mother of his three children. And sometimes, when he is playing live, you will hear him mumble, almost to himself.

"This one's for Kathleen," before he eases into a slow and tender rendition of "Jersey Girl."

I've never met the woman, and I know nothing for certain about her, except what her husband has told me. Which means she is a person thoroughly composed, in my mind, of Tom Waits's words. Which means she's the closest thing out there to a living Tom Waits song.

He has called her "an incandescent presence" in his life and music. She's "a rhododendron, an orchid and an oak." He has described her as "a cross between Eudora Welty and Joan Jett." She has "the four B's. Beauty, brightness, bravery and brains." He insists that she's the truly creative force in the relationship, the feral influence who challenges his "pragmatic" limitations and stirs intrigue into all their music. ("She has dreams like Hieronymus Bosch. . . . She'll start talking in tongues and I'll take it all down.") He says "she speaks to my subtext, not my context." He claims she has expanded his vision so enormously as an artist that he can hardly bear to listen to any of the music he wrote before they met. "She rescued me," he says. "I'd be playing in a steak house right now if it wasn't for her. I wouldn't even be *playing* in a steak house. I'd be *cooking* in a steak house."

"She's the egret in the family," he says "I'm the mule."

"We met on New Year's Eve," Tom Waits tells me.

He loves talking about his wife. You can see it, the pleasure it gives him. He tries not to go too nuts with it, of course, because he does want to protect her privacy. (Which is why he sometimes dodges interviewers' questions about his wife with typical Waitsian nonsense stories. Yeah, he'll say, she's a bush pilot. On a soda jerk. Runs a big motel down in Miami. Or this: He once claimed he fell for Kathleen because she was the first woman he'd ever met who could "stick a knitting needle through her lip and still drink coffee.") And yet he wants to talk about her because—you can just see it—he loves the way her name feels in his mouth.

They met in Hollywood, back in the early 1980s. Waits was writing the music for the Coppola movie *One from the Heart* and

Kathleen Brennan was a script supervisor on the film. Their courtship had all the drunken, spinning, timewarping delirium of a good New Year's Eve party in someone else's house. When they were first falling in love they used to drive wildly around L.A. at all hours and she'd purposely try to get him lost, just for the entertainment value. She'd tell him to take a left, then a right, then another left, then hop on the freeeway, then cross over Adams Boulevard, then straight through a ghetto, then into a worse ghetto, then another left...

"We'd end up in *Indian* country." Waits remembers. "Out where nobody could even believe we were *there*. Places where you could get shot just for wearing *corduroy*. We were going into these bars—I don't know what was protecting us—but we were loaded. God protects drunks and fools and little children. And dogs. Jesus, we had so much fun."

They got married at the Always Forever Yours Wedding Chapel on Manchester Boulevard in Watts. ("It was planned at midnight for a 1 A.M. wedding," says Waits. "We make things *happen* around here!") They'd known each other, what? Two months? Maybe three? They had to page the guy who married them. A pastor who carried a beeper. The Right Reverend Donald W. Washington.

"She thought it was a bad omen that it was a $70 wedding and she had fifty bucks and I only had twenty. She said, 'This is a hell of a way to start a relationship.' I was like, 'C'mon, baby, I'll make it up to you. I'll get you later. . . .'"

There wasn't much of a honeymoon Soon after the wedding, the couple realized they were dead broke. Waits was already a celebrated musician, but he'd made some serious young-artist mistakes with contracts and money, and now it was looking like maybe he was dried-up. Plus, he was on the splits with his manager. And legal headaches? Everywhere. And studio producers trying to put corny string sections behind his darkest songs? And who owned him, exactly? And how had this happened?

It was at this point that his new bride stepped in and encouraged her husband to blow off the whole industry. Screw it, Kathleen suggested. You don't need these outside people, anyhow. You can produce your own work. Manage your own career. Arrange your own songs. Forget about security. Who needs security when you have freedom? The two of them would get by somehow, no matter what. It's like she was always saying: "Whatever you bring home, baby, I'll cook it up. You bring home a possum and a coon? We will live off it."

The result of her dare was *Swordfishtrombones*—a big, brassy, bluesy, gospel-grooved, dark-textured, critically adored declaration of artistic independence. An album like none before it. A boldly drawn line, running right through the center of Tom Waits's work, dividing his life into two neat categories: Before Kathleen Brennan and After Kathleen Brennan.

"Yeah," Waits says, and he's still all dazzled about her. "She's really a radical."

They live in the countryside.

In an old house. They have neighbors, like the guy who collects roadkill to shellac and make into art. And then there are the Seventh-Day Adventists and the Jehovah's Witnesses who knock on the door, wanting to talk about Jesus. Waits always lets them in and offers them coffee and listens politely to their preaching because he thinks they are such sweet, lonely people. He only recently realized that they must think the same of him.

Waits drives a 1960 four-door Cadillac Coup DeVille. It's a bigger car than he probably needs, and he admits that. It devours gas, smells terrible, radio doesn't work. But it's good for little day trips, like visits to the dump. Dumps, salvage yards, rummage sales, junk shops—these are his special retreats. Waits loves to find strange and resonant objects hidden deep in piles of garbage, objects he can rescue and turn into new kinds of musical instruments.

"I like to imagine how it feels for the object itself to become music," he says. "Imagine you're the lid to a fifty-gallon drum. That's your job. You work at that. That's your whole life. Then one day I find you and I say, 'We're gonna drill a hole in you, run a wire through you, hang you from the ceiling of the studio, bang on you with a mallet, and now you're in show business, baby!' "

Sometimes, though, he just goes searching for doors. He loves doors. They're his biggest indulgence. He's always coming home with more doors—Victorian, barn, French. . . . His wife will protest, "But we already have a door!"' and Waits will say. "But this one comes with such nice windows, baby!"

The Waits household has a family dog, too. Waits feels a special affinity for the animal and believes the two of them have a lot in common: Like "nerves," he says. "Barking at things that are inaudible. A need to mark territory. I'm kinda like that. If I've been gone for three days, come home, first thing I have to do is take a walk around the house and establish myself again. I walk all over, touch everything, kick things, sit on things. Remind the room and everyone else that I'm back."

He's home almost all the time, because—unlike other dads—he doesn't have a day job. Which is why he's known by the local schools as the guy they can count on whenever they need an adult to do the driving for a field trip.

"I'm down with the field trips." Waits says. "I got the big car. I'm always looking for a nine-passenger opportunity." Recently, he took a group of kids to a guitar factory. It was a small operation, run by music types. "So I'm waiting for somebody to recognize me. OK. I think, someone's gonna come up and say, 'You're that guy, right?' Now. I've been there for, like, two hours. Nothing. *Nothing.* Now I'm getting pissed. In fact, I'm starting to pose over by the display case. Still waiting, but nothing all day. I get back in the car. I'm a little despondent. I mean, it's my *field.* I expect a nod or a wink, but nothing."

Waits takes a pause to stir his coffee.

"So a week later, we go on another field trip. It's a recycling thing. OK, I'm in. We pull up to the dump and six guys surround my car— 'Hey! It's Tom Waits!'"

He shrugs wearily, like he's telling the timeworn story of his life.

"Everybody knows me at the dump."

Perhaps the most singular feature about Tom Waits as an artist—the thing that makes him the anti-Picasso—is the way he has braided his creative life into his home life with such wit and grace. This whole idea runs contrary to our every stereotype about how geniuses need to work—about their explosive interpersonal relationships, about the lives (particularly the women's lives) they must consume in order to feed their inspiration, about all the painful destruction they leave in the wake of invention. But this is not Tom Waits. A collaborator at heart, he has never had to make the difficult choice between *creativity* and *procreativity*. At the Waits house, it's all thrown in there together—spilling out of the kitchen, which is also the office, which is also where the dog is disciplined, where the kids are raised, where the songs are written and where the coffee is poured for the wandering preachers. All of it somehow influencing the rest.

The kids were certainly never a deterrent to the creativity—just further inspiration for it. He remembers the time his daughter helped him write a song. "We were on a bus coming into L.A. And it was really cold outside. There was this transgender person, to be politically correct, standing on a corner wearing a short little top with a lot of midriff showing, a lot of heavy eye makeup and dyed hair and a really short skirt. And this guy, or girl, was dancing, all by himself. And my little girl saw it and said, 'It must be really hard to dance like that when you're cold and there's no music.'"

Waits took his daughter's exquisite observation and worked it into a ballad called "Hold On"—a song of unspeakably aching hopefulness that was nominated for a Grammy and became the cornerstone of his album *Mule Variations*.

"Children make up the best songs, anyway," he says. "Better than grown-ups. Kids are always working on songs and then throwing them away, like little origami things or paper airplanes. They don't care if they lose it; they'll just make another one."

This openness is what every artist needs. Be ready to receive the inspiration when it comes; be ready to let it go when it vanishes. He believes that if a song "really wants to be written down, it'll stick around in my head. If it wasn't interesting enough for me to remember it, well, it can just move along and go get in someone else's song."

"Some songs," he has learned, "don't want to be recorded." You can't wrestle with them or you'll only scare them off more. Trying to capture them sometimes "is trying to trap birds." Fortunately, he says, other songs come easy, like "digging potatoes out of the ground." Others are sticky and weird, like "gum found under an old table." Clumsy and uncooperative songs may only be useful "to cut up as bait and use 'em to catch other songs." Of course, the best songs of all are those that enter you "like dreams taken through a straw." In those moments, all you can be, Waits says, is grateful.

Like a clever kid with a new toy, Waits is always willing to play with a song, to see what else it can become. He'll play with it forever in and out of the studio, in ways a real grown-up would never imagine. He'll pick it apart, turn it inside out, drag it backward through the mud, ride a bicycle over it—anything he can imagine to make it sound thicker, rougher, deeper, different.

"I like my music," he says, "with the pulp and skin and seeds."

He's always fighting for new ways to hear or perform things. ("Play it like your hair's on fire," he has instructed musicians in the studio, when he can't explain his vision any other way. "Play it like a midget's Bar Mitzvah.") He wants to see the very guts of sound. Just as the architect Frank Gehry believes buildings are more beautiful when they are under construction than when they are completed, Tom Waits likes to see the naked skeleton of song. This is why he finds one of the most exciting sounds in all of music to be that of a symphony orchestra warming up.

"There's something about that moment, when they have no idea what they sound like. . . ," he rhapsodizes. "Someone's tightening up the heads of the timpani, someone else is playing snatches of an old song he hasn't played in a long time, someone else is playing scales, someone else is going over that phrasing she keeps tripping on. It's like a documentary photograph—everyone is doing something without knowing they're being watched. And the audience is talking and paying no attention because it isn't music yet, right? But for me, there's lots of times when the lights go down and the show starts and I'm disappointed. Because nothing can live up to what I've just heard."

He abhors patterns, familiarity and ruts. He stopped playing the piano for a while because, as he says, his hands had become like old dogs, always returning to the same place. Instead, he had fantasies of pushing his piano down the stairs and recording *that* noise. He is known to sing through a police megaphone. He once recorded a song in which the primary instrument was a creaking door. And on *Blood Money*, one of his new albums, he actually recorded a solo on a calliope—a huge, howling, ungodly pneumatic organ, best known for providing music for merry-go-rounds.

"I tell you," Waits says, "playing a calliope is an *experience*. There's an old expression, 'Never let your daughter marry a calliope player.' Because they're all out of their *minds*. Because the calliope is so flaming *loud*. Louder than a bagpipe. In the old days, they used them to announce the arrival of the circus because you could literally hear it three miles away. Imagine something you could hear three miles away, and now you're right in front of it, in a studio. . . playing it like a piano, and your face is red, your hair's sticking up, you're sweating. You could scream and nobody could hear you. It's probably the most visceral music experience I ever had. And when you're done, you feel like you probably should go to the doctor. *Just check me over. Doc, I did a couple numbers on the calliope and I want you to take me through the paces.*"

He likes a day in the studio to end, he says, "when my knees are all skinned up and my pants are wet and my hair's off to one side and I feel like I've been in the foxhole all day. I don't think comfort is good for music. It's good to come out with skinned knuckles after wrestling with something you can't see. I like it when you come home at the end of the day from recording and someone says, 'What happened to your *hand*?' And you don't even know. When you're in that place, you can dance on a broken ankle."

That's a good day of work. A bad day is when the right sound won't reveal itself. Then Waits will pace in tight circles, rock back and forth, rub his hand over his neck, tug out his hair. He and Kathleen have a code for this troublesome moment. They say to each other, "Doctor, our flamingo is sick." Because how do you heal a sick *flamingo*? Why are its feathers falling out? Why are its eyes runny? Why is it so depressed? Who the hell knows? It's a fucking flamingo—a weird pink foreign bird. And music is just that weird, just that foreign. It is at difficult moments like these that Kathleen will show up with novel ideas. (*What if we played it like we were in China? But with banjos?*) She'll bring him a Balinese folk dance to listen to, or old recordings from the Smithsonian of Negro field hollers. Or she'll just take the flamingo off his hands for a while, take it for a walk, try to put some food into it.

I ask Tom Waits who does the bulk of the songwriting around the house—he or his wife? He says there's no way to judge it. It's like anything else in a good marriage. Sometimes it's fifty-fifty; sometimes it's ninety-ten; sometimes one person does all the work; sometimes the other. Gamely, he reaches for metaphors:

"I wash, she dries."

"I hold the nail, she swings the hammer."

"I'm the prospector, she's the cook."

"I bring home the flamingo, she beheads it. . . ."

In the end, he concludes this way: "It's like two people borrowing the same ten bucks back and forth for years. After a while, you don't even write it down anymore. Just put it on the tab. Forget it."

*　　*　　*

Now. About those two new albums.

They are called *Alice* and *Blood Money*. They are recordings of songs Waits has written in recent years for the stage, in collaboration with the visionary theater director Robert Wilson. *Alice* is a dreamy, haunting cycle of love songs based on the real-life story of a middle-aged Victorian minister who fell obsessively (and perhaps pruriently) in love with an enchanting 9-year-old girl. The little girl's name was Alice. The minister's name was Reverend Charles Dodgson, but he is more widely known by his pen name (Lewis Carroll) and for the surreal, not-totally-made-for-children children's story (*Alice's Adventures in Wonderland*) he wrote as a valentine to the girl he adored. On *Alice*, Waits uses his voice as if he were singing tormented lullabies. But singing those lullabies to somebody who's dying, or leaving forever, or growing up too fast.

The second album, *Blood Money*, is completely different. It's based on the German playwright Georg Büchner's unfinished masterwork, *Woyzeck*, about a jealous soldier who murders his lover in a park. (Waits was considering calling the album *Woyzeck*, but then he figured, Jesus Christ, who the hell would buy an album with a name like *Woyzeck*?) This album is all rich, complex, mysterious, dark tomes about the concussion of hatred against love. The sound is not quite industrial or grating, but there is a discord to these songs, an almost physical discomfort. These are dirty little dirges, with gritty titles like "Misery Is the River of the World" and "Everything Goes to Hell."

The good people at Waits's label, Anti, struck on a bit of genius when they decided to release these two albums simultaneously. Because the contrasts of *Alice* and *Blood Money* perfectly highlight the two aspects of Waits's musical character that have been colliding in his work for decades. On one hand, the man has an unmatched instinct for melody. Nobody can write a more heartbreaking ballad than Waits. On the other hand, he has shown a lifelong desire to unbuckle those pretty melodies, cleave them into parts like a butcher, rearrange the parts into some grotesque new beast and then leave it in the sun to rot. It's almost as if he's afraid that if he stuck to writing lovely ballads, he might become Billy Joel. Yet he loves beauty too much to write purely brainy experimental music like John Cage, either. So he does both, going back and forth, some-times on the same album, sometimes in the same song, sometimes in the same phrase. (In the past, he's explained this schizophrenia as some musical version of the alcoholic cycle—first you're nice; then you punch a hole through a wall; then you sober up and apologize by giving flowers to everyone; then you crash your car into the swimming pool. . . .)

This tempestuous struggle with music is the story of his life. Because while Tom Waits and sound have always been infatuated with each other, their relationship has never been a simple one. On the contrary, it's the kind of relationship that leaves broken china and split lips and lost sleep in its wake. There was a time, back when Waits was a child, when he had not yet made any kind of peace with sound and he was veritably tormented by the drunken disorderliness of it all. He remembers that the noises of this world felt like insects to him—insects that burrowed through every wall, crawled under every crack, penetrated every room, making absolute silence an absolute impossibility. With hypersensitivity like that (added to his inherently dark nature), Tom Waits could so easily have gone mad. Instead, he embarked on a mission to arrange a truce between himself and sound. A truce that, over the years, has become something like a collaboration and—with these two new albums—finally feels like a real marriage. Because here, on *Alice* and *Blood Money*, you can see it all together, side-by-side. All that Tom Waits is capable of. All the beauty and all the perversity. All the talent and all the discord. All that he wants to honor and all that he wants to dismantle. All of it gorgeous, all of it transporting.

So gorgeously transporting, in fact, that when you listen to these songs, you will feel as if somebody has blindfolded you, hypnotized you, given you opium, taken away your bearings and now is leading you backward on a carousel of your own past lives, asking you to touch all the dusty wooden animals of your old fears and lost loves, asking you to recognize them with only your hands.

Or maybe that's just how it felt for me.

*   *   *

At the end of it all, the dining room in this old inn has emptied and filled and emptied again several times around us. We've been sitting here talking for hours. The light has changed and changed again. But now Waits stretches and says, gosh, he feels like he knows me so well now that he's almost tempted to take me on a visit to the local dump.

"It's not far from here," he says.

The dump! With Tom Waits! My mind thrills at the thought—the two of us banging on sheet metal or blowing songs into old blue milk-of-magnesia bottles. Sweet Jesus, I suddenly feel like there is nothing I have ever wanted more than to go to the dump with Tom Waits. But then he notices the time and shakes his head. A trip to the dump is impossible today, it turns out. He was due home hours ago. His wife is probably wondering where he is. And, anyhow, if I'm going to catch that flight out of San Francisco, shouldn't I get moving?

"I still have fifteen minutes before I have to leave!" I say, not yet letting go of the dream. "Maybe we could run over to the dump real quick!"

He gives me a grave look. My heart sinks. I already know the answer.

"Fifteen minutes would not be fair to the dump," Tom Waits pronounces, proving that he is above all things a fair and respectful man. "Fifteen minutes would be an insult to the dump."

MICHAEL HALL

Mack McCormick Still Has the Blues

Mack McCormick loves to tell the story of Joe Patterson and the quills. Patterson was a musician from Alabama, who had performed at the Newport Folk Festival in Rhode Island in 1964. He played the quills, or panpipes, like the ones the dancing goat-god Pan is always pictured waving. But Patterson, a childlike man who sometimes threw violent tantrums, wound up in an Alabama asylum, where McCormick went to visit him in 1968. He had no quills to play, so McCormick paid two guards to go down to a nearby river and cut some reeds. As rural musicians have done for ages, Patterson trimmed and hollowed the reeds, holding them together with white hospital tape instead of the bright rag strips he once favored. Then he played his quills as he did growing up, just as people had played them for generations. To McCormick, listening to Patterson's "lovely jumble of sound"—he also whooped and banged a tambourine—was like hearing the first music ever played. "People had to invent music to suit themselves and their community," McCormick says. "It's the purest kind of tradition."

Sitting in his northwest Houston home last September, McCormick pulled out ten reeds held together by faded brown tape. They were Patterson's, and McCormick handed them to me. Instinctively I held them to my lips and blew a disastrous tune. McCormick didn't mind; actually, he seemed pleased. For a few sec-

onds I was directly linked to Patterson as well as to Texas quills
player Henry Thomas and thousands of unknown pipers. For
McCormick, who has spent the better part of his 71 years chasing
down singers, songs, stories, games, recipes, and other folklore, it's
all about connections—between citizens, between artists, between
ideas, and between the stories that bubble in his brain after a lifetime of collecting: how he wrote songs with Lightnin' Hopkins,
how he unplugged Bob Dylan, how Mance Lipscomb made him
weep. One story inevitably segues to another, often in unpredictable
ways. At one point McCormick told me about a version of the cro-
quetlike game roque that was played in oil fields with a ball and
giant mallets, and before long he was talking about Lipscomb, who
had lived in Navasota. Then he paused, as if looking for something
in a pocket in his brain, and said, "Oh, I know, *this* is the connection," and he was off again.

"Mack is one of the most important Texas-vernacular-music historians," says Arhoolie Records president Chris Strachwitz, himself
a collector for forty years. McCormick "discovered" and recorded
living musicians, like Lipscomb and Hopkins, and reimagined the
lives of dead ones, like Robert Johnson. He's written dozens of magazine articles and album liner notes. He's worked for the Smithsonian Institution. He's knocked on more doors than a traveling
salesman, seeking . . . connections. "Mack set out to live his life on
his own terms with all the passion of someone who has made a voca-
tion of his avocation," says Peter Guralnick, the author of many
acclaimed music books, including two about Elvis Presley and several about the blues. "He pursued it in territories where there were
no maps and no rules."

After McCormick's decades in the field, he has amassed one of the
most extensive private archives of Texas musical history in existence.
He has hours of unreleased tapes, perhaps twenty albums' worth of
field and studio recordings by Hopkins, piano players Robert Shaw
and Grey Ghost, Lipscomb, zydeco bands, and the polka-playing
Baca Band. He took pictures everywhere he went and owns some
10,000 negatives, many of famous artists and many more of the
army of unknowns he rescued from oblivion. Then there are his

notebooks, which are like the Dead Sea Scrolls, holding thousands of pages of field notes and interviews testifying to the amazing diversity of Texas music, not just blues. Maybe the most important thing McCormick did was to document the lives and music of a broad group of some of the American century's most-influential musicians, people like Lipscomb, Thomas, Hopkins, Blind Lemon Jefferson, Leadbelly, and Blind Willie Johnson. Much of the archive sits in storage in Houston, much more at a place McCormick owns in the mountains of Mexico. And it's in danger. The pages are fading, the tapes need restoring, and McCormick is sufficiently hoary to worry about dying suddenly with no home for it all. As Strachwitz says, "It would be a horrible tragedy if all his stuff disappeared."

McCormick calls his archive the Monster, a term of both affection and fear. Inside the Monster are secrets—on the origin of the blues, on the story of Texas music, and on the lives of some of the greatest musicians in American history. But the Monster holds secrets about McCormick too, about "some destructive block," as he puts it, that has kept him from completing the many history books he has begun over the past half-century. "I'm the king of unfinished manuscripts," he told me with a self-conscious, pained laugh. Maybe it was the agony of writing. Maybe it was the seclusion. Maybe it was just the blues.

McCormick shuffles around the home he's lived in for thirty years with a cane, favoring a bad left knee. Last fall he suffered an aneurysm in his left leg, and it still hurts. He has snowy white hair and big glasses; he looks a little like crime writer James Ellroy, though without the bulldog ferocity. He has a reputation for being a crusty, reclusive old crank, and he rarely sits for interviews. Indeed, it took several phone calls and a long letter expressing my interest in doing a story on his search for Robert Johnson before I received a reply. No, he was not interested in the story I proposed, but he would cooperate on one that called attention to his collection. He was looking for a benefactor, someone to save it, and he invited me to see it firsthand. I jumped at the chance.

I spent several days with him last fall and winter and though he can be irascible, he is also sweet and generous to a fault, sharing history, tips on research techniques, and a somewhat holistic wisdom about the world. "All I learned," he wrote me later, summarizing his life as a folklorist, "was what others found staying home with the neighbors. Each of us are connected by an infinite number of threads." Though he has spent his life illuminating those threads for everyone else, sometimes he himself has lost sight of them.

"He's a strange guy," says Guralnick. "He's an honorable guy." Both traits have gotten McCormick in trouble.

"Have you ever heard the lyric 'If you get your business in a fix/You better go see Dr. Dick'?" McCormick asked as we drove down a street near his house. "Well, Dr. Dick was my grandfather." Richard McCormick was a Waco doctor who ran the city health clinic, where he treated venereal disease. His nickname became well known and eventually found its way into local folklore and song verses sung by Blind Lemon Jefferson, among others.

Dr. Dick's grandson, Robert Burton McCormick, was born in 1930 in Pittsburgh to Gregg McCormick, a DuPont factory rep who traveled the country showing doctors how to use x-ray machines, and his wife, Effie May, an x-ray technician. They divorced two years later, and their son grew up shuttling between them, living at various times in Texas, Ohio, Alabama, Colorado, and West Virginia. Robert's father, an informal folklorist, would drive him around Dallas, pointing out history and characters, including street musicians in Deep Ellum. "Everywhere we went, he knew something," McCormick remembered. His father took him on demonstration trips to West Texas, talking about local lore and music heroes. The shy, bookish boy found adventure in the stories and meaning in their telling.

In high school McCormick was a jazz and swing fan, and in 1946 he got a job at a ballroom in Cedar Point, Ohio, as a gofer for Buddy Rich, Stan Kenton, and other musicians who came through to play a radio show that was broadcast nationally twice a week. Later that year, on a trip to New Orleans, he met Orin Blackstone, who was compiling a four-volume discography called *Index to Jazz*. Blackstone was so taken with the young jazz buff, who was by then

living in Houston with his mother, that he made him the Texas editor for the final two volumes. In 1949, at age nineteen, McCormick
became the Texas correspondent for *Down Beat* magazine, inter-
viewing everyone from Louis Armstrong to Frank Sinatra. "Mack,"
as he became known, began promoting big jazz shows, managing
and booking bands, and producing recording sessions.

One afternoon in 1949, in downtown Houston near Union Station, McCormick quite literally heard his calling. He wasn't in the
habit of stopping strangers, but something about a tall, old black
hobo carrying a banged-up guitar and a busted kazoolike whistle
made him curious, so he asked him questions and then asked him to
play. The man's words and music were gibberish, but his vigor was
contagious. McCormick didn't realize it at the time, but he was
doing his first field research.

He worked all over—as an electrician on an offshore barge, as a
short-order cook, as a carny in Oklahoma, as a taxi driver and an
aspiring playwright in Houston. "In each job," he told me, "I found
myself intrigued by the virtually unknown, unexplored body of lore
that characterizes a working group"—the limericks, betting games,
initiation rites, and especially music. Driving the cab in Houston
opened McCormick's eyes to the diverse sounds of the state:
acoustic blues, Czech songs, Texas swing, conjunto. "People
thought folk music was over," he said. "I realized that wasn't true."
He began recording ballad singers, fiddlers, and bluesmen. He even
managed Lightnin' Hopkins, or tried to. The mercurial bluesman,
who had made scattered recordings for a dozen labels in the forties
and fifties, had disappeared in the haze of the desultory blues life.
McCormick found and recorded him in 1959 for *Autobiography in
Blues* and brought him back, and for the rest of his life Hopkins was
known as a giant of the Texas blues.

In 1960 McCormick brought together and edited nine years of
country, folk, blues, and zydeco songs that he and other folklorists
had collected. He whittled them down to two albums, *A Treasury of
Field Recordings, Volumes 1* and 2, and wrote long, detailed notes in
booklet form at a time when most albums had cursory back-cover
liner notes. The albums were a revelation, showing how musically

rich Houston and East Texas were—*Saturday Review* called the first
volume "one of the most exciting and valuable folk music collections in years"—and established McCormick as a leading American
folklorist.

"The way to do field research," he told me, "is always from a stand-
point of ignorance. Don't decide beforehand what you want to
find—leave your preconceptions out of it. I've always found it exhil-
arating to knock on doors. I'd stop in a town, knock on someone's
door, and say, 'I'm lost.' Or people would be playing dominoes and
I'd say, 'Can I watch?' Get friendly with people. After awhile, ask a
bunch of questions at once, get them agitated, sit back, and they
start answering them."

His method involved what he called a grid search: He would take
a block of four or eight counties, start in one, head east, return via
the next county north, and then crisscross counties in subsequent
trips, stopping in every grid on his map. He'd go to the county seat
first, find some men talking on the front porch of a store, assume
the guise of innocent ignorance, and ask questions. "As soon as
enough people tell you about something or someone," he said,
"*click*, you've got it." Back in the car he'd jot notes and move on. At
the motel that night or back at home, he'd type or write up his
notes. Later they'd go into one of his many file cabinets.

One name that kept coming up on grid searches in Grimes
County was a sharecropper named Mance Lipscomb. With the help
of Strachwitz, McCormick found the never-recorded Lipscomb in
1960 at his two-room Navasota home and got him on tape.
McCormick talked Strachwitz into making Lipscomb the first
release for his new label, Arhoolie, and the debut featured
McCormick's exhaustive liner notes, showing how the artist was a
connection to the pre-blues past—a "songster" who had been playing ballads, reels, hymns, dance tunes, and blues for most of his 65
years. McCormick had a real rapport with Lipscomb, and while
Lipscomb's wife, Elnora, kept their grandchildren quiet in the other
room, McCormick recorded him in the bedroom, so close their
knees were touching. A year later, in a Houston studio, the two

recorded again as McCormick's mother lay dying in a hospital a few blocks away. When Lipscomb sang "Motherless Children," McCormick began weeping and ruined the take; Lipscomb did the song twice more, though both men had a hard time keeping their composure.

In 1960 McCormick signed on with the U.S. Census Bureau and asked to cover Houston's Fourth Ward. When his day working for the government ended, he would pound the pavement for another four hours, and soon he had uncovered a fascinating pattern: In one urban neighborhood there were two hundred professional piano players. They played a style of rollicking barrelhouse that, McCormick found, went back to a man named Peg Leg Will, who used to play for people on the porch of an Italian grocery store. Young folks would hear Will play and hop up on the piano, imitating him and eventually coming up with their own neighborhood style, one that was different from the barrelhouse playing in the Fifth Ward, just a few miles away. It was what McCormick later called a "cultural cluster—an outburst in place or time when something previously unknown becomes part of our culture; that point where innovators bring forth a new language, slang, music, religion, game, ritual." McCormick had something of an epiphany about the distinction between neighborhood and state, how a local style will become a regional characteristic—"The thing," McCormick wrote me later, "that visitors sense when they say to themselves, 'This is Texas, this is not Vermont, and it is neither the weather nor the rocks which make it so.'"

Where do things come from and why? Drunk with the music and the stories he was hearing, McCormick began to hatch grand plans: a massive book on the origin of the blues and another on the Texas blues. He had a co-writer on the latter, English blues scholar Paul Oliver, and throughout the sixties the two sent research and chapters across the Atlantic. In his fieldwork McCormick was finding that the trails of many of the dead Texas bluesmen were still warm. For example, he found and interviewed the family of Blind Lemon Jefferson, who had died in 1929. Jefferson's sister, Carrie, who lived in the tiny north-central town of

Wortham, told McCormick that her brother didn't want people to know he was blind, so he would nonchalantly escort her around Dallas, plucking the guitar he carried as an echo device to guide him. She gave McCormick a real treasure, a photo of her brother that had never been published (only one picture of him has been). In it, Jefferson is leaning against a building, plump and relaxed, his tiny glasses on his face.

McCormick literally picked up Leadbelly's trail in the little communities at the end of the dead-end roads along the Red River where the folk singer lived as a young man in the early 1900's. Most Leadbelly scholarship concerns his life as a New York folk hero after he was famously pardoned twice—for murder in 1918 and attempted murder in 1930. McCormick talked to the relatives of two people Leadbelly had killed long before that: "He would go down those roads, get a woman, settle down for awhile, then get into a pattern. Drink, pick a fight, hurt a man. Drink, pick a fight, kill a man. He'd just get into fights all the time."

When McCormick wasn't taking notes or working on the book, he was making tapes: prison work songs, bawdy folk songs, truck-driving songs, cowboy songs. He began collecting things other than music, like toasts (the black poetry that would one day become rap), recipes, and oral histories. He took pictures of the work of visionary artists and chronicled local rituals. McCormick would buttonhole anybody who looked promising. At his home office he opened a file and showed me a page of typewritten field notes ("page 2096") that tells of his stopping in Fayetteville in 1962 and speaking to three musicians in a pickup truck on their way to play a dance. The leader, Lee Wormley, age fifty, "has only been playing a short while; then hired 2 youngsters to make rock and roll; Wormley keeps the kids in line and buys the hit records he wants them to imitate." Though McCormick didn't learn much from them (or from a former member of the band, who was "inarticulate, near moronic and almost certainly an inept musician"), the trip allowed him to write about the excellence of most Texas farm-to-market roads and then speculate that this had something to do with the great ease with which rural blacks were moving to cities. Even when he struck out with music, McCormick would score some history.

In 1964 he married a Houston girl, Mary Badeaux. While she worked as an administrator in the microbiology department at the Baylor College of Medicine, he wrote for magazines, newspapers, and educational TV shows in Houston and made a little money from the occasional folklore-society grant or wealthy patron. Throughout the decade, McCormick also booked some of his artists at clubs and helped them make records. He took Mance Lipscomb to play in Corpus Christi and also produced three of his albums for Reprise Records. He co-wrote some songs with Lightnin' Hopkins—one, called "Happy Blues for John Glenn," became a minor hit. Working with McCormick, though, wasn't always smooth. According to Strachwitz, "Mack could be gruff, almost dictatorial. He'd say, 'That's not the way it should be.' When he recorded Mance for Reprise, he made him do 'Trouble in Mind' several times. Mance got mad and said, 'I'll never sing that goddam song again.'"

In 1965 Revered folklorist Alan Lomax, aware of McCormick's work, asked him to bring a Texas prison gang to the Newport Folk Festival to sing work songs. The Texas attorney general wouldn't permit it, so McCormick found a few ex-cons who wanted to go, including Chopping Charlie Coleman, known throughout the Texas prison system for his strength in the fields with a hoe, and drove them there himself. The singers had never sung together in front of a microphone, much less in front of 20,000 people, and McCormick was anxious to give them a brief onstage run-through. But the previous act wouldn't get offstage: It was Bob Dylan with his first electric band. In a matter of hours, Dylan would offend the folkies with loud rock and roll and change popular music forever, but McCormick didn't care about that: "I was trying to tell Dylan, 'We need the stage!' He continued to ignore me. So I went over to the junction box and pulled out the cords. Then he listened."

Later that year McCormick started a label of his own, Almanac Records. His first release was by Robert Shaw, a Fourth Ward piano player who had been playing since the twenties but had never recorded. McCormick again wrote a detailed booklet, connecting Shaw to Peg Leg Will. Nat Hentoff named the album "Best of the Month" in the December 1966 issue of *Hi Fi/Stereo Review*, noting, "McCormick promises more illumination to come from Almanac on such relatively unexplored themes as The Negro Cowboy; Truck Drivers: Songs, Lore, and Hero Tales; and the Legacy of Blind Lemon Jefferson." But Almanac never released another album, and those tapes remain in storage.

McCormick's field research brought him to the attention of the Smithsonian, and he began working there in 1968, when Texas was the featured state in the summer Festival of American Folklife in Washington, D.C. His title was "cultural historian," and he sought anything and everything of interest: quilts, dolls, recipes, games, handcrafted chairs. McCormick even wrote to Lyndon Johnson and asked if he'd like to do a workshop on telling tall tales. "I knew he liked to do that," McCormick remembered. The president said no but showed up anyway, and for fifteen minutes told whoppers. ("He went over great with the crowd," McCormick told me.) Each year the festival featured a different state, and McCormick traveled there to do grid searches beforehand, knocking on doors and looking for people to bring to Washington: a silversmith, a sand-caster, a garlic braider, a cowboy singer, a dulcimer-maker. "It's healthy to have an idea who lives with us," McCormick said of his diverse finds. "You get an enhanced sense of who your neighbors are."

During this time, McCormick was filling file after file with titles like "Bottlenecks and Hang-ups" (about the erroneous idea that Mississippi is the only place where people played bottleneck guitar; they did in Texas too) and "Wild Ox Moan" (about the unicorn legend reappearing as a West Texas myth). But all was not well with one of his biggest projects, *The Texas Blues*, for which anticipation had been building for more than a decade. By 1971 McCormick and Oliver had 38 chapters done, but their relationship was breaking down. One problem, says McCormick, was they were collaborating long-distance without the benefit of copiers, fax machines, or computers. Oliver says it was also a matter of different working methods. Plus, he says, "Mack could be insistent about saying, 'You will do such and such by such time.' I don't work that way." Both got so burned out that they stopped working together. They haven't spoken to each other in thirty years.

McCormick, however, had other things to think about. In 1971 his daughter, Susannah, was born, and he was in the middle of tracking down the most iconic American roots musician of the century, Robert Johnson, a dead bluesman about whom nobody knew much of anything—not even what he had looked like. He was thought to have lived and died in Mississippi, where he was poisoned by a jealous woman or an angry husband, and other folklorists had been on his trail. In 1970, while working for the Smithsonian, McCormick came across a copy of Johnson's death certificate. He found the names of a couple of witnesses to a murder that could have been Johnson's. An interview with them led him to the actual killer, but McCormick wouldn't write about it just yet—it was to be the last chapter of another book he was planning. He spent many more hours in Mississippi, knocking on doors, asking questions on the Rolling Store, a bus that served as a shop for sharecroppers. He eventually tracked down Johnson's two half sisters near Baltimore in 1972 and got the first known photos of the bluesman as well as first publication rights to use them and other family memorabilia. It was the find of a lifetime. Guralnick is still in awe of what McCormick did: "He never would have found Johnson had he been limited by the conventional approach. His work is a tribute to the untrammeled imagination."

So when the two-CD Robert Johnson box set came out in 1990, the one that has sold more than 600,000 copies, why wasn't McCormick's name mentioned in the 48-page booklet that accompanied it—and why didn't he, of all people, write the liner notes? No one knows for sure. (McCormick refused to talk to me about Robert Johnson.) But it has something to do with a blues fan named Steve LaVere, who located one of the half sisters in 1973, a year after McCormick did, and got her to assign to him the rights to administer Johnson's estate. LaVere subsequently went to Columbia

Records with photos and his own story about searching for Johnson, and the label committed to releasing an anthology with him as a co-producer. When McCormick heard the news, he notified Columbia about his prior deal with the half sisters, and the project was put on hold, remaining so for sixteen years.

In the meantime, McCormick worked on his book about Johnson, tentatively titled *Biography of a Phantom*, and he finished one of his masterworks, the album *Henry Thomas, "Ragtime Texas."* Thomas was one of the grand old names McCormick had sought for *The Texas Blues* for decades—a mystery man who had recorded in the late twenties. Thomas' music, like Lipscomb's, wasn't purely blues but lay in the DMZ between blues and the music that came before—reels, ballads, ragtime, and gospel songs from the 1880's through the 1920's, many with the chirping sound of those quills. If McCormick was going to write the definitive guide to the origin of the blues, he had to know where it came from, and Thomas seemed to be a guy to follow. McCormick's interest became a mild obsession over the years, and as he did his grid searches, he asked questions about Thomas. He played Thomas' 78's for people, and some identified his accent as coming from northeast Texas. He got a tape of a Thomas song called "Railroadin' Some" that listed town names along the Texas and Pacific Railroad stretching from Dallas to the hills of East Texas, and he knocked on doors along the route, talking to old-timers who remembered the colorful guitar-and-quills-playing hobo nicknamed Ragtime Texas. McCormick tracked down a second cousin living in East Dallas whose sister had a battered family Bible, and there it was: Henry Thomas, born in 1874 on a farm in Upshur County.

As the Herwin label collected the 23 songs Thomas was known to have recorded, McCormick wrote a 10,000-word evocation of the man. "That essay," says Guralnick, "has such imaginative breadth and scholarly research. Mack went beyond the facts and reimagined the world and music of Thomas—it's one of the most extraordinary pieces of writing on blues I've ever read." McCormick not only came close to finding the source of the music but also had an epiphany of sorts that transported him back to the beginning of his career. While researching Thomas, he saw a picture and a drawing from newspaper ads, one of which looked remarkably like the tall hobo he had stopped near the train station in Houston in 1949. When the Thomas anthology finally came out, in 1975, it was clear that McCormick's first field research had led to one of his greatest achievements.

The publication of *Biography of a Phantom* was announced for the following year, but no book materialized. McCormick took his research and various other manuscripts and moved to another house in Mexico to get some work done. For a decade there were rumors about the book, exacerbated by growing anticipation of the Johnson box set. In 1988 McCormick wrote in the Smithsonian's *American Visions* magazine that he had promised Johnson's killer that he wouldn't publish until the man died. The next year, Guralnick, to whom McCormick had shown much of his research in 1976, published *Searching for Robert Johnson*, a book heavily indebted to his fellow historian. "My entire purpose in writing it was to announce the imminent arrival of Mack's book and perhaps spur him on," Guralnick says now. The gambit didn't work, and when the box set came out, in 1990 (Columbia finally decided to go ahead with the project), McCormick was, as he had once called Johnson, something of a phantom.

Indeed, McCormick was the forgotten folklorist. He was spending his time working on various projects—articles, albums, a family history, a little fieldwork here and there—but he had alienated many in the music world (and perhaps possible benefactors of his archive) when those books never came. Some thought he was playing games or hoarding information. McCormick says he wasn't, that he had always been addicted to field research and it just kept piling up. Also, he had a family and needed to make a living. "It was always something," he told me. "Most of the time it was some museum or the park service calling, asking, 'Do you want to go do this?'" Strachwitz, who had had a falling-out with McCormick in the mid-seventies, knew him to be a champion procrastinator. McCormick rationalized his limitations and began withdrawing. He became reclusive and hard to get hold of. His home was robbed a couple of times, which fueled his mistrust. He declared himself retired. *LA Weekly* writer Robert Gordon says that after he spent two weeks trying to get him to agree to an interview, McCormick finally answered the phone but claimed to be a nonexistent brother. (McCormick denies this: "I told him, as myself, I did not want to contribute.") After a lifetime spent making connections, he was letting them go.

What no one knew was that McCormick was ill. "A great part of the reason I haven't published anything in years," he told me, "is I developed a manic-depressive illness. I'll have states of grandiosity and then a short time later no energy at all. I'd get started on something and then wake up a few days later and say, 'I don't see the point anymore.' It's a crippling and destructive disease." McCormick said that after trying twenty different antidepressants over fourteen years, he finally found the right medicine only four years ago. As for those stories of his self-imposed seclusion, he said, "People call and ask me things all the time. I've helped something like a thousand people. I'm not a recluse—I don't know how I got that reputation." When pressed, though, he admitted, "I think it's because people know I've started and not finished these books."

Indeed, the manuscripts sit where they've sat for years, silently goading him, especially because a few need only a good, passionate editor or co-writer to finish them. *The Texas Blues*, all 500,000 words of it, is 80 percent done (McCormick said it grew far beyond being merely a blues book long ago, expanding through the years to include all Texas music), and *The Aggressive Birth of the Blues* is researched, with maps, fieldwork, and interviews—it just needs to be written. (All McCormick will say about the Robert Johnson manuscript is that it has been abandoned: "It ain't happening anymore. I lost interest.") If these works were completed, they would be the most anticipated music books in years and McCormick's reputation as a hermit would be moot.

At an age when most people are retired, McCormick is still addicted to research, still adding to the Monster, still in love with the chase. Lately he has been mildly obsessed with Emily Dickinson, another semi-recluse, whose life he's probing for a play he's writing. "She's so inspiring," he said. "All I have to do is go to one of her poems for hope. 'This is my letter to the World' is the most heartbreaking poem and the closest to my own lonely feeling sometimes." That feeling got him to join a support group for manic-depressives: "I tell people who are suicidal, who call at three a.m., 'Of course it's hopeless. Who told you it was any different? It's only hopeful in those few moments when you're delusional.'"

But McCormick's life belies such playful cynicism. Only a believer, a person with hope, would spend so much of his life knocking on doors, talking to strangers, seeking connections, even if they sometimes seemed to last for just a few moments, like when Joe Patterson played a jumble of sound on some reeds bound together by white hospital tape.

PAUL BESTON

Life and Death
on "The Late Show"

It is not often that television has anything of import to tell us, and even less often that it is able to arouse genuine emotion, as opposed to manufactured sentiment. And it goes without saying that these rare occasions do not take place on the sets of late night talk shows, which are usually home to triviality and self-promotion.

But recently, David Letterman did something that has perhaps never been done on television. On October 30th, he devoted his entire program to a terminally ill musician, Warren Zevon. The show was a celebration of Zevon's music—he performed three songs—but it was also a public goodbye. It was a remarkable and moving program, and Letterman deserves credit for pulling it off so gracefully. So does Zevon, of course. Those who saw the show are not likely to forget it anytime soon.

Warren Zevon is a rock singer/songwriter who has never sold many records. With the exception of "Werewolves of London," he's never had a hit. But he is known and respected among his fellow songwriters for his barbed take on life and his unusual subject matter. His song catalog is rife with colorful titles like "Monkey Wash Donkey Rinse," "Sentimental Hygiene," "Things to Do in Denver When You're Dead," and "Roland the Headless Thompson Gunner."

He has made a career out of the unusual, and his persona is that of the wild eccentric, an "excitable boy" always perched on the edge

of danger. Ignoring the usual subjects of pop music fare, Zevon has
tended to focus on the obscure and the weird, populating his songs
with headless mercenaries, outlaws, serial killers, boxers, unscrupu-
lous pharmacists, sinister doctors, and "Liz and Liza," who keep
him company on his blistering "Detox Mansion."

Because he has been anything but a mainstream taste, Zevon
has walked a lonely road in the music business. He was without a
recording contract for a time in the 1980s, and his albums are
rarely consistent from start to finish. Rather, they are like conversations in a bar with a neighborhood character — some extraneous,
wandering observations surrounding a few tales you won't soon
forget.

He may not have had many of the suits on his side, but Zevon has
been fortunate to have at least one powerful backer: David Letterman. He has appeared on Letterman's program just about every
time he has a new album, and it is clear that Letterman's affection is
real. Perhaps the late night host, who started out as something of a
rebel himself and has long been conflicted about his career choices,
admires Zevon's resolute staying power, his refusal to go middle of
the road.

And so there he was again on the Letterman set, walking out
somewhat gingerly to generous applause. He would sit for a talk
first, and one wondered how this would go. In the past, Zevon has
indulged the very tired rock convention of obscurity in response to
interview questions. But now, as would befit a man in his predicament, all pretensions were dropped. He did retain his crackling wit,
as when he told Letterman that his "tactical error" in refusing to see
a doctor for 20 years was "one of those phobias that really didn't pay
off." At other points, the gallows humor was a bit too close to the
bone, and even Letterman winced:

Letterman: What was the diagnosis?
Zevon: It's lung cancer that's spread.
Letterman (pause): That's tough. . . that's tough. . .
Zevon: Well, it means you better get your dry cleaning done on
    special!

Unlike many celebrities who live recklessly and spend their waning days campaigning against their former behavior, Zevon accepted his illness as the likely result of choices he had made. "There are always consequences," he said, refreshingly. Letterman asked if his illness gave him any insights into life and death. Zevon shrugged and said he didn't think so, "Not unless I know how much you're supposed to enjoy every sandwich." There was a hush in the audience. And then Letterman did the most difficult thing, which was to conclude the interview. How to do that? Television is not designed for such situations. It is made to show images, not to comment on them. It turns most human sorrow to the mush of sentiment.

So Letterman simply said, "Thank you for being here, and thank you for everything." With that, the segment ended, and the show returned for the performances.

Zevon sang two fairly recent songs, "Mutineer" and "Genius," before concluding with one of his classics, "Roland the Headless Thompson Gunner." One of Zevon's well-kept secrets is tenderness and a gift for gorgeous melodies, and both were in evidence on "Mutineer." What was also in evidence was the slow decline of his voice. The song's lovely chorus requires the singer to go up high, and Zevon made a brave attempt at doing so. He didn't quite get there. Yet the performance was spellbinding—a dying man performing at a kind of public farewell, singing a gentle song of companionship and trust: "You're my witness, I'm your mutineer."

Midway through the song, Zevon turned from his piano and looked at his musicians. He would repeat this gesture in each song he played. In "Roland the Headless Thompson Gunner," he looked over his shoulder at Paul Schaefer, who was leading the band with great gusto behind him. The men exchanged a glance of recognition, and joy. Musicians often exchange glances like this when they are playing and the playing is going well. But here those glances carried much more than pleasure—it was difficult to shake the sense that Zevon, like Letterman earlier, was saying "Thank you for everything."

At the conclusion of the final song, Letterman had a second chance to say goodbye. Standing with Zevon at the piano, his arm around him, he said, "Warren, enjoy every sandwich." To some, this might sound flippant, cold. But it was true to both men's desire to avoid weepy spectacle, and it was true to Zevon's defiant attitude. It was so much more honest than some cheap line like, "Warren, I know you'll beat this thing," that one can readily imagine other hosts uttering.

Zevon will not beat this thing, and he knows it. The entirety of the Letterman program was played out against that realization, without the slightest attempt to paper over the grim reality of his imminent death. This, and Zevon's compelling musical performance, made for a truly moving hour. It is unlikely that television has ever handled something like this with such maturity. Terminal illness has long been a staple of made-for-television movies, which are almost without exception weep-fests, and add nothing in the way of understanding.

Like most people do in cases like this, Zevon has responded by focusing on the essentials—spending time with his children, and doing what he loves, in his case playing music. In one sense, there is nothing remarkable about such choices. What else would you do, after all? But in stepping out into public view and letting us see him, Zevon has been courageous. He has given people a look at what an encounter with death looks like, and an example of how to meet it— with stoicism, with humor, above all, with dignity.

Critics who have followed his music point to its fascination with death, and its many hints at impending demise. They will, naturally enough, search the songs for the lyric that is most fitting for his epitaph. But watching his performance on Letterman, a different epitaph comes to mind—Yeats's "Under Ben Bulben."

That poem famously concludes thus:

> *Cast a cold eye*
> *On life, on death*
> *Horseman, pass by!*

Over the years, many have puzzled over the meaning of that last line, but I would bet that Warren Zevon isn't one of them.

37 Record-Store Clerks Feared Dead in Yo La Tengo Concert Disaster

ATHENS, GA—Thirty-seven record-store clerks are missing and feared dead in the aftermath of a partial roof collapse during a Yo La Tengo concert Monday.

"We're trying our best to rescue these clerks, but, realistically, there's not a lot of hope," said emergency worker Len Guzman, standing outside the 40 Watt Club, where the tragedy occurred. "These people are simply not in the physical condition to survive this sort of trauma. It's just a twisted mass of black-frame glasses and ironic Girl Scouts T-shirts in there."

Also believed to be among the missing are seven freelance rock critics, five vinyl junkies, two 'zine publishers, an art-school dropout, and a college-radio DJ.

The collapse occurred approximately 30 minutes into the Hoboken, NJ, band's set, when a poorly installed rooftop heating-and-cooling unit came loose and crashed through the roof, bringing several massive steel beams down with it.

Andy Ringler, an assistant manager at Wuxtry Records, sustained head trauma when he ran back into the building to rescue a fellow clerk.

"I just had to help," said Ringler, listed in stable condition at a nearby hospital. "I saw all these people coming out bleeding and dazed. I gave up my vintage Galaxie 500 shirt just to help some guy bandage his arm. It was horrible."

Added Ringler: "I just pray they can somehow get this club rebuilt in time for next month's Dismemberment Plan/Death Cab For Cutie show. That's a fantastic double bill."

Joe Gaer was among the lucky record-store clerks who escaped unscathed.

"I was in the bathroom when it happened," said Gaer, a part-time cashier at School Kids Records. "There was this loud crashing sound, followed by even louder crashing, and then all these screams. If I hadn't left to take a leak during 'Moby Octopad'—to be honest, never one of my favorite songs on *I Can Hear The Heart Beating As One*—I'd probably be among the dead."

"It's just tragic," Gaer continued. "I heard they were going to play Daniel Johnston's 'Speeding Motorcycle.' They almost never do that one live."

Devastated by the disaster, Athens record-store owners are still holding out hope that their employees are still alive.

"All I can do is wait and pray they'll find them," said Bert's Discount Records owner Bert Halyard, who lost clerks Todd Fischer and Dan Harris in the collapse. "They were going to start an experimental/math-rock band together. Dan had a really nice Moog synthesizer and an original pressing of the first Squirrel Bait EP."

As of press time, police and emergency rescue workers were still sifting through the wreckage for copies of *Magnet*, heated debates over the definition of emo, and other signs of record-store-clerk life.

"I haven't seen this much senseless hipster carnage since the Great Sebadoh Fire Of '93," said rescue worker Larry Kolterman, finding a green-and-gold suede Puma sneaker in the rubble. "It's such a shame that all those bastions of indie-rock geekitude had to go in their prime. Their cries of 'sellout' have been forever silenced."

MICHAEL CORCORAN

Exhuming the Legend of Washington Phillips

The mystery begins the first time you hear the flowing gospel of Washington Phillips, whose entire recorded output consists of 18 tracks recorded from 1927–1929. His sacred porch songs, bathed in a celestial haze of notes from a strange instrument identified as a dolceola, sing out the existence of a higher power, for how could man alone create music for the angels?

After just five sessions in a Dallas studio, where he'd been summoned by Columbia Records field recorder Frank Walker, Phillips faded back into obscurity. Ry Cooder led a slight revival in 1971, when he covered Phillips' "Denomination Blues," and newer bands, such as Austin's Knife In the Water, have interpreted moralistic lullabies like "A Mother's Last Words To Her Daughter" for the art rock crowd. For the most part, however, Phillips is virtually unknown except to a cult of rabid musicologists who revel in the mystique of the man who emerged out of nowhere as a fully formed artist — and just as quickly disappeared.

The liner notes to Phillips' only American CD, "I Am Born To Preach the Gospel," on the Yazoo label, provided a biographical explanation in 1991, reporting that the singer was committed to the state mental institution in 1930 and died there of tuberculosis eight years later. The All-Music Guide, a favorite Internet reference source for critics and fans, repeats the information, taken from the death certificate of a Washington Phillips of Freestone County.

The truth, however, is that another man of the same name, from the same place, is the one who made that mesmerizing music. The "real" Washington Phillips returned to the farming life in the black settlement of Simsboro, 60 miles east of Waco, content to play for neighbors and churchgoers until 1954, when, at age 74, he died of head injuries suffered from a fall down the stairs at the welfare office in nearby Teague.

I didn't know about this case of mistaken identity in November 2002, when I stood over a grave on the old "colored" side of the Austin State Cemetery, thinking that I'd found the final resting place of the man who helped create modern gospel by putting religious lyrics to 12-bar blues. "It's gotta be this one," said Dave Roup, the hospital's director of maintenance, who led me out to the site where only numbers mark many of the graves. "We know that No. 1692 died in early December '38 and No. 1694 died in April '39." The information on the death certificate, which said a Washington Phillips had been buried at the state cemetery Jan. 2, 1939, placed him in grave No. 1693.

Later that day, Roup called with some interesting news. It turned out that the body had been exhumed the day after it was buried and taken back to Teague, near Simsboro, by brother Sim Phillips.

A few days later, I was making the same trek. According to the liner notes, the parents' names were Houston Phillips and Emma Titus Phillips, which gave me a place to start. Before I left, I sent a few e-mails to historians of Freestone County (also the home of 1920s blues legend Blind Lemon Jefferson) and soon received a phone call from Wilbur Titus of Fairfield, whose grandfather was Emma Titus' brother. Wilbur had traced the Titus roots from the slave depots of the Caribbean to South Carolina, then to Arkansas and finally to Fairfield, Texas, in 1852. What's more, three of Sim Phillips' children were still alive. A volunteer with the Freestone County Genealogical Society, meanwhile, e-mailed me to say she'd found that a Washington Phillips was buried in the Cotton Gin Cemetery near Teague. This search was going too easily, I thought.

The main challenge would be to find out how an uneducated black man from rural East Texas managed to get his hands on a dolceola, a strange keyboard instrument produced in Toledo, Ohio, from 1903 to 1908 and sold almost exclusively in the Northern states as a "miniature grande piano."

Phillips' accompaniment was identified as a dolceola in the '60s by noted British musicologist and author Paul Oliver, who said he got the information from a Columbia executive. Through the years, the dolceola (fewer than 50 are known to exist today), has been such a part of Phillips' lore that modern Memphis dolceolist Andy Cohen told me, "Without Phillips, the instrument would be completely forgotten today." Until Cooder tinkered with a dolceola, Phillips was believed to be the only artist to ever record with the instrument, which measures 16 inches wide and 22 inches long and weighs about 15 pounds.

'You mean, my cousin Wash'

Still on the trail of the wrong Washington Phillips, the one who died at the state hospital, I found his nephew Cleo Phillips in Oklahoma through directory assistance. Born in 1940, he never knew his uncle, but he said he did have a cousin named Wash who used to preach and sing a bit. "He had this trick," Cleo said, "where he'd eat a fish like a sandwich and spit the bones out the side of his mouth." Cleo gave me the number of his sister Annie Mae Flewellen, who lives in California. When I asked her if she remembered anything about her uncle, the gospel singer, she corrected me.

"You mean my cousin Wash. He's the one who sang." Flewellen says she remembers her father going to Austin to bring back the body of his brother when she was a young girl. "I never knew him. They said he drowned in a water tank." But she had lots of memories of Cousin Wash. "He used to dip snuff, right, and when I was small I'd always ask him if I could have some," she recalled. "So one time he finally gave me a little pinch and showed me how to spit it out, but I just went to the floor. Passed out cold."

Giving snuff to a child? That didn't sound like the Bible-thumper who preached good parenthood on "Train Your Child."

But then a lot of things didn't make sense in the Washington Phillips story I was pursuing. For instance, how could someone's mental faculties deteriorate so quickly, so noticably in 1929 Texas, that they could record eight masterfully played and sung tracks in a single day and then be sent to an asylum eight months later?

I returned from my first visit to Freestone County without finding a single person who knew Wash Phillips, the son of Houston and Emma, as the singer who recorded a few 78-rpm records.

Three days later I would find what I hadn't been looking for: eyewitness evidence that Washington Phillips, the gospel pioneer, was not the one who died in Austin on the last day of 1938. While looking over my notes one Monday night, I saw that I hadn't yet talked to Wilbur Titus' cousin Virgil Keeton, who used to sing in a gospel quartet. Since he's also related on the Phillips side, he could be a good source. It was 9 p.m., borderline cutoff for calling a stranger, and the voice at the other end of the line said she thought Keeton was asleep. "Wait, I hear him stirring," said Keeton's wife. "Virgil! Come get the phone." After a couple of minutes came a tired hello.

"Oh, yeah, I knew Wash Phillips, the gospel singer," Keeton said when I told him what I was calling about. "He used to live in Simsboro with his mother, my Aunt Nancy. He used to play this harplike instrument that he made himself. Sang like a bird, man." Born in 1920, Keeton said he first saw Phillips perform in the mid-'30s ("I was a teenager") and visited him and his mother in Simsboro regularly. "He gave one of his '78s to the Titus family and it eventually passed on to us," Keeton said, starting the chorus of "Life Him Up That's All." Virgil and his wife, Jewell, said they last remember seeing Phillips a couple years after they married in 1946.

At the Freestone County Clerk's Office the next day, I searched death records from the late '40s until I came to the date Sept. 20, 1954, and saw the name George Washington Phillips. According to the death certificate, he was born on Jan. 11, 1880, which means he was 47, not 36 as previously believed, when he made his first recordings. Just as Virgil had said, Phillips' mother's name was Nancy (Cooper). His father's name was Tim Phillips.

Next stop was the Keetons' house, where Virgil had just returned from his weekly cancer treatment in Temple. He demonstrated, with a thumb-plucking motion, how Phillips played the strings on his instrument. Showed a picture of a dolceola, Keeton said, "No, that's not it."

Even with this new eyewitness account, some Phillips fans maintain that only a dolceola could make the heavenly accompaniment found on Phillips' recordings. "I'm 100 percent sure it's a dolceola," said Memphis producer Jim Dickinson, who played the "completely illogical instrument" on Ry Cooder's "Crossroads" soundtrack. "The way it sounds like part of it is going backwards, that's a dolceola," he said.

The debate has even carried over to academia. At the 1991 International Conference of African American Music and Literature in Belgium, Dutch musicologist Guido van Rijn ended a lecture on Phillips with an argument for the dolceola theory.

Is it possible that Phillips played a dolceola in the '20s, but then lost it or broke it and switched to a "harplike" instrument in the '30s? But what about the 1927 photo of Phillips, discovered in 1983? It shows him in the recording studio holding two zithers, which look like autoharps and are played in a manner consistent with Keeton's recollection.

Ex-Simsboro resident Doris Foreman Nealy finds it curious and somewhat amusing that musicologists would be giving lectures or arguing over details about her neighbor Wash almost 50 years after his death. "He was what they called a 'jack-leg preacher,' " she said. "He didn't have a church, so he'd kinda roam the town looking for someplace to preach. In Simsboro, we had a big picnic every June 19, and Mr. Wash would always start it off with a song. But none of us kids knew he ever made any records."

He belonged to the Pleasant Hill Trinity Baptist Church in Simsboro, but May Nella Palmore, 82, of Teague recalled Phillips also preached and performed at the "sanctified" St. Paul Church of God In Christ. "His singing really fit in with that crowd," she said. "He had such a strong, powerful voice." The Keetons said they last saw him doing the devotion at St. James African Methodist Episcopal Church in Teague. "I am born to preach the Gospel," he used to say, "and I sure do love my job."

That Phillips was well-versed in the varying beliefs and customs of different churches is evident in "Denomination Blues," his most famous song via covers by Sister Rosetta Tharpe (who renamed it "That's All") and Cooder. Coyly denouncing hypocrisy in organized religion, Phillips mocks six different black denominations before launching into the verse: "You can go to college, you can go to school/ But if you ain't got Jesus, you a educated fool."

The lyrical bitterness, perhaps born from too many Sundays waiting to be called while less-pious men hogged the pulpit, didn't seem to apply to a musical career that never took off. "He knew he had talent," Keeton said. "But he was just ol' Wash Phillips, you know? Don't nobody get famous from Teague."

He was known more for his mule cart, from which he sold homemade ribbon cane syrup, than for a handful of records that gave him a blip of recognition many decades ago.

But where the memories of the man fade, the musician's work is stuck in time, vibrant and eternal. "Without knowing much about him, I feel that his recordings tell his story," said Knife In the Water guitarist Aaron Blount, who became acquainted with the songs six years ago when the grieving father of a friend gave him a Phillips tape and asked if he knew anyone who could play that kind of music at the funeral. "His music is so simple, yet highly developed to the point that it's almost psychedelic," Blount said. "You can hear the essence of a true artist, creating against all odds."

Phillips had some success with his first 78 record, which had the updated church song "Take Your Burden To the Lord" backed with "Lift Him Up That's All." The record sold just over 8,000 copies in 1928. Then came the stock market crash of 1929 and the Great Depression. The scouts and field recorders stopped coming from New York in search of raw talent, and the labels instead focused on making more refined records that would comply with the escapism sought by a dour populace. In the 1920s, Texans such as blind

Pentecostal pianist Arizona Juanita Dranes of Dallas and Marlin's Blind Willie Johnson, whose classic compositions have been covered by Led Zeppelin ("Nobody's Fault But Mine") and Eric Clapton ("Motherless Children") were spicing "Negro spirituals" and songs of praise with barrelhouse piano and slide guitar before anyone else. But the innovative recordings from Texas suddenly stopped. Like Phillips, Dranes made her last recordings in 1929 and Johnson never stepped inside a studio again after April 1930.

How Phillips spent the first 47 years of his life remains a mystery. He was a brilliant instrumentalist, but did he receive formal training or was he self-taught? And what was his relation to the Wash Phillips who was 11 years younger and died 16 years sooner?

The two men named Washington Phillips are buried in the Cotton Gin Cemetery in the countryside six miles west of Teague. But an hourlong search could locate only the tombstone of the Phillips who died in Austin State Hospital. That the Washington Phillips who was gospel's great disappearing act would take his eternal nap in an unmarked grave seems about par for this course in music history.

Sixty-two-year-old Durden Dixon is one of the few black people still living in Simsboro. "They knocked down all the houses and put together these big ranches," he said, waving his arm across the horizon. From '44 to '54, a young Dixon lived down the road from the man he described as "kind of a hermit." Sometimes the old man would bellow neighborhood boys away from his dewberry bushes. Other times he'd invite them up to his porch, where he'd sing and strum a boxlike instrument Dixon said Wash "made from the insides of a piano." Dixon didn't know Phillips made records, so as he rode shotgun to show me where Phillips used to live, I played him "A Mother's Last Words To Her Daughter," a song about shirking temptations to become a child of God. Dixon's face lit up. "That's Mr. Wash all right," he said, in full-beam delight. "I remember he used to sing us that one."

The shack is gone, but Dixon showed me where it used to sit, about 20 yards in from the road. Aside from a few bottles of Coors Light discarded under a tree, the land seemed untouched in the 48 years since Phillips was called home. There are old pieces of tin and some rusted buckets. There was also a little brown bottle, half-buried where the porch used to be. When I picked it up and showed Dixon, he laughed.

"That's his snuff bottle, man." The next day an appraiser at Rue's Antiques in Austin confirmed that the bottle once held Garrett's snuff circa the early '50s.

What do you know? Annie Mae Flewellen's 74-year-old memory was on the mark. If there's anything the story of Washington Phillips has told me, it's that sometimes what's true and what's false come from where you least expect it.

The great musician Wash Phillips didn't die in the insane asylum. And his instrument almost certainly was not a dolceola. The legend lessens with the mundane facts. It's comforting to know, however, that the singer who has affected so few people so profoundly didn't live out his last few years in mental torment, but surrounded by the people who respected him for who he was. "Leave it there, oh leave it there," he used to sing in his sweet tenor of the truth. "Take your burden to the Lord and leave it there."

Sometimes it can be as simple as that, knowing when and where to let go. Sometimes 18 songs is the whole shot and you accept that and just go on living the life you sing about.

PHILIP GOUREVITCH

Mr. Brown

Forty-seven years ago, at a radio station in Macon, Georgia, five young men stood around a microphone and sang a song. One played guitar, another played piano, but the station's recording equipment picked up the instruments so faintly that the tape they made that day is often recalled as an a cappella performance. The lead singer was shorter than the others. He had to stand on an over-turned Coca-Cola crate to get his mouth level with the mike. When the tape started rolling, he cried out the word "Please" with an immensity of feeling that might, more conventionally, have been reserved for a song's climax. Then he cried out again, "Please," and again and again, "Please, please," at heartbeat intervals. With each repetition, he invested the monosyllable with a different emotional accent and stress—prayer and pride, impatience and invitation—and although there was ache in his voice, he did not sound like a man pleading so much as commanding what was rightfully his. After his fourth "Please," the rest of the group filled in softly behind him, crooning, "Please, please don't go," until the lead singer's colossal voice surged back over theirs: "Please, please, please." That was the name of the song, the same word thrice, and, like all truly original things, this song had a past to which it simultaneously paid tribute and bid adieu. Its genesis lay in a rearrangement of the standard "Baby Please Don't Go," so that the rhythmic backup line became the lead, and the melodic lead was relegated to the chorus. A simple gimmick; but, as "Please, Please, Please" progressed, the lead

singer's initial passion only intensified, and it became clear that the
reversal of foreground and background voices reflected a deliberate
emotional attitude that brought a bold new energy and freedom to
the spirit of black popular music. Instead of describing feelings in
the smooth lyrical surface of a tune you could whistle or at least
hum, the singer created the impression of sounds rising untamed
from the rawness and obscurity of a soul that refused all masks.

The song was over in less than three minutes, but that time had
the sense of compressed eternity which one experiences in the
memory of dreams. Transcribed as text, the words suggest a man
gnawing at the last frayed ends of his tether, yet the febrile repeti-
tions, elongations, and elisions of the singer's phrasing make of
these words not a lament but a rhapsody, even an ecstasy:

> Please. Please. Please. Please. Please. Please. Please. Honey,
> please! Don't. Yeah! Oh, yeaah. Oh. I love you so. Baby! You
> did me wrong. Whoa! Whoa-oh. You done me wrong. You
> know you done! Done me wrong. Whoa. Oh yeah! You took
> my love. And now you're gone. Please! Please. Please. Please.
> Please. Please. Please. Please. Please. Please. Honey, please.
> Don't! Whoah. Oh, yeah. Lord. I love you so. I just want to
> hear you say, I . . . I . . . I . . . I . . . I . . . I . . . I . . . I . . . I! Honey,
> please. Don't. Oh! Oh, yeah. Oh. I love you so. Baby! Take my
> hand. I want to be your lover man. Oh, yes. Good God
> almighty. Honey, please! Don't. Ohhh. Oh. Yeahh. Lord. I love
> you so! Pleeeeeeeease. Don't go. Pleeee-ee-ee-ease. Don't go.
> Honey, please don't go. Oh. I love you so. Please. Please.

The song doesn't tell a story so much as express a condition. The
singer might be speaking from the cradle of his lover's arms, or
chasing her down a street, or watching the lights of her train dimin-
ish in the night; he might be crouched alone in an alleyway, or wandering an empty house, or smiling for all the world to see while his
words rattle, unspoken, inside his skull. He could be anyone anywhere. His lover might be dying. He might be dying. He might not
even be addressing an actual lover. He could be speaking of some-

one or something he's never had. He could be talking to God, or to the Devil. It doesn't matter. Despite the implication of a story, a specific predicament, the song is abstract. The words jockey for release and describe the impossibility of release, yet the singing is pure release, defiant, exultant. Speech is inadequate, so the singer makes music, and music is inadequate, so he makes his music speak. Feeling is stripped to its essence, and the feeling is the whole story. And, if that feeling seems inelegant, the singer's immaculately disciplined performance makes his representation of turmoil unmistakably styled and stylish—the brink of frenzy as a style unto itself.

A few months after the Macon recording session, Ralph Bass, a talent scout for King Records, heard a copy of the tape in Atlanta. King was one of the country's leading independent labels, with a particularly strong catalogue of what was then known as "race music"— the music produced by black artists for black audiences which, despite its ghettoized marketing label, was already widely recognized by the mid-fifties as the defining sound of the twentieth century. In the early postwar years especially, King played a big part in bringing rhythm and blues to a national audience, recording and publishing the work of such now largely forgotten acts as Bull Moose Jackson and Eddie (Cleanhead) Vinson, as well as more enduring names: the Five Royales, Little Willie John, and Hank Ballard and the Midnighters. So Ralph Bass knew the repertoire; he'd heard more gravel-voiced shouters, high-pitched keeners, hopped-up rockers, churchy belters, burlesque barkers, doo-wop crooners, and sweet, soft moaners—more lovers, leavers, losers, loners, lady-killers, lambasters, lounge lizards, lemme-show-you men, and lawdy-be boys— than any dozen jukeboxes could contain. But he had never heard a voice that possessed the essence of all these styles while moving beyond them toward a sound at once more feral and more self-assured, until he heard "Please, Please, Please."

The tape identified the singers collectively as the Famous Flames. That was it: nothing more about them, or where they might be found. The Flames, however, had been performing nearly constantly around Georgia, where they were known as "house-wrecking" showmen who danced as they sang, in paroxysms of astounding acrobatic agility. Bass, a white man who always stayed in black hotels along with the musicians, promoters, and disk jockeys who best knew his terrain, soon tracked down the group's manager at a barbershop in Macon. He brought two hundred dollars in cash and a contract, and declared, "I want them now." The Flames were summoned, they signed, and left for a gig. "I still didn't know who the lead singer was," Bass later told the writer Geoff Brown, but he figured it out that night when he stopped in at the club where the Flames were billed to play at ten o'clock Right on time, Bass said, "out comes this guy, crawling on his stomach, going from table to table, wherever a pretty girl was sitting, singing, 'Please, Please, Please.'"

This guy was James Brown. He was twenty-two years old, a lithe, rippling sinew of a man, on parole after three years in the state-penitentiary system. He had been locked up at the age of fifteen for stealing from parked cars in Augusta, where he was raised in a whorehouse run by his Aunt Honey. He was a middle-school dropout, with no formal musical training (he could not read a chart, much less write one), yet from early childhood he had realized in himself an intuitive capacity not only to remember and reproduce any tune or riff he heard but also to hear the underlying structures of music, and to make them his own. He had started singing in church, not long after he began walking, and the hand-clapping, stomp-and-shout, get-all-the-way-down-on-your-knees spirit of the Baptist gospel pulpit formed the bedrock of his musical impulse. But his attunement to the sacred never inhibited his appetite for the profane. He claims to have mastered the harmonica at the age of five, blowing "Lost John," "Oh, Susannah," and "John Henry," and one afternoon, when he was seven, he taught himself to play the organ by working out the fingering of "Coonshine Baby." Before long, he was picking up guitar licks to such songs as "(Honey) It's Tight Like That" from the great bluesman Tampa Red, who was dating one of Aunt Honey's girls. By the time he was twelve, the young prodigy was fronting his own group, the Cremona Trio, and winning talent shows with a romping rendition of Louis Jordan's "Caldonia (What Makes Your Big Head So Hard?)." In reform school in the tiny north Georgia town of Toccoa, his nickname was

Music Box, and he returned to singing for the Lord, forming a
gospel quartet that made its own instruments: a paper-and-comb
harmonica, a drum set of old lard tins, a broomstick-and-washtub
bass. The warden was impressed, as was a young gospel singer in
Toccoa named Bobby Byrd, who'd heard him sing at the prison
gate, and offered to give him a home and find him a job if he could
win his release. "I want to get out and sing for the Lord," James
Brown wrote to the parole board, and although these words suggest
an act of a rather different order than the one he and Byrd eventually put together with the Flames, nobody could deny, as he slith-
ered among the ladies on night-club floors, that he sang as if he'd
burn in Hell if he stopped.

In February of 1956, the Famous Flames crossed the Mason-
Dixon Line for the first time, and drove into Cincinnati, where
King Records had its headquarters in an old ice factory. When they
were shown into the studio, King's founder and president, Syd
Nathan, was seated in the sound booth—a fat little man with a big
cigar, a shouter and a bully, who reminded James Brown of Edward
G. Robinson in "Little Caesar." Nathan's first impression of his new
talent was equally unflattering: the Flames were barely a minute
into "Please, Please, Please" when he exploded from his chair, hollering, "What in hell are they doing? Stop the tape," and "Nobody
wants to hear that noise," and "It's a stupid song," and so on, until
he stalked out. In his autobiography, the singer recalled protesting
to King's music director, "Mr. Nathan doesn't understand it. Everybody's music can't be alike."

The tape got made, and Nathan still hated it. When Ralph Bass
heard of the debacle, he was in St. Louis. "I get Syd on the phone,"
he told Geoff Brown. "He's yelling . . . 'That's the worst piece of
shit I've ever heard! He's just singing one word. It sounds like he's
stuttering.'. . . Before I could say anything, Syd says, 'You're fired!'
But I knew what I had. I had been playing the dub from town to
town, in every hotel I stayed. And the women would go crazy. I told
Syd, 'Don't fire me. Put it out in Atlanta, test it. You'll see.' He says,
'Fuck it, I'm putting it out cross-country, just to prove what a piece
of shit it is.'"

Within a year, the song had climbed to sixth place on the R&B. charts, and was on its way to selling more than a million records; the band had a new manager, Ben Bart, of Universal Attractions in New York, who began booking the act—and its recording and publishing credits—as James Brown and the Famous Flames. The rest of the group, embittered at being upstaged, quit, leaving James Brown feeling both bereft and liberated. "I was sorry," he wrote. "I was heartbroken. . . . They couldn't see that we were really just getting started. There's not much more I can say about it except that they went home, and when they went home I kept going."

I'm Back!

Mr. Brown, as he insists on being addressed, has described himself as "the Napoleon of the stage," and, like the French emperor, he has a compact body, with a big head and big hands, and a taste for loud, tightly fitted costumes. One evening not long ago, in a dressing room at the great Art Deco pile of the Paramount Theatre in Oakland, California, as his valet Roosevelt Johnson ironed a gold lamé suit with heavily fringed epaulettes for the night's performance, Mr. Brown sat before a mirror contemplating his reflection. His totemic hair—an inky, blue-black processed pompadour, "fried, dyed, and laid to the side"—was bunched up in curlers, awaiting release. A black silk shirt hung open from his shoulders, baring a boyishly smooth and muscular torso for a man who says he's sixty-nine and is alleged by various old spoilers down South to be as much as five years older. He had just finished refurbishing the thick greasepaint of his eyebrows and, wielding a wedgeshaped sponge, was lightening the upper edges of his high, flat cheekbones with some latte-colored paste. He studied his smile, a wide, gleaming streak of dental implants whose electrifying whiteness might have made Melville blink. In show business, he has said, "Hair is the first thing, and teeth are the second. Hair and teeth. A man got those two things, he's got it all." Still, he looked tired and lonely and even smaller than he is, as old men tend to look when applying their makeup.

In performance, however, he makes the stage look small, and wears his years with a survivor's defiant pride. James Brown is, after all, pretty universally recognized as the dominant song-and-dance man of the past half century in black-American music, perhaps in American popular music as a whole: he is the source of more hits than anyone of any color after Elvis Presley. He stands virtually unrivalled as the preeminent pioneer and practitioner of the essential black musical styles of the sixties and early seventies—soul and funk—and the progenitor of rap and hip-hop. Since 1968, however, he has had only one Top Ten hit, "Living in America," from the 1985 soundtrack to Sylvester Stallone's *Rocky IV*, which was followed by a period of seeming ruin, marked by serial scrapes with the law on charges of spousal abuse (later dropped) and drug possession, and a return to jail, from 1988 to 1991, after he led a fleet of police cars on a high-speed chase back and forth across the Georgia-South Carolina border. Yet his iconic stature as an entertainer has steadily increased in the decade since his release, and his return to the stage.

He still performs about fifty concerts a year, and, while his sound and style are always unmistakably his own, he manages in the course of each evening to present a sweeping retrospective not only of his own vast repertoire but of all the musical genres to which his originality pays homage: from the field hollers of slavery, the call-and-response, organ-surging exultation of gospel, the tragicomic clowning of minstrel shows, and the boastful reckonings and imploring incantations of the blues, to the sugary seductions of country balladeers and cosmopolitan crooners, the horns of jazz, the guitars of rock and roll, and the percussive insinuations of a thousand local beats from across America, Africa, and the Caribbean. He has repeatedly revolutionized these traditions, discovering in them previously unexpressed possibilities. In turn, his music and dance moves have been so widely studied, reinterpreted, ripped off, and sampled by so many artists of so many different musical dispositions throughout the world that it has become nearly impossible to say, "This is where James Brown's influence ends and the rest of music begins."

By the time he appears onstage, the show is well under way. If there is a curtain, it has risen (and, if there is none, the lights have done the rising) on his band, the Soul Generals—at last count, fourteen men, ten black, four white—four guitarists, two bassists, two full drum sets, a percussionist, a trumpeter, three saxophonists, and an organist. The players wear uniforms with thigh-length blazers and matching trousers (the color varies from night to night cherry red or pool-chalk blue), and white shirts with Chippendale collars folded over bow ties, a look that places them about midway on the sartorial trajectory between zoot-suiters and riverboat gamblers. They come on full tilt, cranking a sassy medley of funk hooks for several minutes before a deep, commanding voice with the drawling singsong excitement and syllable-parsing precision of a carnival barker rises over the music: "Ladies and gentlemen, James Brown Enterprises is proud to present the James Brown Show!"

The voice belongs to a diminutive man who stands backstage with a cordless microphone, clad in tails, a high-buttoned vest, a bunched silk cravat, and, on some nights, a cocked fedora. This is Danny Ray, who has been Mr. Brown's master of ceremonies for thirty-eight years. As the band ratchets up to a crescendo, he steps jauntily into view—an astounding apparition, natty as Cab Calloway, with a face as hard-lived and angular as Keith Richards's. "And now," he proclaims, "the Bittersweets." A quartet of lady backup singers saunter onstage, identically and snugly sheathed in black, ankle-length gowns, banded in overlapping, wedding-cake tiers of fringe that ripple to their every twitch and undulation. Two are white (a willowy, porcelain-skinned brunette and a glowing redhead); and two are black (a bouncy, radiant woman with cornrow braids and a massive, heavyset dame hooded in a processed, pumpkin-colored mane). They assemble downstage left, cock their hips, extend their arms with pointed fingers, and coo, "Ooooh, ahhh, gimme some more."

Danny Ray rocks and grins. "And now," he says, holding the "now" for a full second, "let me tell you this." A beat elapses in silence, and Danny Ray continues, "I want to ask you one thing. Are you ready for some su-per, dy-no-mite soul?" The house answers with a deafening "Yes!" "Thank you," he says. "Because right about now it is star time." The band kicks back in, playing canonical riffs from James Brown crowd-pleasers, as each of the Bittersweets takes a turn naming the songs in a lilting arpeggio: "I Feel Good" ... "Papa's Got a Brand New Bag" ... "Try Me" ... "Doin' It to Death." Danny Ray picks up where they leave off— "'Please, Please, Please' ... 'Sex Machine' ... 'I Got the Feelin'" ... 'Living in America'"—and with that he starts chanting, "James Brown! James Brown!" The house chants back, full bore, hands clapping, bodies swinging, and, lest anybody out there still be seated, the Bittersweets start a cheer of their own: "James Brown, git up, git up. James Brown, git up."

Mr. Brown has always regarded his public with an attitude akin to that of a politician on the campaign trail: by their adulation, he says, "the people" made him, and to keep them he must serve them. At the same time, he has the peculiar idiomatic habit of describing himself as a slayer of audiences. "Normally, I just go out there and kill 'em," he declared in the Oakland dressing room. What he means by such remarks is that, for as long as the price of a ticket brings you to him, he will transport you so totally into the grip of his groove that you will forget your mortal coil in eager surrender, and, if he does his job well, he will literally control your breathing as precisely as if he had his hand clenched around your trachea. So the relationship is symbiotic: he gives his all, and asks for nothing less in return. He was in particularly high swagger in Oakland, after leading his band through an afternoon rehearsal of the overture to his entrance. "You gotta hear the new opening," he said. "When I get up there— the audience, they already dead. I just stand there and look around."

This is precisely what he does, and the ebullient commotion of singers and musicians onstage is such that it's easy not to notice him strolling on from the wings until, all at once, there he is: arms out from his sides as if to welcome an embrace, dentistry blazing in a beatific grin, head turning slowly from side to side, eyes goggle-wide—looking downright blown away to find himself the focus of such a rite of overwhelming acclamation. He lingers thus for several seconds, then, throwing his head back, he lets out a happy scream and rips into the song "Make It Funky." Within seconds, he has sent his microphone stand toppling toward the first row of orchestra seats, only to snatch the cord and yank it back, while spinning on the ball of one foot in a perfect pirouette, so that his mouth returns to the mike and the mike to his mouth in the same instant. He howls. The crowd howls back. The music is irresistibly danceable; the whole house is churning, and the Bittersweets are setting the pace, pelvises swivelling, arms cycling, chanting, "Make it funky," while Mr. Brown, whose microphone is lashed to its stand with a fat snarl of electrical tape, drags the whole assembly with him like a mannequin dance partner, as he stalks the edge of the stage, barking, "Tell me. Uh! So it is. Ha! Got to do it now. . . . Oh, yes. Take me home. To the bridge. To the bridge." He screams, he spins, he does the mashed potato— gliding several yards on one foot. He starts the second song with his back to the crowd, then wheels to face it, and cries, "I'm back, I'm back, I'm back, I'm back. . . ," and screams again.

James Brown screams in nearly every song he has ever recorded or performed. He also grunts, honks, yowls, and hoots, and there are long stretches in many of his songs where he does little else. When he chooses to, of course, he can also sing melody and enunciate lyrics with a piercing clarity. In the space of a sixteenth note, his voice can shift from a honeyed falsetto to anguished lamentation or bellowing bombast. There is very little, if anything, in the range of vocal emotion that he cannot express, and the same can be said of his almost perpetual motion on a stage: although his dance routines are briefer than they once were, and he no longer does splits, or falls to his knees so hard or so often as to draw blood, as he used to, his energy still seems radically at odds with the conventional limitations of human biology. He is a showman of the old school, equal parts high artist and stuntman, and his boldest moments leave art and stunt indistinguishable.

This is never more evident than at the point in his show—during "Please, Please, Please"—when he cuts from the peak of a feverish vocal and instrumental crescendo and collapses to his knees in stunned silence. His band simultaneously fades to a worried murmur of pulsing rhythms, while the audience, as he puts it, falls "so

quiet you can hear a rat peelin' cotton," and in a high, pleading qua-
ver, he announces, "I feel like I'm gonna scream." The crowd goes
silent as he sinks even lower to the floor and lets the beats pass. "You
make me feel so good I wanna scre-e-eam," he wails. The crowd
roars, he falls still, and when the crowd settles down he wails again,
"Can I screeeeam?" And again: "Is it all right if I
screeeeeeeeeeeam?" The crowd appears fit to riot. He appears fit to
be tied. Then he screams. The scream has a sound of such overwhelming feeling that you cannot believe the man controls it. The
impression, to the contrary, is that he is controlled by it, as if out of
all the throats in the cosmos it had found his, and rendered him
wild: the sound in the wild man's throat from beyond the wild man's
consciousness that is the wild man's being.

As he screams, Mr. Brown uncoils and staggers upright, dripping
sweat. The band cranks up behind him, he resumes singing, and
Danny Ray, who drifted offstage during "Make It Funky," reappears. Under his arm he now carries a bundle, which he unfurls with
a swooping snap of both wrists into a wide, floor-length cape of
sequinned velvet. The cape's design varies from show to show, and
on occasion in the same show from scream to scream; sometimes it
is red, sometimes green, sometimes black, sometimes gold, and
sometimes the sequins spell out the words "Godfather of Soul" or
the acronym "G.O.S." Mr. Brown pays no attention as Danny Ray
stalks him with the cape, but when it is flung over his shoulders he
bows deeply, soaking up the applause, before taking heavy, tentative,
stiff-legged steps. As he starts moving he shrugs the cape off, finally
flinging it aside and prancing free. On some nights, Danny Ray will
come back at him with the cape, and Mr. Brown will shrug it off
once more, or he may drop back to his knees, and work himself up
to scream again.

Take this spectacle as you will—as death or birth; conquest or
surrender; hellfire or apotheosis; sexual climax or heartbreak's abjec-
tion; vaudeville hamming or sublime authenticity—you won't be
wrong. James Brown is a master of the simultaneous suggestion of
opposing possibilities. He is a shaman as much as a showman; but,
while his uncanny melding of church and carnival is akin to the con-

vulsive "speaking in tongues" of gospel congregationists, the impression James Brown creates of a man flying off the handle is just that: an impression.

His performances are, and have always been, orchestrated according to the most rigorous discipline. Although no two nights with him are the same, and much of what you see and hear when he's onstage is truly spontaneous, the dazzle of these unpredictable moments is grounded in his ensemble's equally dazzling tightness. He proceeds without song lists, conducting fiercely drilled sidemen and sidewomen through each split-second transition with an elaborate vocabulary of hand signals. "It's like a quarterback—I call the songs as we go," he says, and players whose attention wanders, who miss a beat, or trip into the wrong key, or who merely show up onstage in rumpled uniforms or scuffed shoes, may be fined on the spot, a punishment that is also communicated with hand signals: five fingers suddenly flashed five times, for instance, means twenty-five dollars' docked pay. "I gotta keep order," he explains. "They don't spank children no more, that's why there's no order."

Even in his earliest, wildest days, when his determination to kill an audience was such that he would swing from the rafters, cut flying splits from atop a grand piano, and even leap from a theatre balcony into the orchestra pit, his outrageousness was carefully calculated to convey that, while he cannot be contained, he is always in control. In contrast to the appearance of effortlessness that so many performers strive for in their quest to exhibit mastery, James Brown makes the display of effort one of the most striking features of his art.

In the greatest of his dance performances to be preserved on film—the made-for-television "T.A.M.I." show, of 1964 (in which he stole the thunder from the headline act, an up-and-coming British band called the Rolling Stones, leaving Mick Jagger to complain that it was his greatest mistake ever to follow James Brown)— he hurls himself about, a frenetic dynamo, feet blurring, sweat flying, arms pumping, hairdo collapsing. He is the image of abandon, yet his precision remains absolute, his equilibrium is never shaken, there is no abandon. Even at his most unleashed, he moves like a captive of his body, frantic to shake free, and coming closer than one might have imagined possible.

"Time made me the Godfather, continuous and continuous doing it," Mr. Brown said one afternoon last summer, as he rode in a chauffeur-driven white stretch limousine through the slums of Augusta, where he spent his boyhood—a neighborhood known as the Terry, short for Negro Territory. Beyond the limo's one-way windows, the season's first tropical storm, Allison, was blowing sea-green clouds and rain across a wide street lined with blighted-looking shops and slum dwellings. The street sign said James Brown Boulevard, and James Brown said, "But what made me want to do it? My daddy couldn't do it, his daddy couldn't do it, and his daddy better not tried it."

James Brown Boulevard

We have this idea in America that pedigree doesn't matter. Never mind your ma and pa, set your own sights, and you are what you make of what God made you—that's the idea. The ancestors held its truth to be self-evident, but we have come to call it our dream, and it follows that our inclination to be entertained by success, to be inspired by excellence and enterprise, and to heroize genius increases in direct proportion to the inauspiciousness of an achiever's origins. So it should probably come as no surprise that the man who is very likely better known to more of the world by more fabulous titles than any other American—His Bad Self, Mr. Dyna-mite, Soul Brother No. 1, the Sex Machine, the Hardest-Working Man in Show Business, Mr. Excitement, the Ruler of R&B, the Godfather of Soul, King of the One-Nighters, the Minister of the New New Super-Heavy Funk, the Forefather of Hip-Hop, Mr. Please Please Please, James (Butane) Brown—was not only born dirt poor and black (with a heavy dose of American Indian blood) at the height of the Great Depression, in the depths of the Jim Crow South, but also claims to have been born dead.

"I wasn't supposed to be alive," he declares in the first lines of his autobiography. "You see, I was a stillborn kid." One can't start out any worse off than that. In fact, one can't start out that way, period; stillborn means you're finished. ("Compare live-born," Webster's suggests.) Never mind: in dealing with James Brown, we are not operating in the conventional show-business realm of legend but in that zone of mystical, folkloric, and allegorical interpretations of life's molding forces which can only be called myth. So the story goes that he emerged lifeless from the womb, and remained that way, unresponsive to the paddlings and proddings of his mother and a pair of aunts, who had attended at his birth (in his parents' one-room shack, without windows, plumbing, or electricity, in the pinewoods outside Barnwell, South Carolina), until they gave up on him. One aunt told his father, "He never drew a breath, Joe," while his mother wept. But the other aunt, Minnie, was moved to keep at him, lifting him up and blowing into his mouth. In this way he was resurrected, and promptly issued his first scream.

One of his earliest memories is of his mother leaving his father for another man: his mother in the doorway saying goodbye, his father telling her, "Take your child," his mother saying, "You keep him." He was four years old, and he didn't see her again for twenty years. His father was a second-grade dropout who subsisted by tapping the surrounding pines for pitch to sell to turpentine mills, and by brewing moonshine. He was rarely at home, and although as an adult James Brown cannot stand to be without company, in his autobiography he credits the solitude of his earliest years—"Being alone in the woods like that, spending nights in a cabin with nobody else there"—as an enduring source of inner strength. "It gave me my own mind," he says. "No matter what came my way after that—prison, personal problems, government harassment—I had the ability to fall back on myself." Still, he was relieved, in his sixth year, when his father decided to move across the Savannah River to Augusta in search of steadier employment, and deposited him in the care of Aunt Honey.

Thereafter, his father kept in touch, but they never again lived at the same address. Mr. Brown remembers him as an inspiringly tireless worker, but also as a depressingly angry man, particularly when it came to race. "Where white people were concerned, I would

say my father threw a rock and hit his hand," he says in his autobiography. "He'd call white people 'crackers,' curse 'em and everything when they weren't around, but when he was in front of them,
he'd say, 'Yessir, nawsir.' That's when I lost respect for my father." A
frightened man, in his view, is a cowed man, and a cowed man is a
frightening man. For his own part, he comes across, offstage and on,
as fundamentally fearless. "I fear God," he told me. "I fear a man
with a gun. I fear a man with a knife. I fear a fool behind the wheel.
That's what I fear. I fear death." Then he remembered that he
feared something else even more. "Death may come to me," he said.
"I may not run from it like a lot of people if my rights is there. I put
my rights first, 'cause if I can't live then I'm already dead . . . If I'm
already dead, how can I live? I mean, my daddy was a dead man. He
walked around, he gone into the service, he did everything he could.
He was the bible of the dead man. He come back, he never said a
voice. Dead man."

Race, poverty, and exclusion were the defining features of James
Brown's childhood world, and he might easily have seen himself as
cursed. Instead, he seems to have understood himself to be a free
agent—denied the comforts of a conventional home, but also spared
its constraints—with no choice but to fight for emancipation however he could. If anything, he can sound nostalgic for the harsh but
tight-knit community of his childhood in the Terry. "Age mellowed
me. Yeah, success mellowed me," he said as we rode around. "'Cause
now I look and see people that ain't got nothing, and I got *everything*
and a sense of what they got. I say, You know what? You know why I
say everything? 'Cause I got bein' poor as well as bein' wealthy. A
man who's been always richer than I, he's in worse shape than a cat
who never had nothin'. Cat never had nothin' got a dream. Cat
richer than you'll say, What can I do now?"

After a while, he said again, "I got everything I could ever have
wanted. Well, I thought it was everything I could want. What I
wanted was peace and happiness, and a little success. I don't want
hell and happiness. I got a hell of a lot of happiness, but I got hell
with it, too."

The limousine tour of his childhood turf was Mr. Brown's idea. We set out from his office, from which he also ran a radio station, in a former H. L. Green department store on Augusta's Broad Street, downtown. He was dressed for the occasion in a throbbingly purple training suit, and at first he seemed quite happy to point out landmarks and reminisce. Here was the corner where he used to work a shoeshine box outside a parlor known as the Shoeshine King: "There was a man used to give us fifty cent and one used to give us a dollar. And we used to almost disjoint that man's arm when we see him coming, trying to hold him till he get to our stand. Oh, a dollar was unbelievable. . . . My daddy didn't make but seven dollars a week." Here was the liquor store where he first outearned his father, delivering whiskey ("Can't do that no more, they don't allow it") for nine dollars and ninety cents a week, "and you keep the bicycle—almost like you give me a home." Here was the fairground where he used to sneak into the circus, here was the railroad siding where he learned to roller-skate, and "On this corner was a warehouse, I used to eat food out of there. . . . The can would be old, it would be popped up, broken, I mean, like just about to blow up. We put a hole in it, let the pressure off it, and then take it home and cook it. We ate that. Lord." Here was 944 Twiggs Street, where he lived with Aunt Honey—now abandoned and bristling with weeds. Here, by these train tracks, he buck-danced for the soldiers passing through town at the start of the Second World War; they'd throw him coins, which he took home to Aunt Honey: "Men made thirty cents an hour, twenty cents a hour, fifteen cents a hour. . . . I brought her back five dollars to pay the rent for a month." Here was the narrow canal where he once took refuge from the law: "Police were running me, and I saw 'em coming, and I made a few turns, jumped in the water, and breathed through a cane. I saw it in a movie." He mimicked the police, "Where'd he go? Where he at? Where he at? I know I saw him. I swear I saw that boy—Gawd damn." Then he recalled telling himself, "'Now listen up, it's either jail, either reform school, or you stay in the water,' so I stayed in the water." And here was an oil company that he used to burglarize when he was nine: "That was wrong, but it was survival."

Taken together, these memory vignettes composed a portrait of an artist as a young entrepreneur. The image pleased him. Alongside his career as a performer, James Brown has consistently promoted himself as an exemplary figure of black capitalist self-empowerment, touting a doctrine of enterprise as emancipation; ownership and tycoondom as the ultimate social justice. In Jim Crow days, he says, whites didn't keep blacks down because they disliked them (some of his most enthusiastic, best-paying audiences, in his early days with the Famous Flames, were at the fraternity houses of all-white Southern colleges); rather, whites kept blacks disempowered in order to exploit them in a system of "economic slavery."

He claims that he never stole from blacks, preferring to operate as a sort of freelance Robin Hood, redistributing white wealth, much as he sought to do when he began to command power in the music business. In 1962, when he wanted to make a live record of his act at the Apollo Theatre, Syd Nathan of King Records opposed the idea on the ground that such a disk would get no radio play. Mr. Brown put up the money himself, and the full record went on to become a fixture on the playlist of many stations; it was also a crossover success, substantially bolstering his burgeoning white audience. It has never stopped selling, and remains to this day one of the freshest, most charged, and most satisfying concert recordings available. Soon after its release, Mr. Brown began waging a dogged and ultimately successful campaign to wrest ownership of the royalty-generating master tapes of most of his recordings from the King archives. This was a measure of creative and commercial control that no popular musician, black or white, had quite achieved, and for years afterward he kept the tapes in a bag that was with him at all times. In 1966, he bought his own Learjet, and before long he had established a restaurant franchise and acquired several radio stations. As he flew from gig to gig on a relentless touring schedule, he spoke of himself as a trailblazing "model man"—self-made and self-owned—in whose wake black Americans could no longer be held back.

At the peak of the civil-rights struggle, Mr. Brown's idiosyncratic rhetoric of business as revolution simultaneously appealed to and appalled ideologues on both the left and the right of the political spectrum, who could never decide whether the man who sang, "You got to live for yourself, yourself and nobody else," was with them or against them. In 1966, the Black Power activist Stokely Carmichael (who became Kwame Ture) called him the man most dangerous to the movement, and two years later, at a Black Power conference, the poet LeRoi Jones (later Amiri Baraka) described him as "our No. 1 black poet." But nobody could question that James Brown's greatest public triumph of the era was a direct consequence of his hard-charging capitalism. On the night following Martin Luther King's assassination, in April of 1968, he was booked to play the fourteen-thousand-seat Boston Garden. Elsewhere, major cities were already aflame. Boston was on the brink, and Mayor Kevin White was under heavy pressure to cancel the concert. Mr. Brown, however, was not prepared to forgo the night's pay. Instead, he persuaded the city to guarantee the money—a staggering sixty thousand dollars—and the show would be televised live, then immediately re-broadcast to keep the city's young blacks in front of their TV screens and out of trouble. Toward the end of the concert, some young fans leaped onto the stage, and cops rushed from the wings to push them off. "Wait a minute," Mr. Brown told the police, his hand raised. The music stopped. "Move on back," he said. "I'll be all right. I'll be fine." The cops shrugged and withdrew, but the fans kept coming, mobbing the singer as he said, "You make me look very bad, 'cause I asked the po-lice to step back and you wouldn't go down. No, that's wrong. You not bein' fair to yourself and me and all your race." When he was alone again in the spotlight, he said, "Now, are we together or are we ain't?" Then he told the drummer, "Hit that thing, man," and he resumed singing: "Can't stand it. Can't stand it. Can't stand your love."

The concert worked. The streets of Boston remained mostly quiet, and Mr. Brown was soon summoned to the smoking ruins of Washington, D.C., to spread his message: "Build something, don't burn something." In that same year, 1968, one of his hit songs, "Say It Loud (I'm Black and I'm Proud)," was embraced as an anthem by the Black Power crowd, and decried as incendiary by white conservatives, while another of his hits, "America Is My Home," was denounced by black militants as a jingoist sellout and acclaimed as a message of interracial healing by their opponents. To James Brown, there was no contradiction. He wasn't just unapologetically black; he was the darkest-skinned American performer to achieve such stardom, and his pride in that fact was to him a fulfillment of the American Dream. (Prior to September 11th of last year, a James Brown concert was the rare place where you could count on seeing someone publicly wrapped in the flag.) Unfazed by his critics on the left, he also went to Vietnam that summer to entertain the troops— one of the few times he has performed for free—then returned home and endorsed the Democratic Presidential candidate, Hubert Humphrey, who had befriended him two years earlier after hearing his hit song "Don't Be a Drop Out," which became the theme of a White House-sponsored stay-in-school campaign. When Richard Nixon won, however, Mr. Brown accepted an invitation to play at his Inauguration, where he made his mark by performing "I'm Black and I'm Proud." (In 1972, he endorsed Nixon's successful bid for reëlection, believing that the President would promote minority-enterprise initiatives, but he skipped the Inaugural festivities, because the Nixon people declined to pay for his act.)

"Is he the most important black man in America?" asked the cover line for a profile of James Brown in *Look*, in February of 1969. The article celebrated Mr. Brown's business empire (eighty-five employees; gross annual income, four and a half million dollars) and his populism (travelling a hundred thousand miles a year to reach three million fans where they lived; capping ticket prices at five dollars for adults and ninety-nine cents for children under twelve), and it said, "James Brown is a new important leader. His constituency dwarfs Stokely Carmichael's and the late Dr. Martin Luther King's. . . . He is the black Horatio Alger." Never mind that all of Mr. Brown's early businesses, save for his performing and recording career, failed, or that the Internal Revenue Service discovered by the early seventies that he had never got around to paying more than four million dollars in income tax. (In his autobiography, he proffers the extraordinary argument that the government was to blame for his tax troubles, "because they didn't allow me to go to school." As a result, he says, "they have no legal boundaries over me. . . . You pay tax when you exercise all of your rights. I didn't exercise rights. I didn't have a chance to. I lived with the word can't, so I can't pay taxes.")

As we turned off Twiggs Street onto a narrow and particularly abject strip called Hopkins Street, Mr. Brown's mood turned sombre. The façade of a brick house on the corner was spray-painted with the words "Fuck the world," and farther along the real estate grew more dismal: tottering clapboard bungalows, half of them burned out, and the rest, he said, "probably crack houses now—you come from that, you use crack." In this setting, the limo looked like a spaceship, but none of the street's ragtag residents expressed any surprise. They waved from sidewalks and porches, and although they couldn't see through the rain-streaked one-way glass, they called out, "Hello, Mr. Brown," and "God bless, Mr. Brown." The vehicle could belong to nobody else: every Thanksgiving, he comes through passing out turkeys, and at Christmas he brings toys. Now he said, "They want me to help build this place back. What can I do? Get on my knees and pray, and ask, 'Mr. President, come—Mr. Bush, come in here and clean it out and put decent homes in here'?"

He told his driver to stop outside a broken-down shack, where an emaciated woman and two young men sat on a porch surrounded by household debris. One of the young men stepped forward in the rain, and Mr. Brown lowered his window and held out a fifty-dollar bill. The man bowed, and withdrew. "Wait a minute," Mr. Brown called after him. "Y'all split that. Give that lady some, too." When he rolled his window up, he told me, "I'm not doin' this because you here. I wasn't gonna do it today. I didn't want you to see me handin' no money out there. I wasn't gonna do it. That's the honest-to-God truth." He sounded embarrassed. "You look at this, it kinda take your breath," he said.

At the end of the block, we reached James Brown Boulevard, and he said, "Out here on these same streets, you may see my daughter, and she has no business out here. She don't have to be there. I give her a home, she got a new Mercedes, and her Mercedes just sitting there. I can't give it to her, 'cause I can't—'cause she shrug off everything I do."

Family life has never been Mr. Brown's strong suit; he has been married four times, divorced twice, and made a widower in 1996 when his third wife died from complications following plastic surgery; he had three children with his first wife, two with his second, none with his third, and on the day before my visit to Augusta his current wife (then still his fiancée), Tomi Rae Hynie, a thirty-three-year-old singer of Norwegian descent, who has performed and lived with him on and off for the past four years, gave birth to a son, James Joseph Brown II. In addition to these relationships, throughout much of his career he maintained a succession of girl-friends and mistresses, with a couple of whom he sired children, including the daughter he was keeping an eye out for on the street named after him. "She's got worse than a habit," he said. "When a person is just spooked, we say she got a monkey on her back. She got a gorilla on her back." He fell silent for a beat, then said it again, "She got a gorilla on her back."

So our journey into his past had brought him hard up against the present, and he did not seem to feel so at home anymore. As he spoke of his helplessness before his daughter's destitution, his earlier discomfort at being seen giving handouts suddenly made sense: he wasn't embarrassed for himself, but for the people who accepted his charity. After all, this was the man whose ultimate civil-rights-era message song was "I Don't Want Nobody to Give Me Nothing (Open Up the Door, I'll Get It Myself)." He had wanted to show me the "nothing-ness" he'd come from, but that nothingness, which had been created by a sense of exclusion, had been a full and vibrant world to him. Now it was gone—the door had been opened, and those who found a way had moved on through it—and he was at a loss to account for the new nothingness of oblivion that had taken its place, a genuine wasteland without the blatant boot-heel of Jim Crow to blame.

"I don't know whether this freedom is as good as segregation," he said at one point. "I'll let you figure that out." And he said, "I got a street named after me, and I'm still riding around—I can't say not one thing."

Back to the Crossroad

Mr. Brown has plenty to say, of course, and he does not hesitate to say much of it. He talked non-stop for more than three hours in Augusta, and once we'd put James Brown Boulevard behind us his mood grew easy again, and his words flowed more freely, in long, looping monologues. In his speech, as in his music and dance, he is at once fiercely controlling and wildly spontaneous, unpredictable even to himself. But, unlike his songs, his conversation can be nearly impossible to follow. The patchwork of his syntax and the guttural slipstream of his diction—a gravelly, half-swallowed slur whose vis- cosity has increased through the decades, in lockstep with his pur- suit of perfect dentistry—are only part of the challenge. After deciphering what he's saying, it frequently remains necessary to determine what he's talking about. And much of the time he appears to be wondering the same thing, because his speech is a form of improvisation. So Mr. Brown speaks with an attentive ear, stringing words and ideas along in contrapuntal themes and variations, at times falling back on reliable old formulations to give the jam shape, until he hears some new riff emerging, at which point he works and worries the key elements, juggling their sequence and refining their emphasis, until they converge in a sudden burst of determined lucidity, or fade out and are forgotten.

In one characteristic outburst, he began by pointing to a block of abandoned buildings that were slated by the city for rehabilitation, and said the only way to go was to tear them down and start over from scratch. "What you see now is a shell of a building," he said. "At least if there was nothing there you could build good. You could imagine. But now you can't imagine—you got to think of how to salvage it and save it." He worked this vein for a while, and it soon broadened out: "America needs an overhaul. Overhaul. Go back. I made a song called 'A Man Has to Go Back to the Crossroad.' So America now needs overhauls. She gotta go back to the crossroad. She gotta go back to the drawing board. 'Cause what is happening to it?" He went on, "I mean, you got to go back to the beginning and rewind yourself. You got to do like a tape deck, you got to

rewind and start all over again." He said, "I don't want to tear nothing up, I want to be able to—I want to own part of it. I don't want to
tear it up, I want to build it up, and then own part of it. Or I want an
opportunity to build one just like it."

He said, "Free enterprise is as good as it can be, but when you
start going with one is educated and the other's not, it's not free
enterprise no more. When one is educated, and the other don't
know A from B, it's not free enterprise no more." He said, "The
same intent they showed to keep us separated years ago, they should
show that same intent to put us together." He said, "America has
committed a lot more crimes on civilization than we committed trying to get into civilization. We was out of civilization. What we was
livin' was not civilization, it was uncivil. Our whole thing was
uncivil. It wasn't even civilized! The people know that. You gonna
let people come in your house and cook for you—Look here, you
gonna let people come in your house and cook food and plan for the
whole family, little babies come and there'd be a nanny and let the
baby suck the titty, and then tell 'em, 'Lady, you can't be eatin' with
them'? Come on. It's crazy."

And he went on, "I ask you, let up a little bit. Let's give the small
man a little more chance to be human. Let's not dehumanize the
man and put him in jail for bein' a criminal. Dehumanize! I mean,
you won't put a dog in jail for tryin' to eat out your garbage can or
eat out your yard. So why you gonna do that to a poor man that has
no guides. More schools. The people in jail need to go to school.
Anybody with any less than a ten-year sentence should stay in
school all the time. 'Cause you know that's a dumping ground. Even
the toilet dumps into a refinery and goes round and back to you as
clean. Even a *toilet*. O.K.? It goes to the reservoir and everything
before it come back to the people as drinkin' water. But you take a
man out of prison, who don't know nothing but killin' and doin'
anything wrong, and put him out and expect him to function with
people, like he can live with them. He cannot *live* with them. He
can't live with nobody. I think of all this stuff, and I see it's a cause
that's called L-O-S-T, lost—unless you put music back in it. Music

right now, whether it's gospel, jazz, you need music. You need to
have a music revolution to get these people's mind right."

Once James Brown gets talking, it is not easy to steer him. You may
ask a question, you may get an answer—there may or may not be
any correlation. I asked if he knew that he was not like other people;
that he had a much higher level of energy. "Mmm-hmm," he said.
After a moment, he added, "I'm not going to endorse marijuana for
sale, but for health I will." He said, "A man should never confess,
but I think that anything that's good for people—gotta do." Besides,
if the alternative is hard drugs and a person needs something gen-
tler, "you better bring marijuana back so you have some place to get
off. You can't jump one-four. You know, one-two. One *and* two. Get
'em on the 'and.' Then we can bring 'em back home."

In the late eighties, Mr. Brown and his third wife were widely
reported to have a habit of getting high on angel dust, or PCP, an
animal tranquillizer that tends to induce paranoid and often violent
psychosis in humans. On September 24, 1988, the singer, dishevelled, enraged, and carrying a shotgun, burst into an office next to
his own in Augusta and accused its occupants—forty men and
women attending an insurance-licensing seminar—of using his
bathroom without permission. After a brief standoff, he retreated.
"God said, 'Boy, go home,'" he later told a local reporter. He drove
off in his pickup truck, and soon found himself pursued by a police
car with flashing lights. He pulled the truck over and stopped, and
when the cruiser stopped behind him he peeled back onto the road.
The police stayed on his tail for four miles, until he pulled over once
more. By now he was heading east on Interstate 20, and this time he
waited for the officer to get out of his car before taking off again.
He entered South Carolina at eighty miles an hour, shot off the
interstate, and almost immediately found himself facing the flashing
blue lights of a police car blocking the road, with the lights of
another behind him. When he stopped, an officer approached and
began questioning him through his window. According to Mr.
Brown, another officer appeared at the passenger door and started
smashing the window in with his pistol. The singer threw the truck

into gear and floored it. By then, there were at least four policemen standing in his dust and they opened fire, striking the truck eighteen times, puncturing the gas tank and all four of the tires. "They act like I done rob ten banks," Mr. Brown said later. "I left to protect my life."

Driving full throttle on his wheel rims, he trundled back to Augusta at thirty miles an hour, and meandered through downtown, trailed by a posse of fourteen cruisers. When he finally lost control of the truck, and ground to a halt in a ditch, he was about a mile from the scene of his first arrest (for larceny), thirty-nine years earlier. This time, he was brought back to South Carolina, where he was convicted of aggravated assault and "failure to stop for a blue light," and sentenced to six years. Once again, he served three.

Mr. Brown keeps the crippled hulk of his truck in a shed at his home, a several-hundred-acre estate in Beech Island, South Carolina. There, behind a wrought-iron replica of the gate at Buckingham Palace, guarded by a bloodhound and a white security guard who addresses him with "Yessir" and "Nawsir," a winding two-lane road leads through a forest of pine and live oak, dipping past a large man-made pond (soon to be banked with "six foot of concrete, so people can stand back off and fish"), to his residence. He has been expanding the building according to his own design in recent years to become "just a monstrosity, it's unbelievable, a pleasure monstrosity—one that's gonna be good for you to show your kids to—and it's gonna be quite a monument, so you'll say, 'You know what, that James Brown got somethin' on his mind.'" He wouldn't allow me inside the house, but he made a point of showing me the truck. He claimed he'd turned down offers of as much as a million dollars for it. "That was the truck that started all my success," he said mysteriously.

"Goin' to jail in the nineties was really a great awakening," he added, "because I didn't know people were still that ignorant." I took him to mean his fellow-inmates, but it turned out he was speaking of the police, who had refused to just let him go home, as God told him to. "I stayed away from the ghetto too long," he said. "You living all this and you think musicians got a umbrella, till they

come pick you up. You don't have no rights." He scoffed at allega-
tions that he was high on PCP at the time of his arrest—"Not in my
life," he said of hard drugs in general—but then he added, "Well, I
wouldn't say as I did buy PCP. It might've been in the marijuana.
And, if it was, I sure wish I had some more."

I started to say something, and he cut me off. "I'm'a say that
again. Whatever I had, I need some more, 'cause everybody else is
insane with them drugs they're using. Now, what was you goin' to
ask me?" I no longer remembered, so I said, "How do you account
for an insane generation?" He couldn't. He could only describe its
insanity. "Black kids shootin' every one of each other, they got a
quick temper. . . . But then the white kids, after they go in the service and all this stuff, come back—they shootin' and nobody cutting
'em, they shootin' at a whole room of people, shootin' at the
teacher, they doin' everything. You know, whites are extremists, they
go all the way with it." And he prescribed a solution: "We need a
substance now to make us afraid. A-F-R-A-I-D. That's what we
need. We need something—the kids need a pessimistic drug to slow
them down, to make them, you know, 'I ain't gonna do that.' Ain't
nothin' these kids wanna do today. Ain't nothin' you wanna do.
They in a different bag. They need somethin' to make them pessimistic, and make them come out of this craziness so we can go to
work and save this country."

There are no computers in the offices of James Brown Enterprises.
"He's got this strange notion that they can see back at you," Maria
Moon, one of his staffers, explained. "I guess he watched too many
Russian-spy movies when he was young or something, but he thinks
that they can see you and that they can track everything that you
do." Mr. Brown put it slightly differently: "I don't want computers
coming feeding direct off of me, 'cause I know what I got to tell a
computer that it ain't got in there, and I don't want to. If the government would want me to be heading up the computer people, I
would give 'em a basic idea what we should put in a computer—not
just basic things, you know, but things that will be helpful in the
future. We don't have that, but I could tell 'em a lot of things." He

didn't elaborate, but he told me that on several occasions, while watching television news, he had foreseen the deaths of people on the screen. President Anwar Sadat, of Egypt, was one. "I looked at him when he got off the plane. I said, 'Oh, Lord.' I looked at the man's eyes. 'Oh, Lord!' I said. 'He's a dead man.' And he was dead." On an earlier occasion, during the Attica prison riots in 1971, he foresaw that the inmates who had taken over the prison would be slaughtered. "I was getting my hair fixed, and I looked up at the television," he said, and again his reaction was "Oh, Lord." His hairdresser asked, "What'd you see?" Mr. Brown told him, "All those dead men. They didn't even have no face no more, far as I was concerned. I looked at 'em, I didn't want 'em to be there no more."

James Brown is rarely unaccompanied; he employs a large court of attendants, whom he summons at all hours to listen as he speaks, and he told me, "I got all the friends in the world. My friends— that's all that matter to me." But he has the air of a man who is eternally alone. Even those who have spent a great deal of private time with him hesitate to describe themselves as knowing him. The Reverend Al Sharpton says, "I probably would have been as close to him as anybody for the last twenty-some years." But he is quick to add, "Close as he lets people get close. There's a zone nobody goes in. He draws a crowd, but then he's also centered, lonely, in the crowd." At his core—"deep down inside his solitude"—Sharpton believes, Mr. Brown is a mystical man who "probably has more faith than most preachers," and he said, "In the middle of the night, when there's no crowd, no nothing, that's all he talks about."

James Brown was living in New York, in a Victorian mansion in Queens, surrounded by a moat and decorated each Christmas with black Santa Claus lawn sculptures, when he was introduced to Sharpton, in the late sixties. (He liked New York, he said, except for one thing. "No wholesome people," he said, although in those days New York was a better place for interracial romance than the South, where if you met "a brunette, a blonde, a redhead, you can't even write to her—they'd hang the letter when it gets there.") Sharpton was nineteen when they met again, an unknown, aspiring black activist, and Mr. Brown, whose firstborn son, Teddy, had just died in a car crash, took him under his wing. Sharpton, who came from a broken home, and whose strongest memories of his father were "that we used to stand in front of the Apollo and he'd bribe the guys so we could get up on line to see James Brown," said, "I became in effect, over the next decade, his surrogate son, and he was my surrogate father." Sharpton, who eventually married one of Mr. Brown's singers (Kathy Jordan, who was a backup on a recording of "Tennessee Waltz"), in turn introduced the Godfather to his third wife, and for many years the Reverend was a regular member of their entourage.

Politically, James Brown and Al Sharpton make something of an odd couple. Mr. Brown has always defended his support for Richard Nixon, and a few years ago, when *Rolling Stone* asked him to name a hero from the twentieth century, he chose the reactionary senator from his home state, Strom Thurmond. He also performed at Thurmond's daughter's wedding, and sang "God Bless America" at a ceremony marking the ninety-eight-year-old senator's plan to retire. "But his style, his soul force, was very much an influence on me—and his whole thing of defiance and standing up against great odds if he believed in something," Sharpton said. "He's the only man I've ever met that doesn't need the acceptance and certification of the external world. He goes by his beliefs. He could care less about everybody else's."

By way of an example, Sharpton recalled accompanying his friend when he received a Grammy Award for lifetime achievement shortly after he got out of jail. Mr. Brown got a standing ovation, returned to his seat, said, "Let's go. I have my award, I'm not sitting here watching everybody," and they walked out. "And where do we have to go?" Sharpton said. "The Stage Deli, and eat Hungarian goulash." Similarly, in 1974 James Brown went to Zaire to play at the black-music festival that President Mobutu Sese Seko sponsored to coincide with the world heavyweight championship fight between Muhammad Ali and George Foreman, and the day after the concert he went home. Sharpton couldn't imagine skipping the fight, but his mentor told him, "Reverend, I'm going to be over here making my next dollar while Ali's making his."

Sharpton doesn't see much of his mentor these days, and when I asked Mr. Brown whether he would ever endorse Sharpton for elected office he said, "I would endorse his intent." But he said he no longer meddles with political endorsements, and he reminded me that, "being an ex-offender," he has never voted. At this point, he said, black people don't need leaders—"We need jobs"—and he'd told Sharpton as much. "'You don't lead us, we know how to lead.' I said, 'We don't need that no more. That was all right when we didn't have the nerve and the ambition, but now you can be anything you want to be, so you your own leader.'" Besides, he said, "leaders become dictators."

Time After Time

In late May of last year, the mayor of Cincinnati, Charlie Luken, asked James Brown for help. Seven weeks earlier, on April 7th, a city policeman had shot and killed an unarmed nineteen-year-old black man named Timothy Thomas, after a foot chase in the ghetto neighborhood of Over-the-Rhine. Thomas was the fifteenth black man to lose his life in a confrontation with Cincinnati police since 1995. His death was followed by several days of protests and rioting. Motorists were dragged from their cars and beaten; stores along a wide swath of the city center were looted; fires were set; a citywide dusk-to-dawn curfew was imposed; and although calm was restored within a week, the city remained deeply riven and on edge. Prominent black churchmen continued to lead protests, and were threatening to disrupt the city's annual Memorial Day outdoor food-and-music festival, Taste of Cincinnati. Mayor Luken wanted the festival to mark a return to normal for the city, and he wanted a musical act to set the tone. That meant he wanted a black act. The rhythm-and-blues band Midnight Star and the Isley Brothers were booked, but local black leaders persuaded them to withdraw. Now, with two days to go, the Mayor asked James Brown to come to town.

As it happened, Mr. Brown had just finished recording a new song, addressed to America's youths, called "Killing Is Out, School

Is In," and he thought the message was perfectly suited to Cincinnati's plight. He said he would not get mixed up in local politics, but for fifteen thousand dollars, to cover expenses, he agreed to give a midday press conference and to sing his new song. The news of his intended appearance was not well received at the New Prospect Baptist Church in Over-the-Rhine, the hub of the peaceful-protest movement that had coalesced since the riots. On the morning the Taste was to open, the pews were filled with several hundred men and women (about a quarter of them white) who sang gospel hymns and listened to the pastor, Reverend Damon Lynch III, rally them to stage a boycott of the food fair. In the atrium, a middle-aged black-enterprise activist named Jim Clingman explained the prevailing attitude. "James Brown is being used. He's just window dressing," he said, adding, "I lived by James Brown for a long time. I don't want to hurt the brother, I want to help him."

Pastor Lynch's rhetoric from the pulpit was more high-flown. He spoke of Cincinnati's "economic apartheid," and said, "Every once in a while we got to rise up. . . . What we got now is a Rosa Parks moment in our lives." He spoke the name James Brown, and said the attitude of the city fathers was "If we can just get 'em dancin'—bring in Negro dancers and just get the Negro dancin', he'll forget about his anger, he'll forget about his pain." He explained that he was going to meet the singer before the press conference, and persuade him to join the boycott, because "he is and has been our brother," and "for him now to be drawn into this—we just gotta tap him on the shoulder."

It didn't happen that way. James Brown rode straight from the airport to the press conference, at a downtown hotel. He wore a gunmetal-blue suit and turtleneck, silver-toed black cowboy boots, and, until the Mayor was done introducing him, heavy dark sunglasses. Then he took the podium, with half a dozen of his loyal retainers arrayed behind him, and for the next twenty minutes he held forth in a characteristically kaleidoscopic manner, full of oblique personal references. He called Cincinnati his second home, on account of King Records ("I wouldn't have a career if it wasn't for God, America, and especially Cincinnati"); and he said he was born dead, but didn't elaborate. He said, "I was out there with Dr. King, I was out there with Malcolm, I was out there with Mr. Abernathy, and I knew a lot of people—trying to make it better." And he said, "I didn't come for the Mayor, I didn't come for the police, I didn't come for the people out in the street. I come for the kids." This was his key point: that children were in peril. He criticized TV violence ("You see a show on television today, they done killed twenty people already, and you ain't even got to the show yet"), put in a plug for school prayer, and said we shouldn't be hiring teachers from overseas. He talked briefly about volunteering to entertain the troops in Indochina, and how hot it was there, and about flying around Russia in an old bomber plane, and about going to jail as a teen-ager. He said he'd never met a person he didn't like, and he said that, whatever Cincinnati's current trouble was, "it's going to end in the courthouse, whether you like it or not, it's never going to end in the outhouse." He invoked Rwanda and Bosnia, and asked, "What are we doing killing each other in our community?" He said, "Ants can work together, why can't people work together?" He cited Scripture—John 3:17 ("For God sent not his Son into the world to condemn the world; but that the world through him might be saved")—and said, "God don't want me to quit it, because Papa got a brand new bag."

Jim Clingman, the activist, ventured a question from the floor. "Brother Brown, one of your records that you made had the words 'Let's get together and get some land, raise our food like the man, save our money like the Mob, put up the factory on the job.' Speak on economic empowerment."

"All we got to do is get black Americans to put in one dollar, and from everybody build a company," Mr. Brown said.

"That's what I'm talking about," Clingman agreed.

"All we got to do is build our own stuff," Mr. Brown said.

"That's right."

"Not whether you're black or white."

"Thank you."

"Just have your own. And it's bad, see, if ballplayers, athletes, can't give one dollar apiece a year. . . "

"Thank you."

"It would be that much. They don't give no money."

"Speak."

He went on for a while longer—"We're all in it together, the Italian, the Jew, the German, nobody but all of us. Who am I? I'm 259–32–3801, not black or white, just that Social Security card"— then he rode the elevator down to his limo, and was driven to the festival stage. A thousand people had gathered in the midday sun to see him, most of them white, and around the periphery marched several hundred protesters, chanting, "James Brown sold out." Suddenly, a very loud, thumping beat blared from the sound system, and Mr. Brown appeared onstage, rapping out a karaoke version of his new song, "Killing Is Out, School Is In," with a vocal accompanist, who barked back, "I don't think they heard you, brother. Say it again." Despite the volume, their voices were barely audible over the chants of the protesters. From here and there in the crowd, people began hurling pennies at the stage. Two young black men looked on, discussing James Brown's presence in tones of disgust: "He's done. . . . He's finished. . . . Out the window with all them records— like Frisbees."

All at once, with the song still playing, Mr. Brown spun around and walked off-stage. He did not wait for applause, or return for it. One second he was there, and the next he was gone. Protesters surged toward him as he climbed into his limo. Mounted policemen moved to hold them back. An old man screamed, "Bring Elvis back—they both dead now." James Brown got back out of the car to hug a well-wisher. A few protesters rushed forward, and he ducked back inside. With the police cavalry as an escort, the car finally began to move off. A new chant began: "Say it loud, we got him out now."

A few weeks later, in Augusta, Mr. Brown told me that he had just received an invitation to the White House to present President Bush with a CD of his new song. "He called me," he said. "I knew it had to lead to that, because when they saw us stop the riots in Cincinnati—that was a good thing." His manager, Charles Bobbit, sustained this fantasy: "It was a repeat of 1968—Boston, Massachusetts—and both cities, both mayors, called for help 'cause they couldn't do it." Mr. Brown chuckled. "You right," he said. "That was a repeat. I didn't think about that." He was moved to declare that the new song, with its heavy rap beat, and its obvious reproach to the mayhem-boosting lyrics of so much hip-hop, would be "the biggest thing ever happened in history." He said, "You know, the President didn't call for us to be talkin' jive. He gonna tie it in. And I don't blame him."

Before America was drawn into war last September 11th, James Brown and his handlers had been talking up the release of the new song in the fall, as a sort of back-to-school special. It was an article of faith among the inner circle at James Brown Enterprises that it would be a hit as big as his best civil-rights-era numbers. Members of his band thought otherwise: the words were too blunt, even mildly scolding, lacking the buoyant bravura of his enduring mes-sage songs; the arrangement was a bit ham-fisted, and audiences weren't taking to it. The consensus among his sidemen seemed to be that Mr. Brown was wasting his time trying to reach today's kids, and should go back to his roots by recording an album of the music he loves to sing best when he's alone with a few friends: his greatest hits, a little gospel, even some ballads—songs of pure feeling. Mr. Brown himself never seemed quite satisfied with the recorded ver-sion of "Killing Is Out," and his producer was constantly reworking the mix, with overdubbed vocals and patched-in instrumentals—a process totally alien to the way the singer has worked for most of his life. "He must've mixed that thing fifty times, trying to come up with something else. I mean, he not really understanding that when it come from me, it's the real thing," he said. "It's God. When I first go in and cut, it's God. If I go back to cut, it's me. You see, God is always right. All the records, I used to always use my first cuts. Bam! Cat say, 'You want to cut it again?' I say, 'For what?'"

I wondered what Syd Nathan, who had so often recoiled from Mr. Brown's best innovations, would think. For all their struggles over the years, it was at King Records that Mr. Brown had done his best work. But Nathan has been dead for more than thirty years, so

I went to see Ahmet Ertegun, the Turkish-born éminence grise of record producers, who started Atlantic Records around the time that Nathan started King, and whose backlist of R&B and soul classics includes the best of Ray Charles, Otis Redding, Wilson Pickett, and Aretha Franklin. Ertegun never recorded James Brown, but he has known the singer on and off for fifty years, and admires him as "one of the great geniuses of this most important kind of music." Rappers, he said, "are all James Brown freaks." (Indeed, James Brown earns millions each year on royalties from rap samplings.) "He's got hooks that will outlive most people's compositions," Ertegun said. "Just his little hooks."

Still, the moment Ertegun heard the title "Killing Is Out, School Is In," he shook his head. "Sad thing is those songs are sure to flop," he said. "The public is not looking to take lessons." (After many delays, the song is set to be released in August on Mr. Brown's new album, *The Next Step*.) In Ertegun's experience, the black public is especially tough. "A black artist cannot keep a black audience," he said. "I mean, black audiences live this music. I mean, black audiences are the ones that create what black artists do, whereas white people imitate that, and they love it forever. We have white kids imitating Tampa Red, and they're playing Big Bill Broonzy, and they're students, they're scholars, who go back and listen to the old 78-r.p.m. records and get heavily into that, like all the English rock and rollers did in the sixties. They went back to that music. But black people, they don't study that music. That's the music they invented, and they don't give a shit about it, and they don't like what their mothers like. Their mothers like Billy Eckstine; well, they laugh at Billy Eckstine."

It's true that James Brown's audiences are now predominantly white, and that he gets his most avid response in Europe and Japan. "I'm ten times bigger over there than I am over here," he told me. Of course, Ertegun said, "they're the opposite of black audiences, they're just finding out about all of this." But, here in America, "there's the real expression of black people through, you know, all the rappers," he said. "It's dirty, but it's reality. It's reality for those people who live in the condition that we have more or less put them in. They can't write songs like Cole Porter, because they don't come from a Cole Porter background. They come from a rat-infested basement place somewhere in Compton, and you know that's a different life than putting on your white tie and dancing at the Savoy."

It wasn't the Savoy, but late one night in San Francisco, after playing a show, Mr. Brown returned to the Ritz-Carlton on Nob Hill, where he was staying, and stood stock-still in the center of the lobby. By the angle of his head, you could see that he was listening, and, sure enough, in the nearly vacant bar, a trio was playing: a gray-haired man hunched over a string bass, a young goateed fellow at the grand piano, and, on a stool, in a black evening gown, a woman singing "Somewhere Over the Rainbow." "Let's get a juice or something," Mr. Brown said to his entourage, which numbered about ten that night. He led the way, attired in a dusky-maroon three-piece suit, a purple shirt, and a necktie of golden silk with a pattern of blue slashes. The musicians beamed at the sight of him, and the dozen or so remaining patrons, scattered on banquettes around the edge of the room, sat up and began poking one another and pointing. When the singer, blushing, finished her song, Mr. Brown had one of his men give each of the trio a hundred-dollar bill. The singer asked for requests, and Mr. Brown said, "Anybody here mind if I do one?"

There was no objection. He conferred briefly with the musicians, grinning and joking, looking out at the room, where the audience of twenty had now grown to twenty-five, with an additional contingent of bellhops and valet parkers standing against the back wall. "Up-tempo or slow?" he said. "Oh, I'll give it to you on the up." He started snapping his fingers, his body swayed with them, the piano and bass came in softly, and he sang, "Time after time, when we're together . . ." There was sweetness in his voice, and grit, and as always, an ache, but, most of all, pure pleasure. He clipped the phrases, and juggled some words, making the song his: "Time after time, you hear me say that I feel alone tonight. . . "

After a verse, he sidled up behind the pianist and, gently nudging him to keep playing at the low end of the keyboard, reached in to pick out a liltingly funky right-handed solo. Back at the edge of the tiny stage, he crouched into the words until, making an abrupt signal to the musicians to cut, he finished, with a soft whispered "Aowh." Then, equally softly, he spoke the word "Scream."

GARY GIDDINS

Post-War Jazz: An Arbitrary Road Map

The initial idea was to create an overview of jazz (and jazz-related) records from 1900 to 2001. After several weeks of revelatory listening to music from the dark ages—rags, marches, cakewalks, minstrel and music hall turns—in an attempt to find appropriate selections for the years 1900–1920, I realized that, for reasons of space and time, the project would have to be abbreviated. I had bit off more than I could chew or the *Voice* could accommodate. Still, having narrowed the scope to 1945–2001, I spent nearly five months groping for solutions to the labyrinth I was intent on building; the writing was, relatively, a snap compared to the process of selecting representative recordings, given my self-imposed rules, about which more anon.

I wanted, for my own illumination, to posit a jazz map. By selecting one track (always a track, never an album, though the album on which the track can be found is included at the end of each entry) to represent each year, I hoped to offer a purview that balanced achievement and innovation. Given my rules, however, I soon realized that nothing remotely like objectivity was attainable. An infinite number of maps were possible, all of them valid. Some years and periods—1928, 1936–41, 1957, 1961–65, 1980, 1988, and 1999, among others—are so bountiful with masterworks that choosing was an exercise in frustration, even heartbreak. What I thought at first had at least a whiff of scholastic gravity revealed itself as a shameless parlor game. (Advanced classes might attempt lists made up entirely of non-Americans or guitarists or under–30s, etc.) Though it gives me pleasure to look over this particular terrain, I refuse to defend it against others I drew, or to those you might design. When you've worn yourself out ranting at the insanity of my selections, you might give it a try.

For me, the key reward was in exploring hundreds of records I hadn't revisited in years. Some records that I expected to include no longer sounded as good; others I had previously neglected now filled me with admiration. Since the final draft says more about me than jazz, it doesn't bear analysis, except to mention the obvious. In narrowing my options, I decided to stick with American jazz, an act of inexcusable chauvinism; also, the ages of musicians skewed older as I closed in on the new century—I can't understand that at all. Choosing the best of anything, let alone the most important, is rarely possible. In the end, I simply settled on 57 tracks I cherish. That they also suggest how we got from there to here is of less interest to me than their consistent excellence, exuberance, and diversity. Jazz's bounty continues to astonish me.

If you want to play, you have to abide by the rules, mainly one big rule: A musician may be listed only once as a leader. The alternative is to allow a musician—an Armstrong or an Ellington or a Davis or a Coleman, etc.—to reappear over and over; that approach might be more suitable if the goal is to identify favorite or historically crucial performances, but I sought variety as well, which demanded frantic juggling and endless compromises. When I began, I dashed off paragraphs on random faves: Duke Ellington's "Harlem," Stan Getz's "Diaper Pin," James Moody's "Moody's Mood for Love," Ornette Coleman's "RPDD," George Russell's "All About Rosie," Sonny Rollins's "Three Little Words," Pee Wee Russell's "I'd Climb the Highest Mountain," Al Cohn and Jimmy Rowles's "Them There Eyes," Count Basie's "Little Pony," Dizzy Gillespie's "Emanon," David Murray's "Blues for My Sister," Thelonious Monk's "I Should Care," Lennie Tristano's "Becoming," John Lewis's "For Ellington," Cecil Taylor's "3 Phasis," Henry Threadgill's "100 Year Old Game," and Arthur Blythe's "Sister Daisy," to mention just a few of the post-war sides that were ultimately discarded because of conflicting dates or second-guessing. The only way to proceed was to organize an overall grid, plug in possibilities for each year, mix and match, and pray for the best.

Supplementary rules: Each work had to be tied to the year it was recorded, not released, which might create a disparity of a few years. Tracks that were not released for decades, however, were not eligible. I knew that I would cross generations, acknowledging masterly performances by older players amid new wrinkles by younger ones, but didn't make that a rule. Anyone who thinks that the following comprehensively depicts the post-war jazz era is not paying attention. But are they great records? Every last one.

1945 Charlie Parker, "Koko"

By no means the first bebop or modern jazz record, this is the one that cracked the firmament. Parker showed how to make music with advanced harmonies and tumultuous rhythms, creating a tuneful new lexicon in the process. He unleashed a virtuoso universe in which post-war musicians could reinvent themselves and their place in society. They could and often did play for dancing, laughs, and entertainment, but they no longer had to. For jazz, the noir years were golden. Not the least amazing thing about "Koko" is that it continues to overwhelm. Only after one has lived with it awhile does Parker's blade-like articulation and incredible velocity give up its melodic secrets; Parker's alto sax was nothing if not a melody maker. Built on the chords of "Cherokee," it opens with a jolting eight-bar unison theme, coupled with exchanges between Parker and Dizzy Gillespie. Then Bird flies: two choruses of staggering invention, his tone fat and sensuous, jagged and hard. Drummer Max Roach holds the fort for a chorus, before the head is reprised. In 2:50, the world is remade. *The Charlie Parker Story* (Savoy)

1946 Woody Herman, "Sidewalks of Cuba"

After leading a band associated with blues for 10 years, Herman suddenly leaped to the forefront of swing's twilight years; like Gillespie, who had written for him in 1942, Herman's big band embraced the modernistic spirit with wit and daring. But where Gillespie turned to modes and Afro-Cuban rhythms, Herman looked to Stravinsky and R&B—and to Parker and Gillespie. Handed a prosaic '30s song, arranger Ralph Burns imbued it with the Herd's trademark fervor, reeds strutting as boldly as brasses and drummer Don Lamond on red alert. Herman plays clarinet, and guitarist Chuck Wayne reveals the influence of Charlie Christian and bop. But the heart of the performance is a crazed "Bumble Bee" break and half-chorus trumpet solo by Sonny Berman, whose drug-related death a few months later, at 21, was the wake-up call no one heeded. Berman had absorbed Roy Eldridge and Gillespie while still in his teens, and his phrasing is emphatic, personal, and wry. *Blowin' Up a Storm* (Columbia/Legacy)

1947 Dizzy Gillespie, "Manteca"

No one accomplished more in the post-war era than its clown prince. Of the founding fathers, only Dizzy could have launched a hot-blooded big band—one that introduced saxophonist James Moody and a foursome later known as the Modern Jazz Quartet. And only he persistently sought ideas beyond U.S. borders. "A Night in Tunisia" established him as the most gorgeously spellbinding trumpet player in a generation, and a composer of promise. With George Russell's "Cubana Be"/"Cubana Bop," he fused jazz, modalism, and Caribbean rhythms. The more accessible "Manteca," however, grounded an enduring Cuban-American merger. Percussionist Chano Pozo brought him the idea for a piece that employs three interdependent vamps, to which Dizzy added a contrastingly melodic 16-bar bridge and two short, breakneck solos. "Manteca" doesn't disguise its dual patrimony—the two cultures exist side by side with equal integrity. Gillespie continued to play it for 45 years. *The Complete RCA Victor Recordings* (Bluebird)

1948 Tadd Dameron, "Lady Bird"

When the Royal Roost, a Broadway chicken joint with music, switched from swing to bop, Dameron was installed as leader. The gig ran nearly 10 months, confirming the composer, arranger, and reluctant pianist as an original who knew how to spur good musicians. "Lady Bird" is only 16 bars, but suggests—with its AABC form—a full-blown song. Unlike his unmistakable bop pieces ("Hot House," "Symphonette"), it has a suave, mellow theme that reflects his apprenticeship with swing bands, yet sounds no less modern. After a tricky intro, the dapper drumming of Kenny Clarke guides the ensemble, which boasts two Lestorian tenors— celestial Allen Eager and earthly Wardell Gray. Dameron's greatest interpreter, though, was Fats Navarro, whose trumpet solo opens with a nine-bar phrase, soaring over turnbacks with matchless ease and grace and a tone of transporting beauty. The careers of Dameron, Eager, Gray, and Navarro were devastated by drugs; jazz was devastated by Navarro's absurd loss, at 26. *The Fabulous Fats Navarro* (Blue Note)

1949 Bud Powell, "Tempus Fugue-It"

As much if not more than Parker and Gillespie, Powell represents a line of demarcation for his instrument. The difference between pre-Bud piano and post-Bud piano is categorical. He played impossibly fast or slow, with obsessive fury or meditative detachment; he used the left hand for bracing, kindling chords that fed the right, which expressed a percussive rage equalled only by his gentle raptures. In its economy, hurtling power, and infallible precision, the minor key "Tempus Fugue-It" (originally released as "Tempus Fugit") is a head-banging wonder: the crashing Lisztian chords in which the relatively conventional melody is swaddled, the close harmonies of the release, the thrilling riff configurations of the solo, the smashed arpeggio just before the out-chorus. Yet each detail rings clear as a bell, with sensational logic. It's not that he plays so fast, but that he thinks so coherently, balanced on a moonbeam. *Jazz Giant* (Verve)

1950 Sarah Vaughan, "Mean to Me"

The voice that dropped a thousand jaws helped pave the way for bop in 1944–45 with her recordings of "East of the Sun," "Lover Man," and this song, backed by Parker and Gillespie; but they were just a whisper of where she was headed. At a 1949 Carnegie Hall concert, she introduced a second-chorus variation on "Mean to Me," a fantastic vocal swan-dive that completely revamped the melody without retouching the lyric—without resorting to scat. A year later, she recorded it with a Jimmy Jones band, allowing Budd Johnson a noble half-chorus before embarking on her embellishments, egged on by Miles Davis's obbligato. Her voluptuous, resolute, winged phrasing adjourns high in the sky. By now management was grooming this formerly gawky, church-trained phenomenon for stardom; but they couldn't temper her musicality, much as they tried. *Sarah Vaughan in Hi-Fi* (Columbia/Legacy)

1951 Stan Getz, "Mosquito Knees"

Having achieved glory with an eight-bar solo on Herman's "Early Autumn," Getz became an overnight star—one of many tenor saxophonists who brought the Lester Young template into modern jazz. He eschewed the heavier attack of, say, Wardell Gray (whose solo this year on Basie's "Little Pony" is itself monumental), in favor of a sighing dry-ice lyricism that was occasionally derided as a "white tenor" sound. Yet no one who heard his live 1951 sides could have failed to recognize that his breezy timbre was backed by heroic force. He was in peak form at Storyville, colluding with a dream team: guitarist Jimmy Raney, pianist Al Haig, bassist Teddy Kotick, and drummer Tiny Kahn. He was also armed with an impressive book, including six pieces by Gigi Gryce; a "Honeysuckie Rose" derivation, "Mosquito Knees," propels him into a blistering rampage, revealing a trove of melodic riffs, capped by exchanges with the rousing Kahn. *The Complete Roost Recordings* (Blue Note)

1952 Thelonious Monk, "Little Rootie Tootie"

Lost between the Blue Notes that established him as a cult figure and the Riversides that would soon win him a popular following were the trio sessions that ought to have closed the case on him as a pianist of nerve and genius. Other pianists are obliged to make bad instruments sound good; Monk, with his clattering dissonances (consider the opening of the incredibly swinging "These Foolish Things"), made good instruments sound unstrung. His train song is typical: funny, rambunctious, and starkly rhythmic, with three dissonant chords clanging at the end of alternate bars. He begins the last chorus with a bearded cliché—deedledee-deedledee up, deedledee-deedledee down—and brings it home with hilarious ingenuity. Art Blakey (dig him on the second bridge) was Monk's perfect drummer. *The Complete Prestige Recordings* (Prestige)

1953 Gerry Mulligan, "My Funny Valentine"

Meanwhile, a new school was born on the left coast, and though much of the attention went to George Shearing's boplite and Stan Kenton's bopballistics, the prince of the realm was an exiled New Yorker who had taken a job at an L.A. club with a bandstand too small to fit a piano. Mulligan's love for big bands was apparent in his charts for Kenton and his own Tentette, but he became famous due to the pianoless quartet with Chet Baker, who never sounded more individual than in those early years, before he became enamored of Miles. The live, extended version of "My Funny Valentine," recorded at the cozy Haig, is more evocative than the studio hit of the year before. After a drumroll and an ominous two-note bass vamp, Baker wanders into the chords and by bar three (no baritone support either) is on the green; Mulligan follows suit, gingerly stepping through the clover. *The Com-*

plete Pacific Jazz Recordings of The Gerry Mulligan Quartet (Pacific Jazz)

1954 Brown & Roach Inc., "Delilah"

The quintet founded by Max Roach and Clifford Brown in the spring of 1954 ended on June 26, 1956, when Brown, pianist Richie Powell, and Powell's wife were killed in a highway accident. Brown was 25, and he is still mourned. "Delilah," the most unlikely of vehicles (an undulating Hedy Lamarr prop), begins single-file—bass vamp, cymbals, piano vamp, tenor vamp—before Brown states the theme as though staring down the throat of the cobra he's charming. Harold Land, who had much of Wardell Gray's sandy sound and finesse, offers a bouquet of melodies; then Brown enters with a three-note figure that he develops through the bridge. He ends the chorus blazing and detonates the next one with a heart-stopping rip. Powell, who wrote the inventive chart, plays trebly chords, neat modulations, and a Grieg finish, followed by fours with Roach, who adds a melodic chorus of his own. *Clifford Brown and Max Roach* (Emarcy)

1955 The Jazz Messengers, "Prince Albert"

For one year and one live recording, Art Blakey pretended non-leadership in the hope of creating a genuine cooperative, like the Modern Jazz Quartet, which had been picking up speed since 1954. With an ideal lineup—pianist-composer Horace Silver, trumpeter Kenny Dorham, saxophonist Hank Mobley, bassist Doug Watkins—the drummer press-rolled the Messengers into a new idiom that established itself as a permanent alternative to cool, modal, and avant-garde, and as a predecessor of soul-jazz and funk. Dorham's much played theme is a variation on "All the Things You Are," and Silver playfully introduces it with the requisite Charlie Parker vamp. Dorham's distinctly smoky tone and sleek phrasing are flexible enough to permit a "Camptown Races" joke, and Mobley's reedy authority steps evenly with the time, then doubles it. *At the Café Bohemia, Volume 1* (Blue Note)

1956 George Russell, "Concerto for Billy the Kid"

A major theorist, instigator, and gadfly, as well as one of the most original of jazz composers, Russell had been making his mark behind the scenes for a decade when he finally got the chance to record his own album. It was a turning point for him and the pianist for whom he conceived his dazzling miniconcerto. Bill Evans had appeared on a few sessions but was virtually unknown until he embarked on the avid, single-handed, stop-time whirlwind cadenza at this work's center. Russell, who preferred modes to chords and published several editions of his explanatory Zen-like treatise, *Lydian Chromatic Concept of Tonal Organization*, aligned each musician like a layer in a cake, making the sextet resound with startling freshness. He and Evans continued to collaborate ("All About Rosie," *Living Time*), and their first meeting—in the same year that Cecil Taylor debuted and Art Tatum bowed out—affirmed the rise of the new jazz intellectual. *Jazz Workshop* (RCA Bluebird)

1957 Charles Mingus, "Haitian Fight Song"

After apprenticing himself in swing, bop, R&B, and pop, Mingus worked his way through a labyrinth of academic compositional techniques, which earned him the accusation of failing to swing. "Haitian Fight Song" was his response. A more thunderous bass intro has not been heard; he sounds like a giant plucking ropes against a tree trunk, albeit with perfect intonation. Leading a solid but hardly all-star quintet with written material that amounts to no more than eight bars (two canonical riffs), plus an orthodox blues for the improvisational grid, he herds (le mot juste) his men through double-time and stop-time rhythms for a riveting 12 minutes that feel more like three. Trombonist Jimmy Knepper makes his bones here; the others

—altoist Shafi Hadi, pianist Wade Legge, and, in a fabled debut, drummer Dannie Richmond—play over their heads. Mingus's astounding solo obviated further criticism. *The Clown* (Atlantic)

1958 Sun Ra, "Saturn"

In the year of Ornette Coleman's debut, no one paid much mind to the former Sonny Blount; critics sniffed at the eclecticism, the cultism, the garage sonics. Who can blame them? Compared to Coleman, Taylor, Russell, and Mingus, his bop was distilled with a touch of corn and more than a touch of doo-wop. He looked forward, back, and across the way to the R&B bars. He wrote painstaking charts and involved good musicians, but was a do-it-yourself type who bided his time until the mountain came to him. His theme song, recorded in different versions, combines a six-beat piano intro, a 14-bar contrapuntal 7/4 setup melody, and the hooky main theme (in four and based on conventional changes). The latter may sound a bit too enchanted, but it generates energetic solos from tenor John Gilmore and baritone Pat Patrick, who along with the ensemble sway merrily. *Jazz in Silhouette* (Evidence)

1959 Miles Davis, "So What"

The track (and album) opens with a hushed prelude, reportedly contributed by Gil Evans; Paul Chambers's bass prompts a three-note Bill Evans phrase, leading to a unison bass-like figure played by those two, followed by Evans's enigmatic Spanish-style chords and, finally, Chambers's introduction of a beat and a theme, which is punctuated by unison chords from the three winds. The head couldn't be more basic: a 32-bar AABA song. But instead of chord changes, it offers two scales for the improvisers—D minor with an E-flat bridge. Modalism has now found an accessible context and will soon be everywhere. Davis's solo sticks to the scales and is a lyrical marvel, immaculate in form and execution. Cannonball Adderley and John Coltrane are far more prolix, but they too are focused by the harmonic austerity, and Evans finishes with tightly ground chords, showing that Monk didn't have a patent on minor seconds. It's the most enduringly popular jazz album of the LP era. *Kind of Blue* (Columbia)

1960 Gil Evans, "Le Nevada"

Speaking of minimalism, Evans, nearing 50 and having gained some marquee value for his work with Miles, initiated a big band "head" arrangement, something that had rarely been heard since Basie's days in Kansas City. All he had for "Le Nevada" was a hooky four-bar riff and a tempo, yet after several unsuccessful tries, he eked out a 15-minute bobbing fantasia with exuberant improvs by Johnny Coles, Jimmy Knepper, and, chiefly, ageless tenor saxophonist Budd Johnson. Typically, Evans had strolled over to the trombone section while the recording was in progress and wrote on a matchbook a riff that sent the performance into high gear. Elvin Jones contributed, too, by shaking shakers throughout. In the year of Ornette's *Free Jazz* and Eric Dolphy's *Out There*, this performance walked a tightrope between old (which bop had become) and new, auguring the spontaneous big bands Evans perfected a decade later. *Out of the Cool* (Impulse)

1961 John Coltrane, "Chasin' the Trane"

Coltrane enjoyed an authentic hit with "My Favorite Things," and would soon foster the apex of boudoir crooning with Johnny Hartman, before achieving mythic standing with *A Love Supreme*. This 16-minute blues in F, though, was the Rubicon many of his old admirers could not cross. Coltrane's break with convention didn't encourage dissertations on modes or free time; it elicited ecstasy or wrath. His battle, during 80 or so choruses, against the 12-bar structure that Elvin Jones and Jimmy Garrison maintain with yeoman determination, is a prodigal display of unbridled emotion: a howl, a mutiny, an invocation in the higher frequencies—the informal beginning of expressionism in jazz, and an unforgettable performance in a year brimming with them. Armstrong and Ellington, Bill

Evans, Davis, Gillespie, Getz and Eddie Sauter, Lee Konitz, Mulligan, Blakey, and others all released classics. *Live at the Village Vanguard* (Impulse!)

1962 Dexter Gordon, "Love for Sale"

In a prominent year for tenors—Sonny Rollins home from the bridge, Stan Getz at home with Brazil—Gordon, relishing one of his many comebacks, helped put the melodic, harmonic, rhythmic, and temporal restraints of bop back on the map, though he, too, was playing long and would soon find himself edging toward modes. He was at a personal peak for two sessions backed by a model trio (pianist Sonny Clarke, bassist Butch Warren, drummer Billy Higgins), and though their music lacked the novel lilt of bossa nova, it had the catalytic power and rousing ingenuity of musicians brimming with ideas and having tremendous fun expressing them. Dexter had Coltrane's authority without the panic. "Love for Sale" is a fast hardball hit way out of the park, yet filled with bemused and melodic details; Gordon's broadsword sound exudes dignity, and not one measure of his long solo is superfluous. *Go* (Blue Note)

1963 Jackie McLean, "Love and Hate"

McLean, a Parker acolyte who had proven his bop precocity in the '50s with pungent timbre and razor-sharp acumen, got caught up in and animated by the turbulence of the '60s. On one of his most dramatic albums, he recorded three works by trombonist Grachan Moncur III (whose *Evolution* is something of a companion disc). "Love and Hate" is the most ardent and compelling. It opens with a mourning gait, accented by Bobby Hutcherson's tamped vibraphone chords. After the memorable theme, McLean's caustic alto saxophone commences with a provocative phrase and then explores the harmonically spare terrain with wounded resolve. He sustains absolute emotional pitch, which is extended by Moncur and Hutcherson, while bassist Larry Ridley and drummer Roy Haynes steer a steady course. One way or another, almost everyone was responding to the new avant-garde. *Destination Out!* (Blue Note)

1964 Wayne Shorter, "Infant Eyes"

Working his way through a Coltrane influence, Shorter demonstrated pensive originality as tenor saxophonist and composer with a stellar edition of Blakey's Jazz Messengers. Then he blossomed with Davis's bruising second great quintet, whose members enjoyed a life apart, mostly at Blue Note—a record label that enjoyed an unlikely flurry of hits with Herbie Hancock's "Watermelon Man," Horace Silver's "Song for My Father," and Lee Morgan's "The Sidewinder." "Infant Eyes," a ballad written for his daughter, brings out Shorter's raw, unaffected tenderness. It recycles a quote from Gershwin's "Soon" in a 27-bar ABA structure with one chord per measure. Shorter's improvisation ranges over three octaves, yet it consists of few notes, and each one counts for timbre as well as melody. He later developed an equally expressive approach to the soprano sax, conspicuously evading Coltrane's shadow, while writing a body of sly tunes unlike anything anywhere. *Speak No Evil* (Blue Note)

1965 Archie Shepp, "Hambone"

Shepp's militancy was too shrewd to be one-dimensional, his music too generous to be exclusively strident. The album that produced "Malcolm, Malcolm—Semper Malcolm," almost certainly the best poetry-and-jazz side ever made (some voice, some reading), also offered sextet arrangements of Ellington and bossa nova, a poised response to Buñuel's *Los Olvidados*, and the multi-themed "Hambone," based on a character in a kiddie show. It begins with a familiar mariachi theme and proceeds to a passage that alternates measures in seven and five. The fine solos by trumpeter Ted Curson, altoist Marion Brown, and Shepp—with his raspy, skittery, anxious tenor sax sound—are subordinate to the ensemble, which comes on like a crazed marching band. Yet the new thing, new wave, new music, or new jazz, as it was variously called, was as much derided as Monk had been a decade earlier. *Fire Music* (Impulse!)

1966 Albert Ayler, "Our Prayer/Spirits Rejoice"

He replaced notes with glossolalia and made a band music out of raucous disharmonies, folk melodies, marches, hymns, and bugle calls; his trumpet-playing brother, Donald, had an appropriately tinny sound for the latter. Ayler's grinding tenor saxophone threatened to burst asunder from the effusiveness of his playing. He scared the hell out of people, yet radiated a wildly optimistic passion. The optimism was manic. Dead at 34, in 1970, he never found the acceptance here that he won in Europe—some folks figured he was putting everyone on, among them true believers who were mortified by his later au courant compromises. Yet even in flower-child mode, he carried a cello and howled at the moon; he was never cut out for the Fillmore. Still, his mid-'60s bands electrify, and his medley of two original themes, complete with an interpolation of the "Marseillaise," suggests an old New Orleans parade band brought to a peak of revivalist hysteria. *Lorrach, Paris 1966* (Hatology)

1967 Sonny Criss, "Willow Weep for Me"

Few people noticed Lester Bowie's *Numbers 1 & 2* or acknowledged *Far East Suite* as one of Ellington's masterworks, both recorded this year. But for a brief span, modest attention was paid a blues-driven altoist who had created his own lapidary version of Charlie Parker, yet had not recorded at home in seven years. The third album of his comeback reflected a siege mentality by covering two hits (jazz musicians and producers always went for the most banal chart toppers). Criss's creamy proficiency had no trouble riding roughshod over the Fifth Dimension, but he was in his glory with great tunes. The pitfall of drenching a ballad in minor-thirds and other blues devices is the potential for cliché. Criss—alertly supported by guitarist Tal Farlow and pianist Cedar Walton—averts the danger with infallible taste and gleaming technique, producing a flawless gem, right down to the lustrous cadenza. *Up, Up and Away* (Prestige)

1968 Jaki Byard, "Memories of You"

Byard and Roland Kirk were made for each other—savoring the past as a cocktail of irreverence and sentiment. Byard contributed to Kirk's *Rip, Rig and Panic*, and now Kirk repaid the favor. The rhythm section brought together for Booker Ervin's *Book* series— Byard, bassist Richard Davis, drummer Alan Dawson—was present on all but one old tune by Eubie Blake, who, at 85, was a year away from his famous comeback. Kirk sticks to tenor and, whether soloing or backing Byard, rarely pauses to breathe. Byard's ebullient take on stride piano is emboldened by his peerless, tumbling arpeggios: Tatum-esque in concept, Taylor-esque in touch. If the most ambitious release of the year was *The Jazz Composer's Orchestra*, this duet was perhaps the most serendipitous. Not much noted at the time, it exercised an influence that would be evident 30 years later. *The Jaki Byard Experience* (Prestige)

1969 Tony Williams, "Spectrum"

As rock pushed jazz aside, a few musicians sought common ground not in dinky tunes or soul-brother affectations, but in energy, electricity, and coloration. Miles's *Bitches Brew* and Williams's *Emergency!* were as shocking to some as Ayler had been, yet for the drummer, born in 1945, fusion held the promise of destiny, if not of commercial salvation. He had joined McLean and Miles at 17, had recorded with cutting-edge players like Sam Rivers; to him, rock was a natural challenge and an opportunity. So he took the standard organ-trio instrumentation and maxed it out, fusing free improvisation to blistering rhythms. It pleased hardly anyone—his Hendrixian singing was ill-advised—yet a track like "Spectrum," admittedly more jazz than rock, suggests exciting possibilities. The cymbals' lightning response to the first figure of John McLaughlin's guitar improv prepares you for the alert vitality that abides during Larry

Young's organ spot as well as in their signature wrap-up crescendo.
Spectrum: The Anthology (Verve).

1970 Art Ensemble of Chicago, "Theme de Yoyo"

In perhaps the worst year ever for jazz records, two of the slyest of
veteran swingers, Bobby Hackett and Vic Dickenson, played the hotel
gig that eventually produced the album that launched Chiaroscuro;
and the 15 or so sessions recorded by the little-known AEC in
Europe began showing up stateside. The AEC's antic score for an
obscure French film (shown here for a nanosecond as *Sophie's Ways*)
treats Monteverdi to a second-line beat and, more predictively, ferments free and funk on "Theme de Yoyo." Lester Bowie pushes
trumpet tonality beyond Miles's jurisdiction, proving along with reed-
men Roscoe Mitchell and Joseph Jarman that this strangely theatrical
troupe could be plenty pithy, while whitefaced bassist Malachi Favors
and drummer Don Moye anticipate *Shaft*. For added measure,
Fontella Bass croons, "Your fanny's like two sperm whales floating
down the Seine." *Les Stances a Sophie* (Universal Sound)

1971 Mary Lou Williams, "What's Your Story, Morning Glory?"

In another dour year for jazz records, Circle united Chick Corea
and Dave Holland (they said they hoped to escape fusion) with
Anthony Braxton; Jimmy Rushing made his last stand, mobilizing a
return of mainstream heroes; and Carla Bley waxed the "Overture"
to *Escalator Over the Hill*. No less striking was the latest comeback
by Williams, who, like Earl Hines, had been playing since the 1920s
and still sounded unequivocally modern. After building a following
at the Cookery, she romped deliriously through the *Giants* concert
with Dizzy Gillespie and Bobby Hackett and four months later
started work on a more meditative solo LP. She begins her best-

known blues (even better known as the plagiarized pop hit "Black Coffee") with a rhythmic vamp, then plays seven comely choruses that combine slow-drag blues panache with fresh chords and a subtly metronomic beat—her penultimate chorus is a knockout. *Nite Life* (Chiaroscuro)

Ornette Coleman, "The Men Who Live in the White House"

Things looked up with Dave Holland's *Conference of the Birds*, Sonny Stitt's *Constellation*, and, in St. Louis, Julius Hemphill's self-produced *Dogon A.D.* But nothing could compare with Coleman's first and—to date—only recorded symphony. The somewhat compromised album was completed in nine hours under constraints that forbade him from using his band along with the London Symphony, which was the initial idea; it was ultimately edited for time and divided into 21 episodes. Yet its power ferments. Nearing the final leg, the orchestra introduces a six-note variation on "The Good Life," the gloriously ribald theme formerly called "School Work" and later adapted as "Theme From a Symphony" on the electrifying *Dancing in Your Head* (1975). Coleman's alto is round and warm as he lifts off for a cadenza that mines that same motif with his shamanistic cry, fading with fragile vibrato, until the spacious harmonies of "Love Life" lead him to the final, rustic urgency of "Sunday in America." *Skies of America* (Columbia/Legacy)

1973 Cecil Taylor, "Spring of Two Blue-Js"

Taylor's two magnificent Blue Note albums of 1966 were followed by a silence of nearly seven years, except for his collaboration with the Jazz Composers Association (and European concerts that weren't issued here until much later). Then, within a year, he released *Indent*, a solo recital from Antioch, where he had been teaching, and the second set of a Town Hall concert dedicated to Ben Webster. The latter has two sections: an epic if largely romantic piano solo, which offers an improvisational coherence his earlier work only hints at, and a meditative quartet variation that captures him in transition before the darker, deeper textures that followed when he launched his sextet. This was bassist Sirone's first recording with him and drummer Andrew Cyrille's last; both are fully committed, as is Taylor's most frequent collaborator, Jimmy Lyons, whose alto mirrors every pianistic conceit. *Spring of Two Blue-J's* (Unit Core/OP)

1974 Modern Jazz Quartet, "Django"

This was the piece that solidified international interest in its composer, John Lewis, and the MJQ in 1954, when Lewis, Milt Jackson, Percy Heath, and Kenny Clarke had been working together for nearly three years. It had been introduced at Clarke's last session; he would soon leave and be replaced by Connie Kay. Two decades later, all four called it quits (until 1981, when they reunited as if they had been enjoying a long vacation). But first they gave a series of farewell concerts. Despite its cool formalism, the MJQ was at its best in the free fall of live recording, and their triumphant evening in New York provided a definitive version of the cortege written in memory of Django Reinhardt—as definitive as possible for a piece Lewis never stopped revising. Here all the elements of his skill and the MJQ's interpretive power are as one: the evocative Gypsy feeling in the main theme, recalling the Adagio of Mendelssohn's octet; the stout bass motif; the mixture of delicacy and force, discipline and spontaneity, tragedy and joy. *The Complete Last Concert* (Atlantic)

1975 The Revolutionary Ensemble, "Ponderous Planets"

Their first studio album was their last; the group disbanded in 1977, ending a six-year run—impressive considering its inability to crack the cult ceiling. TRE often replaced a staunch beat with a mere pulse, suggesting a fusion between classical and jazz practices. But the reflexive interplay between Leroy Jenkins's spry violin, Sirone's redwood-heavy bass (and expert arco technique), and Jerome Cooper's fastidious, if often whimsical percussion was largely consonant and accessible, never more so than on Cooper's by-no-means-ponderous opus. It begins with bowed strings and saw, achieves jazzy frisson with the entrance of plucked bass and cymbals, and finally, having made the case that impassioned improvisation can flourish without swing, swings like a mutha—in waltz time. A good year for Jenkins, who also introduced *For Players Only*, his daring Jazz Composers Orchestra spectacle. *The People's Republic (Horizon/OP)

1976 Anthony Braxton, "Piece Three"

Not exactly typical Braxton, but then, what is? And who else would have tried something as wry and unexpected as this brazen send-up of a march—a piece, incidentally, that actually had everyone taking a position. The jubilant theme, which owes as much to the beer garden (dig that counter-theme by the reeds) as to military needs, modulates to a repeated oompah figure, as though stuck in a rut; into this berserk stasis Leo Smith comes a-burning, playing only those trumpet tones of no use in a march. A surprising interlude introduces the aggressive trombone of George Lewis, who enters with a droll tailgate slide and is soon ripping and snorting, followed by the waspish, perhaps quizzical clarinet of Braxton, who fights against another static riff. Suddenly, the march is restored like a beam of sunshine, as the ensemble waddles cheekily down the pike. *Creative Orchestra Music 1976* (Bluebird)

1977 Hank Jones, "Oh, What a Beautiful Morning"

Jazz records were bullish again, triggered by small labels that suited a horde of unknown talents from the West and Midwest, who also helped establish a loft alternative to nightclub venues. At the same time, there was an invasion of re-energized mainstreamers who required labels, too. Duets and trios were big: Jimmy Rowles serially encountered Al, Zoot, and Stan; McCoy Tyner and Tommy Flanagan tested diverse rhythm-makers; Konitz parleyed with Solal, Venuti with McKenna, and Hemphill with alter ego Roi Boye. Jones's best albums were with Tony Williams and Ron Carter, but it was at a session with Milt Hinton and Bobby Rosengarden that he was talked into going one alone and produced this neglected masterpiece—his quintessential performance. After a laconic vamp, the unlikely melody suddenly spills down in broken chords, and is just as quickly dispensed with as Jones dives deep into its harmonies for a series of blues-driven variations that are infernally clever and utterly lovely. *The Trio* (Chiaroscuro/OP)

1978 Sonny Rollins, "Autumn Nocturne"

Jazz's preeminent concertizer disdains recording, where he usually keeps the lid on his id. So why not record all his concerts and cherry-pick them for albums? Maybe because the ferocity would alienate the faint of heart and leave no possibility at all for radio play. Happily, he does issue some live performances (meanwhile, his fans surreptitiously filch every note), preserving the most charismatic attack in the history of the tenor saxophone—a sound that, having already influenced the playing habits of two generations, reached extrovert heights in the mid '70s. Indeed, not since "West End Blues" had there been a cadenza quite like this, which similarly begins on an odd note before plunging into a grove of euphoric convolutions. When Rollins finally attains the theme, after citations from "To a Wild Rose" and "Home Sweet Home," plus two vocal yawps, the sensation of release is overwhelming. From that point, he exhales a whoosh of melody, radiant and raunchy all at once. *Silver City* (Milestone)

1979 Bill Evans, "I Loves You Porgy"

A musical dybbuk took possession of him in the last two years of his life, unleashing fresh, unexpected powers. The superb new trio with bassist Marc Johnson and drummer Joe LaBarbara revitalized him, too, and he played with the visionary conviction of a 19th-century romantic. Yet few knew about it until after his death, when a stream of concert recordings revealed that the impetuous "My Romance" or the extended "Nardis" you may once have heard were, in fact, chronic parts of his repertoire. These rhapsodies didn't quite dim the reverence for the old days but did put them in perspective: Paris '79 was every bit as imposing as Vanguard '61. His unaccompanied "I Loves You Porgy" trumps the celebrated 1968 Montreux version, from the wary opening tones and patented Evans harmonies and touch to the downright zealous digressions that follow. He's captive to his own command. *The Paris Concert, Edition One* (Blue Note)

1980 World Saxophone Quartet, "I Heard That"

Sometimes simple does the trick. At 3:23, Hamiet Bluiett's elementary blues could have fit on a 78, and it doesn't waste a moment. Most of the WSQ specialties were polyphonic or contrapuntal, and encouraged collective improvisation; the most intricate were by Julius Hemphill and usually featured the quartet—himself, Bluiett, Oliver Lake, and the uncontainable David Murray, who also adapted some of his own best melodies. Here, Bluiett offers a showcase for Hemphill's roiling alto, his huge blistering sound buoyed by precision stop-time chords, as he renovates old licks and bonds them with biting asides and turnbacks. Hemphill sustains the churchy signifying and technical élan that too often took a backseat to his composing, posing, japing. This LP was in the can for two years and yet it still seemed a breakthrough when released in late 1982. *Revue* (Black Saint)

1981 Art Pepper, "Arthur's Blues"

After 16 years of silence due to incarceration and drug addiction, one of the golden boys of 1950s L.A. came back in 1976 with a pressing need to be heard not only as a madly competitive altoist making up for lost years, but as a memoirist and nightclub seer. At first he battled his way through a Coltrane influence, but a year later the old facility returned, sharpened by a new urgency: Every solo was a bloodletting, whether backed with strings handsomely arranged by Bill Holman or loving piano by George Cables. The painstakingly slow but energetic quartet blues recorded a year before his death is typical: Throughout four choruses that Pepper plays before the piano and bass solos and three that he plays after, he constructs a narrative with barks, squeals, and 32nd-note asides, combining bravura technique, sheer guts, and a concerted purpose. *The Complete Galaxy Recordings* (Galaxy)

1982 Air, "Do Tell"

The most durable cooperative after the Art Ensemble, Air achieved nonpareil equity among its members, who could—playing Joplin and Morton or originals—undermine the beat without forfeiting it. Each member possessed grit and wit. Steve McCall's drums were plush and decisive, yet spare and understated. Fred Hopkins's bass fused audacious power with mercurial reflexes. Henry Threadgill wrote most of the material and played reeds, flute, and, briefly, a contraption made of hubcaps. Like Arthur Blythe, whose "Sister Daisy" (same year, *Elaborations*) is another model of loft-era swing, Threadgill's alto is ripe, raw, and focused; they had more in common with the restored Pepper than with the '60s avant-gardists. "Do Tell" has a mellow A-theme and double-time B-theme; each man helps to shore up the backbeat pulse until Threadgill initiates a lusty climax. Air turned out to be a starter band for him, succeeded by such compound ensembles as Very Very Circus, Make a Move, and Zooid. *80 Degrees Below '82* (Antilles)

1983 Craig Harris, "Blackwell"

In the year of James Blood Ulmer's *Odyssey*, when harmolodics ran the gamut from Shannon Jackson's Decoding Society to the acoustical Old and New Dreams, Harris's overlooked tribute to pioneering drummer Ed Blackwell offers a more obscure link to Ornette. More pointedly, it serves as a reminder that the trombonist and composer, who made a splash a year earlier with his "Nigerian Sunset," could conjure up insightful and inventive themes in a neoclassical mode. This one alternates tricky syncopations in eight and six, which support a growly, ripping, timbre-changing trombone solo by Harris, a taut and pointed one by tenor saxophonist George Adams, and— connecting them—an upbeat Cecil-like offering by pianist Donald Smith, all of them kept on track by Fred Hopkins and Charlie Persip, who italicize every beat. Harris is probably the only trombonist ever to double on didgeridoo. *Black Bone* (Soul Note)

1984 Jack DeJohnette, "Third World Anthem"

The drummer's Special Edition was big on saxophonists, and the tidy alliance of a reed trio (suggesting the influence of World Saxophone Quartet), machine-gun stickwork, and Rufus Reid's limber bass has a sharp state-of-the-art clarity. DeJohnette's music usually employs multiple themes and time signatures. This one begins with a staccato rhythm and moves through a sequence of tantalizing melodies and backup figures, welling and waning like a train now approaching, now receding. The alto, tenor, and tuba solos are vividly self-assured. John Purcell, whose alto captures some of the radius of Arthur Blythe's sound, welds short, acerbic phrases into a bold design; Howard Johnson, who doubles on baritone sax, lets loose a welter of double-time passages; and David Murray, whose woolly coilings on tenor personified the era, is enthused, funny, and succinct. *Album Album* (ECM)

1985 Benny Carter, "Lover Man"

The most quietly productive career in jazz began in the '20s, when Carter helped formulate big band music and established a standard—rivaled only by Johnny Hodges—on alto saxophone; he later introduced his own suave orchestra, an introspective trumpet style, and major compositions, peaking in his seventh and eighth decades.

His masterly "Lover Man" solo is a single chorus—32 bars; two minutes, 20 seconds—that, with glancing phrases and melodious arcs, stands as a defining, sui generis statement. After a poised theme recitation by trumpeter Joe Wilder and guitarist Ed Bickert, Carter enters as the embodiment of lucid invention, doubling up the slow tempo, pushing the beat, mixing mincing steps and flowing strides, disguising the melody with blues innuendos, taut riffs, and half-moon melodies. Too bad a subtler pianist than Gene Harris wasn't on hand, but his glib soul-notes underscore Carter's ingenuity. *A Gentleman and His Music (Concord Jazz)

1986 Wynton Marsalis, "Autumn Leaves"

Looking to Marsalis for deep feelings is as pointless as looking to Miles Davis for easy laughs. The nature of his virtuosity is to stand slightly above the chords and rhythmic change-ups, alighting in an expression of kinetic display. In a transitional juncture between the orthodox quintet that (along with classical side-trips) made his name and the self-conscious septet that fixed his direction, he appeared with just piano, bass, and drums, and revealed a lean, aspirate timbre that recalled Kenny Dorham rather than Miles, with whom he was widely compared. Even with a tune and speedy gait closely associated with Davis, he reveals a resolute inventiveness and stylish approach to time: The rhythm section gives the illusion of retarding the pulse, but Marsalis never flags during his seven hurtling turns, replete with raring turnbacks and rugged riffs, notably a 10-bar incursion in the fourth go-round. *Live at Blues Alley (Columbia)

1987 John Carter, "On a Country Road"

The last movement of the fourth of five suites in *Roots and Folklore: Episodes in the Development of American Folk Music* shows how much ground Carter—who taught public school for more than 30 years before committing himself to a career in music—could seed with relatively chaste material. At heart it's a deceptively simple clarinet riff that burbles like a swallow yet requires consummate breath control, two-note chords, and register hopping. In a winning take on musique concrète, Carter employs a tape of his Uncle John telling a story; the cadences of John's voice and his nephew's appreciative laughter—not the tale—are what count. Fred Hopkins picks up on the clarinet riff and Andrew Cyrille (outstanding throughout the album) brings the rhythm home as the piece turns into a big-city blues, featuring growling choruses by trumpeter Bobby Bradford, who is then superseded by a harmonica solo, which, ipso facto, returns us to the country. *Fields* (Gramavision)

1988 Don Pullen, "At the Cafe Centrale"

The year belonged to the 11-volume *Cecil Taylor in Berlin '88*, despite its limited number and distribution—still the most extravagant single-artist achievement of the CD era. But another remarkable pianist associated with the outer fringe suggested a powerful rapprochement with the center, when he teamed with Gary Peacock and Tony Williams. Pullen had journeyed from ESP-Disk to backing pop singers to working for Charles Mingus to co-leading a successful quintet with saxophonist George Adams. He innovated a keyboard technique that obliged him to turn his palms up and rake the keys with his knuckles, while hewing to chordal boundaries and uncovering ecstatic melodies. His opening three choruses on "At the Cafe Centrale," a symmetrical 48-bar flamenco stomp, are parsed in eight-bar segments, shadowed every step by Williams. The harmonic range is narrow, yet Pullen's percussive attack abounds with colors. *New Beginnings* (Blue Note)

1989 Muhal Richard Abrams, "Finditnow"

Guru to the Association for the Advancement of Creative Musicians, Abrams relocated to New York in the '70s and sent the pigeonholers racing for cover. With every recording and concert a discrete project, he produced an immensely varied tableau of works that range from basic blues (not least his homage to Muddy Waters) to cultured orchestration and new-music fusions, often with humor.

Along the way, he emerged as a major force in the preservation of big band jazz—in this instance as played by 18 pieces that trace the instrumental food chain from glockenspiel to synthesizer. Muhal brings out the best in everyone as "Finditnow" blends unadorned swing (the indispensable Fred Hopkins and Andrew Cyrille), four- and eight-bar exchanges (best are Abrams's piano and Warren Smith's vibes), a tidy flute and soprano sax passage, a Bach-inspired cello interlude (Diedre Murray), and rare voicings for xylophone and trombones. *The Hearinga Suite* (Black Saint)

1990 Abbey Lincoln, "The World Is Falling Down"

It had been almost three decades since her last major record when a French-produced album (with perhaps the only unflattering photographs of her ever published) affirmed her return as a matchless singer and songwriter working a terrain bounded by Billie Holiday and Bob Dylan. The title track throbs with backbeat fidelity, a gospelly stoicism that all but disguises the originality of her four-plus-eight-bar verses and a lyric worth hearing. With empathic support from Charlie Haden and Billy Higgins, she articulates every word, jolting the phrase, "We'll follow the breeze." Yet Lincoln accounts for less than half of the Ron Carter-arranged performance. Clark Terry and Jackie McLean abstain from their trademark licks as they exchange 20-bar trumpet and alto solos, plus a chorus of fours and twos (Terry's Schubertian insert is deft and telling), before she returns with the refrain: "The world is falling down, hold my hand." *The World Is Falling Down* (Verve).

1991 Joe Lovano, "Portrait of Jenny"

The only bona fide jazz star in years who enjoyed a serious big band apprenticeship, Lovano worked with Woody Herman and Mel Lewis, then shared center stage with guitarist Bill Frisell in Paul Motian's alluring combos. His consistency as a saxophonist is matched by an evidently limitless fund of conceptual ideas—every album is something new. An impetuous modernist with a mile-long romantic streak, he's an exceptional ballad player, aged and sagacious. His theme chorus on "Portrait of Jenny" recalls Coltrane, but for a warm, breathy vibrato that brings to mind Joe Henderson—who also had a breakthrough in 1991, playing Billy Strayhorn. Backed by pianist Michel Petrucciani, Dave Holland, and Ed Blackwell, Lovano totally stamps the song: the unwavering sustained note in the third bar; the trilling multiphonics as he comes out of his second bridge, propelled by Blackwell's cymbals; the cadenza, gently underscored by Blackwell's mallets. *From the Soul* (Blue Note).

1992 David Murray, "Flowers for Albert"

He introduced this homage to Albert Ayler at his first performance in New York, in 1975. The 20-year-old then returned to Oakland long enough to drop out of college, and was back in a flash—a poster boy for what became known as the loft era, playing in every context, from unaccompanied tenor sax and bass clarinet to the greatly admired octet, followed by the big band, funk, rap, African percussion, etc. Murray may earn an entry in Guinness for the number of albums he's made. A writer of engaging tunes and initiator of challenging projects (like an orchestral transcription of Paul Gonsalves's 27-chorus solo on "Diminuendo and Crescendo in Blue"), he developed an immense network of collaborators. For his fourth big band album, he reconceived his mascot tune as a mirthful dance, conducted by longtime associate Butch Morris, with elatedly cranky solos by Murray, Craig Harris, and (in an especially diverting turn) trumpeter Hugh Ragin. Just when you think it's winding down, Murray reappears for a two-minute cadenza that would've warmed Albert's cockles—Gonsalves's, too. *South of the Border* (DIW).

1993 Lee Konitz, "Exposition"

If anyone rivals Murray in output and diversity, it's the venerable Konitz, whose widely noted solos with the Claude Thornhill band

in 1947 (when he was 20) established him as the altoist who didn't
sound like Bird. He was obviously the cool choice for Miles's nonet,
and subsequent projects with his former teacher, Lennie Tristano. A
committed improviser who shuns cliches and was playing long and
free before long-and-free was a movement, Konitz was inevitably
tagged a musician's musician, though his lilting if acidic timbre and
casual swing, not to mention protorepertory liberality, make him
quite listener-friendly. Working with routine chord changes and
like-minded fellows—clarinetist Jimmy Giuffre, pianist Paul Bley,
bassist Gary Peacock—he makes "Exposition" a 19-minute medita-
tion on instantaneous invention, conversational intrigue, and rhythmic equilibrium. *Rhapsody* (Evidence).

1994 James Carter, "Take the A Train"

A reeds virtuoso who can play anything except subtle, Carter
opened the year with a roar and closed it with a sigh—the former on
behalf of eager little DIW (he looks like a jazz musician on the
cover) and the latter for corporate stepchild Atlantic (he looks like a
movie star). Both discs were mighty impressive, auguring his ability
to make thematic albums. His raptor-like chomping of the Ellington band's theme is a splendidly driven prank. Soloing for nearly
eight minutes, he uses every avant-garde technique Coltrane, Dolphy, and the other anti-jazz felons had employed to wreak havoc on
the shaken '60s, only he swings like a madman and he never misses a
chord. When he comes to ground, popping notes and closing with a
screech, it's OK to guffaw. Craig Taborn continues in the same
riotous vein on piano; perhaps the only prototype for this pair is
Byard and Kirk. *Jurassic Classics* (DIW).

1995 Randy Weston, "Tangier Bay"

In a solid year for records, connections with the Dark Continent
were asserted in Hannibal Lokumbe's *African Portraits*, a stately
oratorio that begins before the middle passage and ends after
52nd Street (and Hannibal's trumpet pyrotechnics), and circum-

navigated in the unexpected techno-funk duets of Kenny Barron and Mino Cinelu's *Swamp Sally*. Weston, a pioneer in African American (or Moroccan-Brooklyn) rapprochement, inducted the best working band of his life, called it African Rhythms, and resuscitated his treasured older pieces, some of which had been around since the '50s. His seductive highflier "Tangier Bay"—A (16) A (16) B (16) C (a kind of eight-bar semicolon with first-beat drone chords)—opens with a suspenseful piano tableau by the composer, until a vamp fires the melody, stated by altoist Talib Kibwe with bebopping insouciance and plummy tone. Weston's two choruses can afford to flaunt his love of Monk, because his reflections soon turn to signature phrases that are pure Weston. *Saga* (Verve).

1996 Uri Caine,
"Symphony No. 1, Third Movement"

Other places and tribal rites also came into view: John Zorn at Masada, Tiny Bell in the Balkans, Roy Hargrove in Cuba, Don Byron on the Lower East Side, Steve Turre on the beach. Caine labored over the persistently fashionable Gustav Mahler and rein- vented him as a suppressed Jewish klezmer. Mahler's soulful minor-key melodies, wrested from aggressive major-key opuses engender a provoking midrash from the downtown elite, includ- ing Byron, clarinet; Dave Douglas, trumpet; Joey Baron, drums; a hand-drumming cantor; and many more. The third-movement themes from the Titan are ideal for Caine, demanding to be played "mit parodie" and offering a wistful canon, a dance tune that might have served *The Godfather*, and crashing cymbals (Bar- ron may be the most strenuous drummer since Shannon Jackson). Caine adds a funeral march, bombshell eruptions, oy vey moan- ing, shrieking textures, a touch of "Autumn Leaves," and superla- tive solos by Byron and Douglas. *Primal Light* (Winter & Winter).

1997 David S. Ware, "Logistic"

There are two themes. A short, repeated saxophone phrase sets off
William Parker's teeming arco bass and Susie Ibarra's precise click-
ety-clack drumming; then an ascending hiccup figure leads to a
galumphing melody, for which Matthew Shipp provides contrary
piano chords, reminding us of the irony that strangely underscores
the quartet's "godspellized" bliss. Ware's tenor had made an unforgettable impression in the '70s and '80s bands of Cecil Taylor and
Andrew Cyrille, with its squalling timbre, its serrated edge—a
sound that could rip phone books in half. If he often seems like a
product of the Coltrane-Pharoah Sanders nexus, he is a phrase-
maker of undeniable individuality, an avant-shocker whose control
is never in doubt. Nor is the reach of his impulsively interactive
quartet, or the freedom with which his bandmates head out for
orbits of their own—alternative jazz of the past 20 years is unimag-
inable without Parker and Shipp. *Go See the World* (Columbia)

1998 Tommy Flanagan, "Let's"

Suddenly, it was about the old Turks: Dewey Redman, Cecil Taylor,
and Elvin Jones recorded the mesmerizing *Momentum Space*, and John
Lewis began preparing a stunning envoi—*Evolution*, two volumes.
Flanagan had been one of many gifted Bud Powell-influenced pianists
in the '50s. But not until the '70s, after a decade as Ella Fitzgerald's
accompanist, did he create the trio that set him apart. He was now
forging standards for group dynamics and discerning repertoire. Who
else would have revived Thad Jones's balmy caper? Based on standard
AABA changes in a configuration that may have stimulated Coltrane's
"Mr. P.C.," "Let's" veers into an old-dark-house digression with blunt
chords and hesitations. In this definitive version, Flanagan bodes the
antic hay with a descending phrase that recalls a song from *The Court
Jester*. Then he goes to the races for half a dozen express laps. Bassist
Peter Washington and drummer Lewis Nash cover him like white on
rice. *Sunset and the Mocking Bird* (Blue Note)

1999 Keith Jarrett, "What Is This Thing Called Love?"

Piano trios were bearish: Barry Harris assumed ever greater sub-
tleties, Roy Haynes created a thrilling context for Danilo Perez,
Cyrus Chestnut solidified his following, and relative newcomers—
Bill Charlap, Jason Moran, Jacky Terrasson, Brad Mehldau—earned
their own. After years of somber and extensive keyboard medita-
tions (standing firm against the Fender plague), Jarrett turned to
standards and convened a trio of extrasensory instincts. Sometimes
he failed to sustain his shiniest conceits, and one wished he had
ducked out of a piece sooner. Yet in Paris, "What Is This Thing
Called Love?" was by far the longest improvisation, and he never
falters. He begins alone, a firm left hand girding lively embellishments played with an oscillating rhythm between baroque and bop.
Gary Peacock's bass knocks twice, followed by a shimmer of Jack
DeJohnette's cymbal, and very soon the trio levitates. * *Whisper Not*
(ECM)

2000 Ted Nash, "Premiere Rhapsodie"

The achievement of a Flanagan or Jarrett derives in large part from
logging numberless miles on the road, inducing among the players a
synergy that borders on clairvoyance. Yet some projects may be
better off as one-shots, conceived for the studio. Nash, the soul of
sideman dependability, presented this memorable quintet at at least
one New York concert, but it survives as a recorded feat of genre-
defying eclecticism—a bright idea, brightly done. Debussy's clarinet
exercise is augmented by Nash's resourceful voicings and an instrumentation that cannot help evoking tangents. Wyclife Gordon's
plunger trombone calls to mind Tyree Glenn's fruitful stay with
Ellington and proves that bygone techniques can be revitalized without pomo condescension, while Nash's clarinet implies a rapprochement between France and Weimar and his tenor pushes at the
parameters of free jazz—to say nothing of evocations summoned by
accordion, violin, and drums. *Sidewalk Meeting* (Arabesque)

2001 Jason Moran, "The Sun at Midnight"

A student of Byard and protégé of altoist Greg Osby, who has mus-
tered several important talents, Moran incarnates the state of a
music that often seems weighed down by its own history. He has
assimilated piano techniques of eight decades, from stride to free,
devising a personal music that refuses to acknowledge stylistic prej-
udices. The past cannot suffocate him and musicians as varied as
Stefon Harris, Mark Turner, Vijay Iyer, or the insatiably productive
Matthew Shipp, among many others, because they've been there.
Moran brought off a small miracle in specifically making common
cause with the unwavering maverick Sam Rivers. His "The Sun at
Midnight," pretty in a stark and unsentimental way, is ideal for
Rivers's flute, which amplifies the melody, forging ahead like a
scout, spotted every step by drummer Nasheet Waits, bassist Tarus
Mateen, and Moran, whose spiky, luminous elaboration continues
the mood right through to a pedaled crescendo that brings Rivers
home for the reprise. You might think that an individual keyboard
attack is no longer possible, but you would be wrong. *Black Stars*
(Blue Note).

MITCH MYERS

A Lone Star
State of Mind

In the old days, unless your name was George Bush, Texas kids (even the white ones) would rarely dream of growing up to be president of the United States. Of course, Texas has always had its fair share of idyllic wealth and golden opportunities, but it was one tough place to live in the early 1950s. And for an all-American boy to imagine escaping the pervasive barrenness, narrow-minded intolerance and soul-killing humdrum of everyday Texas life, dreams just needed to be a little bit more down to earth.

A San Antonio kid might fantasize about being a country-music legend like Hank Williams. A few years later, that same kid might grease back his hair and imagine being Elvis Presley or a local hero like Lubbock's Buddy Holly. Or maybe he'd learn to play the devil out of the guitar and dress to the nines like Aaron Thibeaux "T-Bone" Walker, a pimped-out blues pioneer from Linden. Later still, that very same kid could fantasize about being in a group like the Rolling Stones or singing like Bob Dylan or maybe jamming with the Grateful Dead.

Doug Sahm dared to dream all those different dreams, and he grew up to be all those different people. He traversed the realms of country, jump blues, honky tonk, primal rock 'n' roll, Cajun, San Francisco psychedelia, all sorts of roots music (including Tex-Mex, Conjunto and two-step polkas), as well embracing sophisticated jazz, soul, R&B and Dylan. Sahm met most of the famous artists he respected, shared in the joys of their music and delved into their unique lives. But he always moved on.

Sahm played American music. He mastered the steel guitar by the age of five and soon played fiddle, electric guitar, bass and mandolin; he could also sing his ever-loving ass off. Sahm epitomized the complex traditions of Texas music in a way that Willie Nelson never could. Of course, Nelson was smart. Smart enough to emulate Sahm's redneck-hippie persona and doubly smart to hook up with Waylon Jennings, another Texas rebel. Still, when it came to Texas, Sahm was the man.

Sahm was the hometown boy made good. He earned his own living on his own terms, was fanatical about baseball and wrestling, brought his reefer with him everywhere he went and loved Texas as much as he loved music. A fast-talking cosmic cowboy, Sahm performed and recorded prolifically for more than 50 years, until his death on Nov. 18, 1999. Still, the Sahm discography remains splintered and disorganized, with several of his finest recordings lamentably out of print. In a world where American music martyrs like Townes Van Zandt and Gram Parsons command respect in terms of comprehensive reissues, there's no retrospective boxed set being planned for Sahm.

There are, however, two new tribute albums. The Bottle Rockets' *Songs Of Sahm* and Eugene Chadbourne's *Texas Sessions: Chapter Two* were made on minuscule budgets and released on indie labels. There are no special duets or alt-country superstars paying homage—just bright new versions of wonderful songs written by Sahm.

"Doug's an example of why music is interesting, and it's not about accumulating large amounts of money," says avant/jazz/psych guitarist Chadbourne. "The guy was into so many styles of music; it's too much for most people. Going from psychedelic rock to country and then a heavy blues thing, he kept jumping around the whole time."

While he may be the polar musical opposite of Chadbourne, Brian Henneman—frontman of alt-roots-rockers the Bottle Rockets—agrees. "The first time I heard Doug Sahm, our friend put on (1969's) *Mendocino*," he says. "From note one, the sound of that record was cooler than anything that I'd been listening to. I wasn't even wise enough to formulate the reasons why I loved it. I didn't realize that it was country and blues and Mexican music and psychedelic rock. I didn't separate it like that yet. I was still digging Aerosmith."

Catch A Man On The Rise

Born Nov. 6, 1941, Douglas Wayne Sahm began making Texas music at a very early age. With his parents' encouragement, Sahm was touted as a child prodigy playing a triple-neck Fender steel guitar. An instrumental wunderkind, he appeared on radio and television and went by the stage name Little Doug. Something of a novelty, Little Doug performed on *Louisiana Hayride* (a popular live radio show), played with local Western-swing bands and began supporting big-time country acts like Webb Pierce and Hank Thompson. Little Doug even appeared onstage with Hank Williams in Austin in 1953, just two weeks before Williams' death.

A smattering of black blues bars on San Antonio's East Side had a huge impact on Sahm as a teenager. Sneaking into the Eastwood Country Club near his home, the underage Sahm would watch and listen to mature R&B performers like T-Bone Walker, Bobby "Blue" Bland, Hank Ballard and Clarence "Gatemouth" Brown. Drummer Ernie Durawa met Sahm in 1957 and gigged with him sporadically over the next four decades. "We bounced around all of the clubs on the East Side," says Durawa. "That was our education, learning to play blues shuffles. We had a gig playing in a black band led by a tenor player named Spot Barnett at a club called the Ebony."

Attending high school by day and playing shows at night, Sahm also worked at a nightspot called the Tiffany Lounge in the Chicano-dominated West Side, where shootings were common and a breed of rough-and-tumble musicians was getting its start. The brusque mixture of white, black and Hispanic culture was a natural part of life in downtown San Antonio, and it soon became a component of Sahm's own sound.

Sahm made his recording debut in 1955, but it took a few years
for his local appeal to take hold. Now leaning toward San Antonio's
Hispanic "West Side Sound," replete with a bruising horn section,
he enjoyed regional success with the Little Richard-inspired
screamer "Crazy Daisy." By the time Doug Sahm & The Mar-Kays
(featuring tenor saxophonist Rocky Morales) hit it big with "Why,
Why, Why" in 1960, his celebrity within San Antonio's Chicano
population was well established.

As a hip-shaking-cat-gone-rock-'n'-roller, Sahm provided South
Texas with a local alternative to the growing number of entertainers
inspired by Elvis Presley. During this time, Sahm became aware of a
Tex-Mex recording artist called EI Be-Bop Kid. The Kid was born
Baldmar Huerta but became forever known as Freddy Fender, and
like so many musicians Sahm met during those days—Barnett,
Morales, Durawa and drummer Johnny Perez among them—he
would be pulled into Sahm's musical whirlwind for decades to come.

Sahm's next group, the Sir Douglas Quintet, was born of the
British Invasion; just as the Beatles and Stones captured the imagination of teenagers on both coasts, they inspired the racially mixed
R&B groups thriving in San Antonio. Original SDQ bassist Jack
Barber remembers things this way: "The type of music we played in
San Antonio was rhythm and blues like Bobby Bland, with horns
and a lot of chord changes. They had these battles of the bands, and
everybody had to kick butt or you weren't in the clique. The Quintet came in 1964; Doug came up with the idea after the Beatles
came out. He knew Huey could help us."

Enter Huey P. Meaux, a.k.a. "The Crazy Cajun." A self-styled
hustler who owned a barbershop in Houston, Meaux had his fingers
in countless pies and made contacts in the course of his work behind
the barber chair. Just why Sahm was so excited to make records with
Meaux is something to consider, but their unusual business alliance
proved to be successful beyond anyone's expectations. The key to
their success lay in the hands of a childhood friend of Sahm's named
Augie Meyers. Meyers owned a Vox Continental organ (the only
one in Texas at the time), and it became the jewel in Sahm's ornate
musical crown.

"Doug and me grew up together since we were 10 years old and met at my momma's grocery store when he was looking through all the baseball cards," recalls Meyers. "I had my band and he had his band until we were in our 20s, then we got together for the Quintet. I opened a show for the Dave Clark Five, and Doug's band came on afterward. Huey Meaux was there, trying to see what all the commotion was about with those English bands. Huey said, 'Man, you got long hair, and Doug, you got long hair—you all got to put a band together. Let's get an English name and go with it.' So that's what we did, but it was really hard to pull off because we had three Mexican guys in the band."

Masquerading as an English group with Prince Valiant haircuts, the Sir Douglas Quintet didn't receive a royal-reception with its first single, 1964's "Sugar Bee." But the group's second effort, "She's About A Mover," broke things wide open later that year. Powered by Sahm's bluesy voice and Meyers' monomaniacal Vox pulse, "Mover" borrowed from Ray Charles' "What I Say" while adding the demented context of infectious greaser garage rock. "We were doing things different way back when," says Meyers. "'She's About A Mover' was a polka with a rock 'n' roll beat and a Vox organ. I played what a bajo sexto (a 12-string bass guitar) player in a Conjunto band would do."

Sahm, Meyers, Barber, Perez and saxophonist Frank Marin were soon touring America, opening for the Rolling Stones, James Brown, Otis Redding and the Beach Boys, as well as appearing on television programs like *Hullabaloo* and *Shindig*. It was around this time Sahm met Bob Dylan, who insisted he wasn't fooled by the SDQ's English façade on *Shindig*.

The SDQ released more singles and scored again with "The Rains Came," but the band's momentum came to an abrupt stop when its members were arrested at the Corpus Christi airport for possession of marijuana. Pot laws in Texas were unusually harsh during this time, and the bust didn't bode well for the SDQ.

Not to be deterred, Meaux released the band's debut full-length, *The Best Of The Sir Douglas Quintet*, in 1965. The "best of" title was a particularly confusing claim for a group's first record, but Meaux was unsure of the Quintet's future after the bust. So unsure, in fact, that he designed an album cover featuring the band in silhouette in an attempt to extend its *faux*-British mythos. The anonymous group photo also allowed Meaux to package phony versions of the SDQ for concert appearances while Sahm and the boys were out of commission.

Steve Earle grew up in Texas and remembers the impact of the Sir Douglas Quintet. "The Quintet were *the* local heroes," he says. "'She's About A Mover' happened while I was in grade school and I was pretty plugged in to it. In those days, there were local teen shows, and the Quintet did all that stuff. Then they moved to California."

Groover's Paradise

There were two bands from Texas with long hair in the mid-'60s: Roky Erickson's 13th Floor Elevators and the Sir Douglas Quintet. Sahm claimed his band was unfairly set up for its drug arrest and that he was really just being harassed for his rebel-hippie stance. Soon after, Sahm decided to move with wife Violet and their two young sons, Shawn and Shandon, to the more tolerant environs of Northern California. Living in Salinas and spending much of his time in San Francisco during its '60s heyday, Sahm immersed himself in the liberated lifestyle of the Haight-Ashbury elite.

"When I met Doug, his little son Shawn walked in while we were talking and Doug handed him a joint," says Denny Bruce, a producer and manager who now runs the Takoma label. "It was the first time I had seen an adult give pot to a kid, and Shawn took a toke and his eyes started spinning. Doug was a real free spirit and probably took advantage of the hippie thing. He liked the notoriety and the acclaim."

Reforming the Quintet without Meyers (who initially stayed in Texas), Sahm began what many consider his most adventurous musical period. Performing at the Fillmore Auditorium and the Avalon Ballroom with the likes of Big Brother & The Holding Company, Quicksilver Messenger Service and the Grateful Dead,

Sahm became close with Jerry Garcia and partied with fellow Tex-patriots like Chet Helms and Janis Joplin.

Thriving in San Francisco, Sahm was featured on the cover of *Rolling Stone* in 1968 and again in 1971. George Rains, a drummer from Fort Worth, played for the SDQ during this time. "Doug was such a promoter of San Francisco," says Rains. "He considered himself a hippie, the whole thing of getting loaded and free love. He felt it was just heaven, and for a musician, it was. That's all he talked about, 'Man, you gotta go up to San Francisco.'"

His first California album, 1968's *Honkey Blues*, was credited to the Sir Douglas Quintet + 2. The record displays a jazzy, experimental and strangely psychedelic R&B that was undeniably brilliant, but it confused both his record company and his fans. Sahm reunited with Meyers and his Vox for the Quintet's next effort, *Mendocino*.

Former Uncle Tupelo singer/guitarist Jay Farrar recalls the mercurial magic of *Mendocino*. "There is an elusive quality to it that drew me in and never let go," he says. "The ease at which Doug moved around and blended styles from Tex-Mex to Texas R&B to psychedelia and country are what kept me a devotee."

The California edition of the SDQ recorded two more masterful albums (*Together After Five* and *1+1+1=4*, both from 1970), but Sahm was ready to move back to Texas.

Texas Me

The cover of Sahm's next record, 1971's *The Return Of Doug Saldaña*, said it all. "He's sitting on my front porch (in Bulverde, Texas), leaning back in a chair holding a bottle of Big Red," says Meyers. "He owes me enchiladas for that." For the uninitiated, Big Red is an all-the-sugar-and-twice-the-caffeine soda that originated in Texas and is usually consumed by kids too young to know better. Still, Sahm always enjoyed the stuff, and the elixir probably took the edge off of the copious amounts of weed he was smoking. Hyperactive with or without Big Red, Sahm moved home to San Antonio only to quickly leave again. This time he headed to Austin, where he helped blaze the trail of so-called redneck rock.

Divorced and living down the road from the Soap Creek Saloon, Sahm grooved into another essential phase of his musical sojourn. Between Soap Creek and the Armadillo World Headquarters club, there was an assortment of cosmic cowboys hanging around—including Jerry Jeff Walker and the newly arrived Willie Nelson, who was eager to reinvent himself after a decade of songwriting in straight-laced Nashville. Sahm established a weekly gig at Soap Creek and set about gathering his troops. Jack Barber moved up from San Antonio, and George Rains followed Sahm from San Francisco. Old pals like Rocky Morales and trumpeter Charlie McBirney gave Sahm the toughest horn section in town, reviving memories of the fabled West Side Sound.

Austin also allowed Sahm to be supportive of musicians less fortunate than himself. By reviving Fender's classic tune "Wasted Days And Wasted Nights" during his Soap Creek sets, Sahm showed empathy for a forgotten compadre who'd been imprisoned for marijuana possession and had withdrawn from the music business. He eventually coaxed Fender out of retirement, securing the singer a reassuring comeback gig within the friendly confines of Soap Creek. Sahm also produced the "Red Temple Prayer (Two-Headed-Dog)"/"Starry Eyes" single for Roky Erickson, who'd fallen on hard times due to a nasty combination of schizophrenia and drug abuse.

In 1973, Atlantic Records honcho Jerry Wexler produced *Doug Sahm And Band* in New York City. The star-studded album featured Meyers, Dr. John, David "Fathead" Newman, an obscure accordion player named Flaco Jimenez and the very famous Bob Dylan. "In many ways, Doug and Bob were flip sides of each other's personalities, which is why they were so musically compatible," says Chet Flippo, Sahm's friend and a veteran music journalist. "Each perhaps secretly envied the other a little bit and hoped that some of that particular magic would rub off."

Wexler had signed both Sahm and Willie Nelson to recording contracts, but neither artist fared well with Atlantic. (Nelson's success came soon after leaving the label.) Speedy Sparks, a roadie for Sahm and sometime bassist with the SDQ, remembers the influence

Sahm had on Nelson. "Willie wanted that rock 'n' roll crowd, and Doug had them," he says. "Willie would come out and watch Doug and figure out what Doug was doing. Willie got the hip rednecks, and then he won everybody else over. At first, Doug was the king, not Willie or Jerry Jeff or Waylon."

Using leftover tracks from Wexler's Manhattan sessions, Sahm pieced together a 1973 album called *Texas Tornado*. "*Texas Tornado* is one of the records that made it hip to play country music in Texas," says Steve Earle. "There used to be a dividing line between musicians that played pop music and the musicians that played country. It was a social line, too. That whole Armadillo World HQ/Soap Creek Saloon thing in Austin, it changed Texas." 1974's *Groovers Paradise* was a passionate homage to Austin and featured the former rhythm section of Creedence Clearwater Revival. Sahm was still making great music, but his commercial success was dwindling.

The Rains Came

A gifted organizer, Sahm wasn't the best businessman. "Doug pulled a lot of stunts in his life, financially," says Denny Bruce. "I'm not saying Doug screwed Augie, but there were so many times that he would take advantage of him. But just when you would count Doug out, he would come up and it would be like, 'Let's go, get on the bus, Augie!'"

Part of Sahm's survival was linked to an enduring popularity overseas. After signing with a Swedish label, Sahm went platinum with the crowd-pleasing "Meet Me in Stockholm" in 1983. Moves to Canada and back to Texas were peppered with the requisite number of baseball games, long nights and musical adventures. Sahm's relationship with sons Shawn and Shandon (the latter played drums in the Meat Puppets) was musical as well. Doug Sahm & Sons appeared on 1990's *Where The Pyramid Meets The Eye* (a tribute to Roky Erickson) and eventually recorded a 1994 full-length called *Day Dreaming At Midnight* (credited to the Sir Douglas Quartet).

Sahm remained a baseball fanatic throughout his life, and there were times when he would refuse to come out of his hotel room—

even to rehearse—when watching a ballgame on television. He declined to tour one fall so he could stay home and watch the World Series. "He liked so many different teams," says Shawn Sahm. "To be a baseball scout would have been his dream. He had a Joe DiMaggio baseball and an autographed menu from DiMaggio's restaurant. He would call me from all these training camps, 'Yeah Shawn, I'm hanging out with the Cubs!'"

Bruce once made a trip to Yankee Stadium with Sahm. "Doug worked his way down to the bullpen and was leaning over and talking to (pitcher) Goose Gossage," he recalls. "He came back and said, 'I knew that Goose got high!' They were talking about pot."

Performing with ensembles like the West Side Horns and the Texas Mavericks, Sahm was never far from his San Antonio roots. But it wasn't until 1989 that his love affair with Tex-Mex and Conjunto music came to full flower. Along with Meyers, Sahm reunited with Fender and Jimenez to form the Texas Tornados. Several Tornados albums and tours followed, highlighted by a Grammy award in 1991. "Doug was a real versatile guy and soulful, of course," says Jimenez. "He was a groover—a super groover—and he played a pretty good bajo sexto, too. There's not too many Anglos doing that."

Forever returning to those intricate blues shuffles and triplets he practiced in San Antonio, Sahm made a 1998 album called *S.D.Q. '98*, which included two collaborations with Texas rockers the Gourds. Gourds frontman Kevin Russell noticed a hint of melancholy in Sahm's manner. "He had a taste of fame back in the day, and I think he was always trying to recapture that," says Russell. "There was always a little bit of sadness about his best days being behind him. He wouldn't say that, but I got the feeling that was how he felt."

Unlike Gram Parsons, who died using drugs and partying with a woman near Joshua Tree, Sahm died alone of a heart attack in a hotel room in Taos, N.M., where he'd gone in hopes of regaining his health. He'd spoken to friends on the phone and complained about pains in his fingers, arm and chest. Although he was clearly sick and contemplated visiting a doctor the night he died, Sahm chose to tough things out on his own.

His final recording, a beautiful country album called *The Return Of Wayne Douglas*, was posthumously released in 2000. Sahm's lyrics have often been quoted over the years, but none as much as those from 1969's "At The Crossroads." I thought I could write Doug Sahm's story without using these words, but I've changed my mind. "You can teach me lots of lessons/You can bring me a lot of gold/But you just can't live in Texas/If you don't have a lot of soul."

Joe "King" Carrasco, a Texas musician who always emulated Sahm, says, "Nobody that had ever come from Texas covered the whole cross-section of what Texas was about except Doug. The biggest funeral they ever had in San Antonio was Doug's, and the next one will be when Augie goes. That's a whole chapter of what's the best of Texas. Once these guys are gone, that's it."

WIL S. HYLTON

The Master
of Everything
(and Nothing at All)

You are something like nothing else. That has always been clear, not least of all to yourself. When you look in the mirror, you see huge blue saucer eyes, empty and blinking on a wide-open face, a flat face almost without eyebrows. You see soft, downy cheeks and bulbous, crimson, just-punched lips. In the morning, at the black upright piano in your dining room, by the seven-foot windows overlooking L.A.'s inky Silver Lake reservoir, you hunch over the keys and blink, and your big lips smirk at the rising sun. You smirk because you have played all night. You have played the night into day. You have always been able to play away time. You are thirty-two years old now, but you could pass for half that.

You stand and stare out the window. You are alone in your jeans. Your skeleton shoulders and bony chest make a ghostly silhouette in the new light. Your waist is smaller than some men's biceps. You are the size of a teenage girl without breasts. Your hair is an unruly knot of yellow (you call it a "Jew-fro"), and your stump of a chin slides down your narrowing neck into the collar of your too-tight T-shirt. Your body cants forward, knobby knees akimbo. Your dangling arms are thin and crooked with too many elbows. Your hands are almost larger than your head. You have Frisbee palms and pipe-cleaner fingers that are gnarled from playing. Your skin is spotty and splotchy and red from no sleep. The music has come and gone.

The music has always traveled in unpredictable orbits around you. You play what you hear, not the other way around. You play because it's there and because you can. Because in silence, you hear sound. Notes and lyrics tumble into your mind like memories. When they come, you open your head and receive them. You do not think about what the words mean. You just say what you see. What you see is true. What you see is somehow you. "Neptune's lips taste like fermented wine / Perfumed blokes on the Ginza line / Running buck wild like a concubine / Whose mother never had held her hand / Brief encounters in Mercedes-Benz / Wearing hepatitis contact lens / Bed and breakfast get-away weekends / With *Sports Illustrated* moms."

You wrote that. You have written some of everything. You have written country music and indie rock. You have done hip-hop and R&B. You have danced across stages in a cowboy hat and tassels, with your thin white arms and legs wriggling in breakdance. You have crooned love ballads and shouted punk anthems. You have no genre. You have gained a mastery of everything, yet you are the master of nothing. The last song on your last album, a soaring falsetto funk called "Debra," could have been made by Prince if Prince had a sense of humor. Your sense of humor is evolving. It is important to you. It is elusive, though. You have been accused of being ironic. You have doubts about that. To you, the word *ironic* has wrong implications. It suggests that you are poking fun at other artists and genres. You are not. You are *having* fun. There is a difference.

When things began, you had less fun. That was your fault. You had an obsession with detail that dragged you toward the self-serious. You were consumed by the first album, *Mellow Gold*. Every song had to be essential and distinct. You wanted desperately to show your range. You included an indie-rock groove called "Blackhole," but you also tossed in a busted old blues sound on "Whiskeyclone, Hotel City" and an industrial-punk mix on "Sweet Sunshine." You rapped on "Loser." You flaunted your versatility like a gold tooth. You played the instruments, produced the album yourself, and recorded it in your friends' houses. You were obsessed. The weight of the thing was oppressive.

But that was a decade ago, and things are different now. Now your career is reinforced by three Grammys, and the success brings out something playful in you. The last album was a show of that. It was a flex of your creative license. Because you had snatched up two Grammys with the 1996 album *Odelay*, another for the soft-channeling *Mutations* in 1998, and by 1999 critics had begun to swoon and write your future for you. They said your music was becoming more refined with each album, less experimental and inaccessible, more personal and intimate. They predicted that you were just one album away from the slow, delicate masterpiece that would define you. And hearing that, you wanted to smack somebody. You knew that you were going in no such linear direction. In fact, what you *really* wanted to do at the time, what struck you most personally and intimately at the moment, was the need to blow off some steam and get in the studio and just have fun. And so you did that instead of making another slow, delicate album. You made a funky album with horns and cymbals and your voice in soprano, and you called the whole thing *Midnite Vultures*. The critics didn't know what to make of *that*. Many of your fans didn't, either. Nobody called *that* album intimate, but you knew that it was. It was all about abandoning the expectations of others. What could be more intimate than that?

And now, perhaps to throw them off again, you have returned to the slow, delicate sound of *Mutations*. But more so. This time, you have built on it. This time, it's even softer and more pacific, almost a translucent sound. And the critics are calling it intimate again. You don't protest. You smile. You understand. They missed it last time; they will miss it now.

You were raised to understand that critics miss the essential things. They missed your grandfather entirely, and his work was seminal. Look around you. Look at your house. His art is everywhere, collages of busty, nude women. The shapes are rough but evocative, made of things like Hershey's candy-bar wrappers. Your grandfather was a fan of the Hershey company because it did not advertise much. He used its wrappers often in his collages. It was his trademark. His other trademark was pushing pianos off rooftops. He did that often, too. He called it performance art. He called it "Yoko Ono Piano Drop." Yoko Ono was his friend. So was Lou Reed. So was Andy Warhol. Your grandfather found Warhol after the shooting. People at Warhol's Factory embraced and understood your grandfather, but most other people didn't. When he finally found a gallery that appreciated him, in Germany in the 1980s, he moved to Cologne and lived there until he died in 1995. But he left his mark behind on you. Your music is your collage. You have pasted together a spectrum of sounds.

His work on your walls is an homage, from your art to his. His collages are just about the only things on your walls. They are just about the only noticeable things in your home. Everything else is stark and scabby and impersonal. There is very little sign that anyone lives there, let alone someone like you. There is a plain olive-green sofa adrift on the hardwood floor of your living room, and there is an orange easy chair squatting alone nearby, with a small blue shag carpet in between. There is temporary shelving by the window, with books and records on it—books like the collected illustrations of George Grosz, and records like Stevie Wonder's *Innervisions*. There is a big white refrigerator with a picture of a typewriter stuck to the front; leftover platters of vegetables are inside. There is a breakfast nook and a worn tile bathroom with old-fashioned, semifunctional faucetry. There is very little stuff to show for your success.

You do not have a fancy stereo, and you do not use the stereo that you have. You play your Al Green and your Rolling Stones albums not on vinyl but on your Mac laptop, trickling through small plastic speakers. You are not concerned with high-fidelity sound. You are, in fact, unconcerned with it. This lack of concern is deliberate and thought-out. It is the result of a *petit* epiphany you experienced while waiting for a stage to be set a few years ago. The construction workers on the job were jamming to a small, shabby radio with shitty speakers, and you noticed that they did not mind or even notice the crackle and fuzz. Something crystallized for you in that.

You realized that sound quality is a luxury that rarely surfaces in real life. You realized that in real life, music usually arrives through a filter of ambient noise. Maybe a faucet is running. Maybe you're in the car, or on a busy street. Maybe the music is droning through the walls of your neighbor's apartment. It doesn't matter what kind of interference you get—just that there *will be* interference most of the time, something between your ears and the speakers to annul the precision of the recording. It was then that you came up with the Other Room Test. Before you can release a new album, you have to give it the ORT: play it on a boom box and listen from another room, letting the sound enter your ears sideways and distorted. Lately, you have been playing the new album that way. You like the new album that way. The new album sounds like the desert. It's dry and dusty, and it crackles with the tension of emptiness. It has no name yet, but that will come. You are still waiting for the right words, the right picture to enter your mind. You are culling it, calling for it, but so far, no luck. You have considered *Golden Years*. That's the name of a song on the album. But you have a thing about eponymous songs and albums. The thing is that you don't like them. And so you're stuck. The tour starts in a few weeks. You'll need a name by then.

By then, you will have packed up your laptop (with all your music inside) and your instruments and your clothes and your copies of the new album, and you will have traveled to Seattle for the first show in your two-man acoustic tour. The clothes, especially, will be important. You are going to be a folk singer for a while. And so you will leave behind the sequined, urban-cowboy getups and giant sunglasses that you wore during the funk-album period, and you will have flannel shirts and jeans with you instead. You will wear low-top Converse sneakers. You have many pairs of Converse sneakers now in many different colors. You have enough scarves to fill a duffel bag. You have T-shirts and bracelets and watches. You are ready for the next thing. You are ready to travel. You are ready to leave the empty house and the collages of naked women, ready to walk away from the black upright piano and step outside onto the winding street of your evolving image. You are ready for the next sea change.

G. BEATO

Not Bad for a White Girl

The hazel-eyed, curly-haired woman is nervous as she and her manager enter the Manhattan restaurant where they have a dinner date with Eminem. A few months earlier, the 22-year-old rapper, who goes by the name Ivory, signed with Warner Bros.; now she spends most of her time meeting producers and other artists, talking about potential collaborations. And because her attorney is Eminem's attorney—well, who knows?

After growing up in Lowell, Massachusetts, Ivory moved to Hudson, a tiny town in New Hampshire. During high school, she dated an aspiring rapper, and after a few months of listening to him practice, she decided to speak up. Soon, even *his* friends were responding better to her rhymes, and eventually a local producer asked if she wanted to record a demo. That led to the record deal, which led to an abrupt halt to her education (she was a scholarship student at Newbury College with a 3.4 GPA) and a promising job at a Boston club (where she was voted Bartender of the Year by a local magazine).

Now, you'd think that a woman who is a) Bartender of the Year; and b) a former swimsuit model would have no trouble keeping Slim Shady's attention. But after introductions—"Oh, I heard a lot about you," Em says graciously—the conversation dies off. D12, Eminem's boisterous crew, are around, so that's one distraction, and there's a basketball game on a TV in the corner. Plus, both Ivory and Eminem, despite their chosen profession, are essentially quiet people. So they're sitting there, not saying much, and Em's manager is kicking him under the table, as if to say, "Go ahead, talk to her." Ivory's manager is glaring at her, as if to say, "You *better* talk to him." Finally, they chat, and at the end of the meal, the manager shows Eminem a card from Ivory's modeling days. On the front, there's a photo of her face, and on the back, there's a photo of her in a bathing suit, with a very tiny, very sheer bottom.

"Oh," Eminem says, gazing at the portrait. "Can I keep this?"

Despite this promising contact, definitive plans for a collaboration have yet to materialize. "Right now, with D12, he's a little busy," Ivory says. "Plus, we want to be very careful if we go ahead and do that, you know, because he's a white rapper, I'm a white rapper. . . ."

Ivory's voice trails off. No further explanation is necessary. White rappers these days are obviously marketable, especially when paired with established black hip-hop stars like, say, Dr. Dre or Method Man or Timbaland.

But two scoops of vanilla and no chocolate at all? Plus one of them's female? Well, that just might be a little too much marketability to swallow.

"After Eminem sold ten million records? Trust me, every motherfucker in the industry was looking for a good white rapper," says Danté Ross, a longtime hip-hop producer who's worked with Everlast, De La Soul, and Run-D.M.C., among others. "But that's no longer a novelty, so what niche hasn't been touched yet? The white *female* rapper."

Thus, the call went out. In New York City in 2000, the president of a "midsize, poppy label" let it be known that he was looking for Feminem, if you will—a PG–13 party-girl with the looks of Mandy, the hooks of Britney, and at least a passing acquaintance with hip-hop. In Los Angeles, the president of a major label was making similar requests, and across the country, managers and producers started posting messages on the Internet looking for the next white hype:

SEEKING WHITE FEMALE RAPPERS/SINGERS, AGES 16–23, FOR
RECORDING PROJECT. SEND CD AND PICTURE TO SONY STUDIOS,
C/O MIKE MORE MEDIA.

WHITE FEMALE RAPPER NEEDED—UPPERCUT RECORDS AND
AFTADEATH ENTERTAINMENT ARE LOOKING FOR A FEMALE RAP-
PER. IF U HAVE ANY KIND OF SKILLS, PLEASE CONTACT US.

KLD PRODUCTIONS & FORT APACHE ENTERTAINMENT—ONE OF
THE PRODUCERS AND WRITERS FOR R&B/POP GROUP BLAQUE IS
LOOKING FOR A WHITE FEMALE RAPPER.

"There's an obvious void," says Delain Roberts, who runs a music
production company in L.A. and manages a white female rapper
named Gem who signed a demo deal with Interscope earlier this
year. "Everyone's coming out with pop 'tops' and urban 'bottoms':
'N Sync went and got black producers. Eminem and Bubba Sparxxx
are doing their thing. Sooner or later, someone's gonna come out
with a white female rapper, and it's gonna hit."

Of course, there are gonna be a few misses, too. "To find a white
female rapper—of course, you want to do it if she's talented," says
Eric Nicks, senior vice president of A&R at Violator. "I mean, no
question—I would love to find a talented Foxy Brown who's white.
But if a white female rapper walked into my office and wasn't among
the best female rappers out there, I would just pass."

Since most A&R guys are trying to convince the next DMX that
they're down for real hip-hop, none of them wants to be known as
the fool who tried (and failed) to hustle a fast buck off a marginally
talented white girl. But if someone did discover a marketable white
female rapper, it also could be the big score, a multi-demographic
bonanza. The odds are against you, but if it worked, think of the
payday!

Throughout hip-hop history, the white female rapper has been
almost nonexistent. In 1990, Los Angeles' Tairrie B, billed as "the
rap Madonna," was the first to release a full-length album—*The*

Power of a Woman—on Eazy-E's Ruthless Records (distributed by MCA). A year later, a 17-year-old high school cheerleader called Icy Blu released a couple of singles that briefly charted on the *Billboard* Hot 100—"Pump It (Nice an' Hard)" and "I Wanna Be Your Girl." Today she's so obscure that her former label, Giant, has no idea what happened to her. Still, Icy remains the most successful white female MC, unless you count Debbie Harry's unlikely flow on Blondie's 1981 No. 1 hit "Rapture."

Somehow, without even having a chance to honestly establish her supposed ineptitude, the white female rapper has come to serve as the ultimate symbol of inauthentic, culture-stealing, oxymoronic wackness.

"It's inherently cheesy to be a white female rapper," says Princess Superstar, a.k.a. Concetta Kirschner, the only major-label artist who fits that description to release multiple full-length albums in her career. "You hear that label, and you're like, 'Oh, no. . . .'"

"Oh, no" because hip-hop has never even had time for *black* female rappers. Salt-N-Pepa were the first women rappers to earn a platinum album, in 1988, but it wasn't until 1995 that a solo female rapper went platinum (Da Brat for *Funkdafied*). For rappers like Lauryn Hill and Eve to gain artistic *and* commercial respect took a few years more. Now white girls, who symbolically represent malls and suburbia (at least in pop culture), are bum-rushing the stage.

In Princess Superstar's case, she's released four albums and never once mentioned Pottery Barn. And her skills have shown marked improvement. "When I first started out, I couldn't rhyme at all. It was 1995, but you'd think my CD came out in '83," she says, laughing. "It was like 'Bah-bah-bappa-bah / Bah-bah-bah-bah.' That's a problem a lot of white people have."

On her latest CD, *Princess Superstar Is* (featuring cameos by respected underground figures Kool Keith, the High & Mighty, Bahamadia, and others), she delivers hilarious boasts ("I got sexists begging to make me breakfast") and spits pop culture references faster than a *Jeopardy!* writer. But she still struggles for respect.

"I was playing this show in Winnipeg," she says. "And as soon as I got onstage, this white guy in a Wu-Tang T-shirt starts heckling me: 'You ain't hip-hop. You ain't keeping it real.' I was on a 30-date tour that I booked myself! I put out my albums on my own label. How much realer can you get?"

It must be hard to keep the faith when even Canadian wiggers say you're fronting.

"When I see someone like [black veteran L.A. rapper] Medusa perform, I see histories of black people and enslaved women coming through her soul and her spirit," says Rachel Raimist, whose documentary *Nobody Knows My Name* profiles six women who are deeply involved in hip-hop culture. "But when I turn on a main stream rap record, I don't feel too much of anything, except maybe I wanna get up and shake my butt around the room. It's pretty much devoid of depth anyway, and I think that's probably going to be magnified in the case of white female rappers."

Maybe. But considering the racial makeup of hip-hop performers at this point, decrying the impact of white girls is like discussing the negative impact of a pimple on Jennifer Lopez's ass.

Tairrie B is now a mid–30s tattooed banshee who leads My Ruin, a metallic "stoner-rock" band (new album: *A Prayer Under Pressure of Violent Anguish*). But in her hip-hop days, she was a creamy cartoon of blonde pulchritude, all bright red Kewpie-doll lips and piled-high material-girl hair. Plunked down in the very black, very male world of Ruthless—home to gangsta rap godfathers N.W.A— she was the ultimate cultural trespasser, as well as a troublesome object of desire. "Yo, Eazy, everyone thinks that I'm rockin' you, and that's why I got a record deal," she says on her debut album. "Fuck nah," replies Eazy. "She won't even give me the pussy."

It's a casual exchange that hints at an underlying tension. "They were like, 'Dre's gonna produce you, Ice Cube's gonna write your lyrics.' But I didn't want that," she says. "I mean, I don't sit in denial—I definitely wasn't MC Lyte on that shit. But I tried to work with everybody, and it just became a nightmare."

Tairrie says ill will between her and Dre exploded at the Grammys in 1990. "He approached me and my manager and was talking shit," she remembers. "He got up in my face and we went toe to toe in front of a whole lot of people—Dick Clark was there, New Kids on the Block. And then he punched me in the eye. When I didn't go down, he punched me again."

According to Tairrie, Eazy-E paid her to stay quiet, and the altercation blew over without much publicity. (She did memorialize it, however, in the lyrics of her song "Ruthless Bitch.") She says it was just one of many incidents that left her doubting her place in hip-hop. (Via his publicist, Dr. Dre had no comment.) Tairrie recorded a track with Salt-N-Pepa for her second album, but the group bowed out at the last minute. "They told me they were getting a lot of flak from their community, and that it wasn't really good to have an association with me, because I was white."

Ruthless never released the second album, and Tairrie B left hip-hop to form the rap-rock band Manhole. "One day I just woke up and told myself I don't like being told I need a bodyguard to come to my own label. I don't like being told I need a gun for protection. People didn't understand that I really loved the hip-hop world. It wasn't something I was faking."

"I see me like a Madonna—sexy, but not raunchy," explains Baby Girl, a 24-year-old with curiously tinted hair (an orangy platinum blonde) and a hardened, hard-bodied bearing that belies her name. It's Saturday morning, fall 2000, as she sits down on a sofa in the sleek Manhattan studio of a commercial music production house. She has come here with her manager to audition for a couple of guys named Steve Mac and Bret Disend.

Mac, 24, works at the studio as an audio engineer, but in his off-hours he produces a teen-pop trio called Trace. Disend, 31, manages a pair of producers whose star is rising in the realm of not-quite-'N Sync hitmakers: they've done tracks for LFO; they've worked with Jennifer Love Hewitt; Atlantic wants them to write with three guys from the show *Making the Band* who didn't make the cut (now part of a "man band" called LMNT). "Can you sing too?" Disend asks Baby Girl. "Are you open to more of a rock or a pop sound?"

"I kinda do want to experiment with some Limp Bizkit shit," Baby Girl answers, glancing at her manager to see if that's the right answer. "I don't want to be too ghetto, and I don't want to be too rock."

When Baby Girl pops in her demo, she shuts her eyes as the track fills up the room. A former stripper originally from Massachusetts and Maine (who now lives in Brooklyn), she has a definite, too-nasty-for-*Jerry Springer* charisma—especially when spitting lyrics that are part bootylicious pussy-power and part hardcore sex video. But this isn't exactly what Disend and Mac are looking for: They want 18-year-olds who could pass for 16-year-old virgins, not 24-year-olds who could pass for 30-year-old porn queens.

A couple of hours later, a rapper named Leah Beabout arrives. A tiny woman with a big voice and smile, Beabout grew up on army bases all over the world, where her friends were mostly nonwhite kids. Now, at 22, her homegirl bravado seems completely natural. "I don't know," she says. "Maybe people think, 'Damn, she's all mixed up,' when they see me. But I love hip-hop culture, and I just want to write songs about life."

Right now, life isn't going too well for her. "I'm kind of struggling," she says with rueful candor. "Actually, I'm *really* struggling."

In fact, she's pretty much homeless, but she says she can deal with it. At 17, she says, she had "domestic problems" and ended up homeless for almost a year, even sleeping under bridges at one point. Now she's spending a lot of nights on Harlem subway trains.

When Disend asks her to rap, Beabout freestyles for a minute, then segues into a piece she has previously written. "They say my ego stay like the tires on a bike be," she declares. "Inflated / They dated / But ain't inspired to make it / Wifey material / Where life is just cereal / I'm gonna milk it / Put on the silk shit / Pluck the eyebrows / Fuck the whys and hows."

Her flow is assured, her lyrics witty but also deeply felt—and probably too smart, soulful, and disenfranchised for what Disend and Mac want. "She's definitely not the Britney Spears of rap," Mac concludes after she leaves. "I don't think it'd work if we were like, 'Hey, Leah, can you put on this shiny dress?'"

Months later, and still searching, Mac says, "It's kind of like you're looking for Sasquatch. You hear things, but you really don't know if she's out there."

Mac and Disend have seen dozens of MCs. There's a girl in the Bronx who's promising. There's the woman who plays a bartender on *The Sopranos*. They've tracked down candidates from Texas, Canada, and Australia. But the white female rapper with decent skills who looks great in a shiny dress eludes them, and they decide to move on. Disend is now working with a group of moronic white-boy rappers called Bad Ronald, who released a record on Warner Bros. this past year, popped up on MTV, then vanished. Mac's teen-pop group, Trace, has a deal with Warner, too.

But if Mac and Disend ever get back in the female rapper game, they'll have competition. In addition to Ivory, Universal's going with a platinum blonde 19-year-old from Orange County named Natasha. She made her public debut as a rapper while modeling a pair of Nike Air Presto Chanjo slip-ons at a product launch held in the Tiger Woods Center in Beaverton, Oregon. (Sample lyric: "When we come into town / We'll be easy to spot / You can hear our sound / Swoosh! Hot!")

RCA is betting on an artist called Wicked Queen—a former beauty pageant prodigy who's tap-danced with Savion Glover, played drums for Timbaland, starred in Lawry's Seasoned Salt commercials, and backed up Ricky Martin on percussion when he performed at the Grammys. She started rapping in an effort to connect with bored students during personal appearances as Miss Boston. Then she started adding rap interludes to karaoke performances of songs like "Sweet Child o' Mine"; now she's planning to bring an old-school female touch to the Y-chromosome genre of rap-rock.

But rapping shoe models? Beauty pageant MCs? Will hip-hop-pers buy into this? Well, a few already have. Ruff Ryder Swizz Beatz is producing Natasha's first single. DJ Lethal (of Limp Bizkit and House of Pain) is producing most of Wicked Queen's album; expect other contributors, including Missy Elliott and Timbaland, who "saw me first," she enthuses.

"My sound is like Pat Benatar meets Kid Rock in Linkin Park, and we're all going on Ozzfest together."

That squeal of joy you just heard was the staff of MTV, where Wicked Queen, also blessed with the sultry features of Angelina

Jolie and the trashy-chic fashion sense of Billy Bob Thornton, seems ready-made to reign supreme.

Believe it or not, it's been more than three years since the Off-spring's "Pretty Fly (For a White Guy)." In his flashy tracksuit hey-day, the slang-slangin' wigger was a favorite of movie directors and trash-TV producers. Now, white interest in hip-hop just doesn't strike anyone as particularly extraordinary.

But that doesn't mean Eminem changed everything.

For more than 20 years, Judith Fontaine operated a Los Angeles modeling agency. But in the mid-'90s, she sold the company and went into music management with her daughter Debbie. Fontaine Music Management has schooled teen acts with names like Street-beat and 23 Blush; its biggest success is the original incarnation of the group Dream, which recorded a platinum album for P. Diddy's Bad Boy Records. (Fontaine filed a suit, later dismissed, against Bad Boy, charging that the label falsely took credit for discovering Dream.) Another Fontaine-groomed girl group, Billie Jean, has recorded an album for Elektra.

But after a record label president told the Fontaines he wanted a white female rapper, they entered the hunt. "We probably looked at more white female rappers than anyone at any record company," says Debbie Fontaine. "It took us over a year to find a girl we felt had the full package." That girl was Natasha, the former Nike shoe model.

Natasha had been dancing professionally in music videos and live concerts since her early teens and rapping for three years. "When she enters a room, you know it," says Fontaine. "And unlike a lot of the girls, she actually writes her own material." But the rapper wasn't an easy sell. "The first question everyone always asked was, 'Where is she from?'" Fontaine recounts. "Because if you come from the suburbs, you're not legitimate. We emailed her photo to one of the labels, and just based on that, they said no. I called up a very well-known producer, and he didn't even want to hear her music. He was very adamant about it. 'I come from the real,' he said, 'and I'm sick and tired of white people trying to pass themselves off as rappers.'"

Everyone proceeds with a measure of caution. "Sure, there's a market for a white female rapper," says Kevin Black, the Interscope exec who helped break Eminem and Bubba Sparxxx, along with many platinum-selling hip-hop artists. "I mean, shit, you could be two roaches dancing and rapping and there'd be a market for it if the music's good. But with a white female rapper, I would dot all of my *i*'s and cross all of my *t*'s, because there'd be no room for mistakes."

Ché Pope, vice president of A&R at Warner Bros., who signed Ivory, echoes Black's sentiments. "I'm definitely not interested in making a packaged, gimmicky album," he says. "Because if we put something gimmicky out, we're coming from a label that doesn't really have the respect in the urban world. We have to be really credible."

"Credibility—that word gets thrown around a lot," says Natasha. "But to me, if you write about who you are and what you do, you're credible."

But will that ever be good enough?

"There's this white girl in New York who's incredible—this girl Invincible," says Danté Ross. "She's fucking ridiculous, the best female rapper I've ever heard. But she's trying to keep it too real for her own good. I tried signing her three times, but she always says no," he continues. "I know Bad Boy tried to sign her too, and Rawkus, and a few others."

Originally from Ann Arbor, Michigan, the 20-year-old Invincible performs with an all-female crew called the Anomolies. In addition, she had a recurring role on MTV's short-lived sketch-comedy series *The Lyricist Lounge Show*. According to Ross, Invincible is wary of how a record company might market her. "Her words to me exactly were, 'I don't want to be that white chick who killed rap music.' On one level, it's kind of beautiful that she sticks to her guns and has integrity like that. On another level, I think she's silly."

When asked if she wanted to talk about her experiences as a white female rapper for this article, Invincible declined. "I don't really have any desire to be in an article like that," she said. "The subject's not that interesting to me."

Her position is understandable. Black filmmakers, for instance, are often burdened with the responsibility of formally addressing the "black experience." In contrast, white filmmakers are never expected to address the "white experience," which allows them to make films about explosions and car chases.

The various expectations and directives that white female rappers encounter often seem more trouble than they're worth.

"I had a hard year," says Leah Beabout in October 2001, almost 12 months after her audition for Mac and Disend. "I was going up in all these pretty little offices, and nothing came of it because I was, like, 'They're trying to make me sell out!' I didn't want to make the wrong move, so I ended up making no moves."

For a few months, Beabout says, she felt like giving up. "I still think the fact that I'm white is one of my main pluses if I'm gonna be taken in by a record company or marketed," she says. "But at the same time, producers know that. And so they don't think you're cultivated. They're like, 'Go ahead, rap, prove yourself.' And that made me lose my momentum—all that proving of yourself. I just wanted to make my music."

Beabout returned to New Haven and joined a rock band. But unlike other women she has followed (such as Tairrie B), and others who will follow her, she just couldn't imagine hip-hop not being a part of her life.

"Now I'm in New York, trying to get back on the saddle, you know? I mean, I've been rapping since I was 12 years old. I've been doing this shit a long, long time. But now I have a plan. I'm getting my own pictures. I'm gonna drop my own marketing scheme. And I'm gonna come in Tims and fuckin' khakis." She laughs. "No dresses."

SUSAN ORLEAN

The Congo Sound

Hervé Halfon, a French person who hates French people, owns a record store on the Rue des Plantes, in Montparnasse, just a few Métro stops from the Eiffel Tower but spiritually closer to Avenue Gambela, in Congo, or to the Mokolo district, in Yaoundé, Cameroon. The store is called Afric' Music. It has a small sign and an unremarkable window display, and it's about the size and shape of a Parisian parking space. Inside, Hervé has spared all expense on the décor. Besides the floor and ceiling and one long counter, the store is nothing but rows and rows of CDs in racks and on shelves and in piles, all of them devoted to African music, except for a section reserved for the music of the Caribbean. A sound system sits somewhere behind the counter, out of view and, more important, out of reach of any customer who might want to, perhaps, switch the new N'Dombolo recording for something by M'Pongo Love. The sound system is on, loud, all the time. If you walk down the Rue des Plantes, you will at first hear just the usual rumbling and tootling and clattering sounds of a Paris street, and then, as you pass the open door of Afric' Music, you will be blasted by a few bars of a Congolese ballad, and as soon as you step past the door the ballad will suddenly be out of earshot and the Paris street sounds will resume, as if you had walked through a harmonic cloudburst.

As is the custom in record stores all over the world, a song rarely gets played in its entirety at Afric' Music. What happens is that Hervé and a customer will be listening to a song—let's say, some-

thing by Wenge Tonya Tonya—and a certain guitar line will make
Hervé think of a cut on an old Franco and O.K. Jazz album, which
he will put on, and then the Franco song will remind the customer
of a song by Les Youles that he heard the other day on the world-
music show on Radio Nova, so Hervé will turn off the Franco and
put on Les Youles, and then another customer will wander in and
suggest that the Les Youles song is a pitiful imitation of a much better song recorded twenty years ago by Tabu Ley Rochereau. Hervé
will have that recording, too, so he will play it, and then the two
customers will start arguing about it, and then Hervé, in his role as a
peacekeeping force, will take off the Tabu Ley record and put on
something uncontroversial, like the new album "Bang Bang," by
Carimi, whose members are Haitian but grew up in Miami.

Afric' Music opened twenty-six years ago. The store was founded by
Hervé's cousin David Halfon, who had picked up a taste for African
music at clubs around town. At the time, David was working as a
salesclerk in a musical-instrument shop in the Paris neighborhood
of Saint-Michel. On a gamble, he asked the owners of the shop to
let him sell African records and tapes out of the back corner of the
store.

There was no store in France devoted to African music in 1976,
even though there were already more than a million Africans living
in the country, many of whom came from the French-speaking
nations of Gabon, Benin, Togo, Mali, Chad, Ivory Coast, and Senegal, as well as from Zaire—the country now known as Congo—
whose music, called soukous, or just *la musique moderne*, was the
least parochial and most widely embraced throughout Africa. Moreover, a number of the Congolese expatriates living in Paris happened to be that country's greatest musicians. And even though
there was nowhere to buy African music in France in the mid-seventies, much of it was actually being recorded in studios in Paris and in
Brussels and shipped back to Africa for release.

This peculiar cross-continental journey was actually in keeping
with the history of soukous—and of all African music, which, in the
words of the Cameroonian saxophonist Manu Dibango, was essen-

tially "a music of encounters." To begin with, soukous was a mélange of indigenous village music and Cuban rumba, which had become popular in Congo through a series of records released there in the nineteen-thirties. Rumba was in fact finding its way back to its origins, since it, too, was a mélange—in this case, a combination of Spanish music and the sounds brought to the Caribbean by African slaves. In other words, soukous had left home, absorbed a new culture, returned home, and was being absorbed and reinterpreted once again. The music that resulted was especially elastic. Its lyrics were almost always sung in Lingala, a trading language of the Congo region and a distinct African dialect, but one that is generic and unprovincial—a sort of lingua franca with no fractious history attached. But what made soukous the preëminent music in Africa was its sound, the voluptuous interplay of three or four or even five guitars, swirling around keening melodies and a dreamy, compelling beat. It is emotional, complex music, with the brightness and propulsion and hot guitars of popular music but with a less hurried, mounting intensity. It sounds neither contemporary nor old; it is melodic and highly structured, even orchestral, but also powerfully rhythmic and cyclic, like a chant. You can dance for hours and hours to soukous music; it has that kind of drive. But it is also strangely, ineffably poignant. Even the biggest, brassiest soukous songs have a wistful undercurrent, the sound of something longed for or lost.

Kinshasa, the capital of the Democratic Republic of the Congo, was once the home of Africa's most energetic recording industry. Gary Stewart, in his authoritative history, "Rumba on the River," recounts how, in 1948, a Greek merchant named Nicolas Jeronimidis opened the Ngoma studio in downtown Kinshasa. Eventually, there were a score of studios, including many owned and operated by Congolese, and soukous's most successful musicians ran studios of their own. Soukous was the sound on every street, in clubs, on the airwaves, even on public-address systems, which blared the music for anyone who didn't have a radio. It became so entwined in the country's sense of identity that in 1960, when its delegates went to Brussels for a conference on independence, the leading soukous orchestra at the time, Joseph Kabasele and African Jazz, accompanied them.

Mobutu Sese Seko, the dictator who ruled the country for thirty-two years, was aware of how directly music communicated to the Congolese. When he took power, in 1965, he demanded that the country's musicians write songs to celebrate his achievement, and then arranged for them to receive generous state sponsorship as a sort of insurance policy against future songs that might question his actions. When he introduced his Authenticité campaign, in 1971, with the aim of ridding the country of foreign influence, he designated the great soukous orchestra O.K. Jazz the official musical medium for conveying his doctrine. He travelled throughout Zaire with the orchestra; after each of his speeches, O.K. Jazz performed, both to sweeten the medicine of Authenticite and to use its lyrics to lecture the crowds, however gorgeously, about Mobutu's programs. It would be like George W. Bush giving a series of speeches about why he wanted to go to war with Iraq, accompanied by foreign-policy songs by Bruce Springsteen.

Official intimacy did have its tribulations. Songs that Mobutu considered controversial or disparaging were banned; musicians who were too mouthy were subtly—or overtly—run out of the country. Even the greatest soukous master of all, Franco Luambo Makiadi, who led O.K. Jazz for thirty-three years, was jailed once, had his songs censored, and several times left for Europe when he felt an official chill. Franco was a huge man with a husky voice and a chiming, lacy style on guitar. His playing was so hypnotizing that throughout his life he was quite seriously accused of being a sorcerer. It is said that Mobutu loved Franco's music so much that each time Franco's left, the dictator would eventually send word that he would be pardoned if he was willing to come home and perform. When Franco died, in Brussels, in 1989, Mobutu declared four days of national mourning and gave him a state funeral.

But Mobutu was responsible for the music business's eventual exodus from the country. By the mid-nineteen-seventies, the price of copper, Zaire's chief export, had fallen dramatically, and the President's totalitarianism and his move toward Mao-inspired nationalization of industry had chased away investors and set off terrible inflation. Before long, almost all of Kinshasa's studios had gone out of business or relocated to Paris or Brussels, and the few that remained had little money for equipment, engineers, or even vinyl. Record sales were also flagging. It wasn't that the passion for souk-ous was fading; it was that people in Zaire were broke. Meanwhile, as the domestic economy worsened throughout the decade, Mobutu and his family skimmed at least five billion dollars from the treasury and from international aid.

One by one, all of soukous's biggest stars made their debuts in Paris: Tabu Ley Rochereau, in 1970; Joseph Kabasele, also in 1970; Franco and O.K. Jazz, in 1978. In Paris you could sing about any-thing you wanted, you could record in the best studios, you could play to the ever-growing population of Africans and West Indians. It was safe; there was money. Night clubs catering to the African com-munity were opening—Keur Samba, a swanky place near the Place de la Concorde, was the first, in 1975, followed by the Black and White Club, the Atlantis, Timmy's, L'Alizé, Au Petit Tam-Tam. By the late seventies, more and more of Zaire's most prominent musi-cians were leaving Africa to tour Europe and weren't coming back. In 1980 came the most symbolic move of all: while touring with O.K. Jazz, Franco bought a house in Brussels and an apartment in Paris, and started spending more time far from home.

David Halfon's back corner of the instrument shop in Saint-Michel quickly became one of the most famous back corners in Paris. Most Africans in Paris lived in other neighborhoods—in the north, in Barbès and Saint-Denis, or to the east, in the "red" suburb of Mon-treuil, which is said to have the largest community of Malians out-side Mali and as a municipality has financed public-works projects in Mali's villages. But the goods to be found in Saint-Michel were worth travelling for—it was the sound of the familiar, of the life that had been left behind. Before long, David had rented a storefront and set up a proper store.

Hervé worked in Afric' Music after school. He was then a teen-ager, mildly disgusted by French pop treacle like Plastic Bertrand

and only occasionally moved by French crooners like Charles
Aznavour. His musical interests were black soul, black reggae, black
blues. Hanging around David, he became fluent in the music of
Congo, Senegal, Nigeria, and Antilles. Fourteen years ago, David
decided to sell Afric' Music and open a chain of fast-food restaurants, so Hervé and a partner bought him out. They also began producing a number of African bands, including the renowned
Congolese guitarist Diblo Dibala and his band, Matchatcha; Les
Coeurs Brisés; Branché; and Flaisha Mani, known as the Diamond
of Zaire.

Hervé is now thirty-six years old, with a sinewy build, receding
dark hair, and the chic, messy look of a tragic intellectual. It has
never struck him as weird or incongruous that he is a white guy, and
a Jewish one at that, selling African music to expatriates. His parents
both grew up in Tunisia and imparted something of an outsider's
perspective to him; as a result, Hervé's outlook on the archetypal
French persona is somewhat negative. One recent morning, as he
was shelving new CDs, he said, "I don't like the narrow-mindedness
of French people. I'm more comfortable with Africans. They have a
different attitude—more open to the world." He is tempted to leave
France altogether. Five years ago, a customer of his who had moved
back to Ivory Coast asked him to come to Abidjan and help him
open a record store. Hervé and his wife visited for two weeks. They
were put up in the best hotel in the country and had a car and driver
at their disposal, but, ultimately, they decided that they felt too out
of place. Hervé now says he is considering moving to Canada or
Israel, but isn't sure how or when he will ever really leave.

Hervé's role in the store is all-inclusive. He orders new music,
arranges it on the shelves, writes the Afric' Music best-seller lists—
African and Caribbean—that hang on the back wall, answers the
phone, writes up sales, and takes out the trash. He also dispenses
opinions and directives to anyone willing to hear them. He has a
generous policy regarding test drives: he is willing to open any CD
to let you have a listen; as a result, about half the CDs in the store
no longer have their plastic wrappers. Hervé likes to steer customers
toward what he calls "hot music." By hot he means sexy, intense,

and exciting, rather than trendy. Only a small amount of dancing occurs in the store, though; the customers, who are overwhelmingly male, usually just lean up against the counter and move only one part of their body—a foot, a hand, a chin—in time with the song. Hervé is less inhibited, and often pounds out the beat on his thighs, or on the counter, sometimes using the plastic cover of a CD. When he's not at the store, he plays drums as a hobby, but the fact that he lives in an apartment with his wife and their two small kids cuts into his rehearsal opportunities.

Hervé is a cheerful person, although he says that being in the record-store business is a living nightmare. For one thing, Afric' Music no longer enjoys the primacy it had when it opened in 1976. African music has become a real commodity in Paris: a number of competing specialty shops have cropped up in the past two decades, and FNAC, the large French music-and-bookstore chain, now features an African section. The specialty-record-store mortality rate is high—Blue Moon Musique, Anvers Musique, and Kim Music, among others, have gone out of business—but new ones open all the time. In the past year or so, five or six tiny stores have opened in Saint-Denis.

One morning in early September, I headed over to Afric' Music. There was a pinch in the air, a scrim over the sun, and smoke-gray clouds scudding across the horizon. Placards advertising Ray Charles's upcoming concert were pasted on every light pole and bus shelter in Paris. When I arrived at Afric' Music, Hervé was chatting with two young men from Benin, who were taken with an album called "Hot Zouk Love." Hervé knows almost all his customers by sight and most by name; some are even second-generation shoppers. One of the young men from Benin was the son of a longtime customer. After a moment, a short, bubbly guy carrying two cell phones and a set of car keys came in, gave Hervé a hug, and started scanning the CD section marked "Nigeria." We started to talk, and I asked him what he did for a living.

"I was a student in economics," he said, "but now I drive a taxi, Madame." He chuckled, and added that he was from Nigeria but was looking for a record by a Haitian band called Digital Express.

"These days, you have to go to London to find really good Nigerian music," he said. He winked at me and then said in a loud voice, "Hervé, he doesn't like Nigerians."

Hervé broke off his conversation with the men from Benin and started hollering in agitated French. He grabbed an album by King Sunny Ade, who is from Nigeria, and poked the taxi-driver with it. "And what about Tilda?" Hervé said. "I have Tilda albums, too."

"She's not Nigerian!" the man said.

"Yes, she is," Hervé said.

"No! She isn't!" the man said, excitedly. "Her father is Nigerian, but her mother is from Cameroon!"

"Well, she's Nigerian, then," Hervé said, pleased with himself.

"No," the cabdriver said. "Half of her is not Nigerian. She sings Nigerian songs, but she's only half."

The men from Benin paid for their copy of "Hot Zouk Love" and quietly edged out of the store.

A young lawyer from Cameroon came in. He shook hands with Hervé and explained that he was going to d.j. at a party that night—the wedding of a French friend and an African friend—so he wanted the best dance music he could find. Hervé put on a singer named Sandra Melody doing a reggae version of the American group T.L.C.'s song "No Scrubs." I mentioned to the lawyer that it was an American song, and he gasped.

"No way is this an American song!" he exclaimed. "Listen!" He rested his right hand on his right hip, held his left hand up, as if he were holding a partner, and then started to shimmy back and forth. Everyone in the store paused as he completed his turn around the floor. When the song ended, he turned to me and said, "See? You couldn't dance to it like this if it were an American song!"

There was a moment when it seemed as if Congo would once again be the home of the Congo sound. In 1997, Laurent Kabila, the leader of the People's Revolutionary Party, marched with his troops into Kinshasa, and the aging Mobutu, who was suffering from terminal cancer, fled the country. Kabila's takeover was celebrated everywhere, including in Paris, where Tabu Ley Rochereau, one of the last members of the generation that had invented soukous, was quoted as saying that it was time for the diaspora to end, for Congo's musicians to go home. Kabila offered him a deputy post in his transitional parliament, and Tabu Ley accepted. A few others followed, most notably Sam Mangwana and the singer Kanda Bongo Man, but soon they returned to Europe: even with Mobutu gone, the country's political and economic turmoil continued. (Kabila was assassinated in 2001; his son, Joseph, is now in power.) And, for their part, the musicians who had lived in Europe had grown used to being able to sing about whatever they wanted, used to forty-eight-track studios and the most advanced synthesizers and drum machines, and to an audience that had spread from the Rue des Plantes all over the world.

While I was in Paris, I visited the guitarist Diblo Dibala, who had moved to Europe in 1989. He said that he was a supporter of both Kabilas but that he still couldn't imagine going back. "When you've been away for fifteen or twenty years, the reality of the place is different from what you remember," he said. "We're much more popular here than in Congo. The people there forget you when you leave for so long." He hasn't performed in Kinshasa since 1995. He said that he finds his inspiration in Paris, because it is where most African musicians are, and he doesn't think that will change. "Everyone comes to Paris," he said.

Soukous has become, then, the music of Africa once removed; it has absorbed yet another new culture, and when you listen to what is being recorded now, you hear a briskness and shimmer, as if the clamor and sleekness of modern Paris were a constant underscore. You might miss the pensive majesty of Franco's orchestra, but it is the nature of Congolese music to reach out, react, and remake itself each time it encounters a different world. One afternoon, Dany Engobo, the leader of Les Coeurs Brisés, stopped by my hotel to bring me the group's latest CD. I was staying in a smart new place in Montparnasse that I had chosen because of its proximity to the record store but that also happened to be decorated in Africa-chic; it had animal-print wallpaper and ethnic knickknacks, and African music—mostly Senegalese and Nigerian—was piped into the lobby all day long, re-creating in this bourgeois arrondissement of Paris a mythic version of pre-French colonial Africa. Engobo has lived in Paris since 1976, and started Les Coeurs Brisés after he arrived. The group—which includes musicians from Algeria, France, and Israel—has played throughout the United States and Europe and in a few African countries, but never in Kinshasa or Brazzaville, where Engobo is from. He doesn't expect that they will play there anytime soon. "It's too dangerous to go," Engobo said, shrugging. "I'd like to go sometime, but . . ." He paused, and the music whirled around us, a King Sunny Ade melody with tinkling thumb piano and the singer's reedy alto spelling out the tune. "I am a citizen of the world," Engobo said. "I don't think I'll ever go back. But in life, you never know."

At Afric' Music, while the Cameroonian lawyer was dancing, a tall man with a hospital-employee I.D. around his neck walked in. "Hervé," he said, "I'm dying for the new Gilberto Santa Rosa. Do you have it?" Hervé pulled several Santa Rosa CDs out of a stack. The man shuffled through them and said he wasn't sure if any of these was the one he wanted. He pulled his cell phone out of a holster, called one of Hervé's competitors, who was unhelpful, and then briefly contemplated calling friends in Martinique for a consultation. While he was thinking, a heavyset blind man from Guadeloupe eased his way through the doorway, folded up his cane, leaned on the counter, and asked Hervé to put on something by the popular young band Zouk Station. Hervé found the album, split the shrink-wrap with a two-euro coin, and put it on. The blind man smiled and said he would buy it. Two elderly women walking past with groceries, their baguettes sticking up like exclamation points, glanced in anxiously as they moved through the blast of Zouk Station. A red-cheeked drunk zigzagged across the Rue des Plantes toward the music, rolled through the door, and came to rest against the counter. Just then, the man who was thinking about calling Martinique realized that it was four in the morning in the Caribbean, so he told Hervé he would take two Santa Rosa albums. As he was paying, a cab pulled onto the sidewalk in front of Afric' Music, and a compact old man from Togo wearing a newsboy cap and a bomber jacket got out of the driver's seat, walked into the store, headed for the rack marked "Congo," ran his hands up and down the CDs, and said, "Franco! Oh, oh, Franco!" After a moment, he walked back out of the store, got into his cab, and drove away.

"He likes Franco," Hervé said.

The Cameroonian lawyer had chosen five albums and wanted more. Hervé removed the previous selection and blasted Fara Fara. The lawyer did a two-step, a tango move, and then shook his head. Off with Fara Fara. On with the new CD by Wenge Musica. The song had a galloping bass line and a bright, chattering guitar, and soon the lawyer was doing a modified cha-cha and Hervé was smiling, beating a tattoo on the counter. The sound was huge, pushing out of the little store and ballooning onto the Paris sidewalk, where the businesspeople and the shop clerks of Montparnasse were striding by in the dull autumn sunlight, smoking and talking on their way to lunch. As the song reached its crescendo, a man from Ivory Coast stepped into the store, slapped Hervé on the back, pulled out his cell phone, called a friend, and when his friend answered, said simply, "Hey. I'm here."

GREIL MARCUS

In the Secret Country: Walter Mosley, Doo-Wop, and '50s L.A.

In 1990, With *Devil in a Blue Dress*, Walter Mosley published the first of a series of crime novels. He meant to rewrite the postwar history of Los Angeles, his birthplace, as a swamp of racism—and as a field of action for his hero, an unlicensed black detective called Easy Rawlins.

When we first meet Ezekiel Rawlins—"Easy" is his street name, he tells us—it's 1948; the next three books, *A Red Death* (1991), *White Butterfly* (1992), and *Black Betty* (1994), carry the story from 1953 to 1956 to 1961. As an investigation into the nature of racism in a big, open, sunny California city full of promises and full of traps, as an investigation of how a black American walks down American streets, Mosley's series paused with its fifth installment, *A Little Yellow Dog* (1996), which ends on November 22, 1963. It was only this July, with *Bad Boy Brawly Brown* (Little, Brown, 320 pages, $24.95), that the story took its next step—a very short step. With *A Little Yellow Dog*, Mosley had stopped short: He stopped the Easy Rawlins series when its place ran away from its hero, two years before the place blew up—with the Watts riots. That event looms just as threateningly today. In six years of publishing time the story has moved forward in historical time only three months, to February 1964.

Easy Rawlins is 70 years old when in 1990 he looks back and begins to tell his tale. He's 28 when the story opens. Born in Louisiana, Rawlins grew up in Houston. In California he is a new man. He has a job at an aircraft factory, and he owns his own house: "I was a man of property," he says with infinite pride. But as a black man in Los Angeles, Easy Rawlins is also under suspicion no matter what he does or doesn't do. His only way out is to be even more suspicious, to interrogate his time and place even more deeply than it interrogates him— "Can I help you, son?" "What're you doing here, boy?"—and to become invisible. Easy Rawlins is Ralph Ellison's invisible man as a strategist, as a black explorer in the jungle of a white city.

"He stopped in the doorway," the story begins on the first page of *Devil in a Blue Dress*. Rawlins is drinking in a bar in Watts, and a white man has just walked in. "When he looked at me I felt a thrill of fear, but that went away quickly because I was used to white people by 1948. I had spent five years with white men, and women, from Africa to Italy, through Paris, and into the Fatherland itself. I are with them and slept with them, and I killed enough blue-eyed young men to know that they were just as afraid to die as I was."

So he says—but a moment a bare 12 pages later says more about where he is and who he is. The white man who has walked into the bar has hired him to look for a white woman who likes the black jazz clubs on Central Avenue, hired Rawlins to go where a white man can't, to talk to people who would never talk to him. It's the first step in a shadow career of taking money from whites to look for people who don't want to be found, mostly white people who have found their way into black Los Angeles—a career that will carry Rawlins all the way through his life. Rawlins goes to an address the man has given him. He hears a voice behind his back. "Excuse me," says the voice.

The voice made me jump.

"What?" My voice strained and cracked as I turned to see the small man.

"Who are you looking for?"

He was a little white man wearing a suit that was also a uniform.

"I'm looking for, um . . . ah . . . ," I stuttered. I forgot the name. I had to squint so that the room wouldn't start spinning.

It was a habit I developed in Texas when I was a boy. Sometimes, when a white man of authority would catch me off guard, I'd empty my head of everything so I was unable to say anything. "The less you know, the less trouble you find," they used to say. I hated myself for it but I also hated white people, and colored people too, for making me that way.

The Easy Rawlins books are written to chart the history of moments like this—these moments of self-recognition, self-hate, and the will to live a different life.

As the '40s turn the corner into the '50s, Rawlins, working off found money from his first case, begins to buy apartment buildings in Watts. He hides them behind a front man, pretending that he is the janitor of his own property, just as later, when he takes into his life two found children—one a boy sold to a pedophile before he was three, another an infant girl born to a murdered white stripper—he will pretend he has legally adopted them. By 1956 he is easily a millionaire in today's dollars. He takes pleasure in the fact that no one knows what he has—not even his wife, whom he tells nothing, not about his work, his finances, where he goes, where he's been. But he has title to nothing; anything can be taken away at any time.

He is there but he is not there. He is a factory worker who's just lost his job; he is a detective. He is a detective; he is a man who sweeps up and fixes stairs. "I felt a secret glee when I went into a bar and ordered a beer with money someone else had paid me," Rawlins says in *Devil in a Blue Dress*, remembering how it felt when he first began to play a role, to assume a mask. "I'd ask the bartender his name and talk about anything, but, really, behind the friendly talk, I was working to find something. Nobody knew what I was up to and that made me sort of invisible; people thought that they saw me but what they really saw was an illusion of me, something that wasn't real."

Mosley's sense of time is magical: the way his hero, and the city around him, change so slightly with each book, as a few years pass;

the way the bitter, thoughtful old man fades into the bitter young man trying to make his way toward the old man's old age, and trying to do it in secret. There are secrets kept from him, too. Watts is the secret country that he is sometimes forced to open to the police, white and black, who cannot reach it. In 1948, black people out in public in Pasadena after dark were arrested. The Los Angeles Police Department shot African Americans and Mexican Americans on the street, or beat them to death in alleys or cells: Rodney King was everyday life, and there were no video cameras. It was against the law for unmarried black and white people, even of the same gender, to share a house. The deep ideology of the city, maintained in the offices of the *Los Angeles Times*, in the offices of the great land companies and law firms, in the city's universities and secret societies, was not ordinary, automatic racism but Aryanism: not the belief in white superiority but the belief that only white people were human. Los Angeles is the greater secret country, certain the likes of Easy Rawlins can never truly find where it is.

By 1956, with *White Butterfly*, in Rawlins's ninth year of living a secret life in the secret country, his own story threatens to dissolve. There are too many bodies. There is too much bad sex. There is too much alcohol. Rawlins begins to scare the reader. He rapes his own wife and can't understand when she tells him what he's done. She tells him that she sees through him—which means she can't see him at all, because he isn't really there. She leaves him for another man, taking their little girl, his only natural child. He goes to see an old Watts jazz musician; he finds him sitting half-naked in a hovel, playing his horn: "The music washed over me like the air at the end of the first battle after D-Day. There were no more bullets or shards of metal flying through the air. The dead lay around in pieces and whole but I couldn't really mourn for them because I was still alive."

I couldn't really mourn for them because I was still alive: That is the sound of a man ready to die. All of Easy Rawlins's wariness, his careful maneuvers down streets that don't recognize him and those that do, his entry into places where he is welcome and those where he does not belong, his confidence and his rage, his will to show only what he wants to show—all of this is gone. Now the invisible man is exposed; the music that described his odyssey through his place and time, that played the journey out as it happened, no longer sounds. Anything can unmask him. And he admits it: "I nodded and bowed. My wife had left me, had taken my child, had gone off with my friend. There was no song on the radio too stupid for my heart."

That stupid song might have been the Jewels' "Hearts of Stone" or the Penguins' "Earth Angel," made in Los Angeles in 1954; Jesse Belvin's "I'm Only a Fool" or Don Julian and the Meadowlarks' "Heaven and Paradise," made in Los Angeles in 1955; Arthur Lee Maye and the Crowns' "Gloria," made in Los Angeles in 1956. But I like to think it was the Medallions' "The Letter," made in Los Angeles in 1954.

It is a profoundly stupid record—and also profoundly strange. There's no instrumentation except for a quietly rumbling piano. A few weak voices go "Oh—uh uh uh—oh" behind the lead singer, Vernon Green. He starts off crooning around one word: "Darling." As the backing singers shift into long "ooos," Green stops singing and starts talking. He speaks in a clipped, almost effete voice, not like a man but like a boy trapped in a fantasy he can't even begin to believe. "Darling—I'm writing this letter—knowing that you may never read it." The listener doesn't believe the person the singer is writing to exists.

As the singer goes on, his voice crumbles with puerile emotion. He seems confused, barely able to remember what he's talking about. He sounds like he's underwater, but he's in love with his own voice. "Darling—what is there words—on this earth—to be unable—to stop loving you," he says, swirling. "*Oh!* my darling!" Then Vernon Green—16, crippled by polio, who would wander the streets of Watts on his crutches, making up songs, trying to find people to sing with him—offered the words that would make him immortal, or at the least unsolvable. "And to kiss, and love—and then have to wait. . . *Oh!* my darling. Let me whisper, sweet words of dismortality—and discuss the pompatus of love. Put it together, and what do you have? *Matrimony!*"

Dismortality. Pompatus. Matrimony! He sounds like a complete idiot. At the same time he sounds like someone who knows something you never will.

This was doo-wop at its limit—and there is nothing like doo-wop. Voices crossing, meeting, separating, meeting again, voices lifting a listener off the ground: the sentimental group harmony sound of the 1950s. It was the first form of rock 'n' roll to take shape; today it is the most distant. Of all the styles of the new pop music, doo-wop was the least mediated and most accessible. Some historians claim that more than 15,000 vocal groups made records in the 1950s; the formulaic nature of so much doo-wop, and the plain unlikeliness of so much of it, make that figure credible. Doo-wop was the closest to a new, common language: To speak it, all you needed were voices.

In Los Angeles, the groups came out of the high schools, most notably Jefferson and Fremont. It was only after the war that the schools achieved anything resembling integration—and that helped set off an explosion of experiment, of people learning to speak each *other's* languages. White students wanted to learn how to sing rhythm and blues; black students like Richard Berry, who would go on to write and record "Louie Louie," were crazy about country music. The blues ballad singer Jesse Belvin, suave, sophisticated, the great songwriter of the scene, wanted nothing more than to match the silky-voiced white crooner Frankie Laine, to do what Laine did with his 1947 hit "That's My Desire," slipping the first line of the song past the country before the country realized just what it was hearing: "To spend one night with you." Twenty years later on *The Ed Sullivan Show* with "Let's Spend the Night Together," the Rolling Stones didn't get away with it.

On the East Coast, doo-wop groups were almost always African American or Italian American. In Los Angeles, as with the Jaguars, with two black singers, one Chicano singer, and one Italian Polish singer, or the Meadowlarks, with three guys who looked like black hipsters and one who looked like a surfer, they were often mixed. "In six semesters we had six student body presidents of different nationalities," said the black singer Sonny Knight, talking about

Belmont High School in the late '40s, where Knight—who would score national hits with "Confidential" in 1956 and the ghostly "If You Want This Love" in 1964—would meet Mike Stoller, who with his future partner Jerry Leiber, Jewish refugees from the East Coast, would remake Los Angeles rhythm and blues song-writing from the inside out. Everyone had to pay his due to the ruler of the scene: bandleader, nightclub owner, and record producer Johnny Otis, a dark-skinned Greek American—his brother, Nicholas Veliotes, would become Ronald Reagan's ambassador to Egypt—who had left his home in Berkeley in the early '40s to pass for black in L.A.

Into the '50s there were different musician locals for blacks and whites, but that stopped nobody. When Leiber and Stoller had their first number one R&B hit, with Willie Mae Thornton's "Hound Dog" in 1953, they were living against the law, part of a black-and-white, male-and-female communist commune, passing out literature on street corners when they weren't writing "One Bad Stud," "King Solomon's Blues," or "Easyville." "How difficult was it for a couple of white teenagers to be taken seriously by these great black artists you wanted to sing your songs?" an interviewer asked Leiber and Stoller last year. "Well," Leiber said. "we weren't white then." He wasn't kidding.

Whatever Los Angeles this was happening in, it wasn't Easy Rawlins's Los Angeles—even if, in *A Red Death*, the case takes Easy Rawlins to the black bar called the Cozy Room, "a shack . . . in the middle of a big vacant lot" with no musicians, just "a radio that played cowboy music." There were record labels with headquarters in abandoned buildings, private homes, the back rooms of legitimate stores, and even actual offices. According to Dave Marsh's *Louie Louie*, there were more labels than in any other city in the country, and they ranged far beyond Capitol or RCA: Modern, Aladdin, 7–11, Philo, Spark, Ultra, Lamp, Score, Specialty, Crown, Flip, Flair, Dig, Dolphin, Dootone, Del-Fi, Original Sound, owned by Italian Americans, Arab Americans, Jewish Americans, African Americans, and that Greek American who was, he says today, "black by choice." Only a small portion of the records that were made were doo-wop, but it was a style that in Los Angeles—where doo-wop was warmer, more ridiculous, more despairing, more emotionally and musically extreme than it was in any other city—reached for places in the heart that elsewhere in the country might not have existed at all.

By 1954, the same year that Elvis Presley made his first records, before Chuck Berry made his first, the music had found itself. As it came forth with the Penguins' "Earth Angel"—stately, hushed, glorious, a little flip of a piano triplet, then a slow but relentless progression into a desire the singers will never realize—L.A. doo-wop was a finished form. "Earth Angel" was only a demo, never meant for release—runaway airplay forced it onto the market before the producer could call the group back into the studio for a decent master—but the fogginess in the sound was part of what made the record irresistible, and bottomless. That was what Philip Roth heard when he was in his early twenties, what he heard as he kept the song playing in his head from 1954 to 1962, when he wove it through *Letting Go*, his first novel, until the tune could seal the deadly last line of the story, as a young woman silently sings the song to herself as she struggles to make sense of her life, and fails: "She could not believe that her good times were all gone."

That is the secret message of doo-wop: Life is full of glory, and that glory will not last. Doo-wop is about the way life makes promises life will not keep. In that sense, the music spoke for the same city Walter Mosley re-created, or made up, but in a different way. There is no wariness, no suspicion, because you already know how the story will turn out, and it is no one's fault, because for everyone the story will be the same.

"The air we breathed was racist," Easy Rawlins says in *White Butterfly* of Los Angeles in the '50s, and that made everything corrupt, and every life a subject for murder. In the Los Angeles that L.A. doo-wop conjured up, there was an awareness of how perfect life could be and an awareness that as soon as you formed the image of perfection, it would disappear. The only way to make it last was to turn it into a song. Such a vision, almost certainly, would only occur once. You could remake "Earth Angel" over and over again, and nothing would happen; you could try to follow "The Letter" with "The Telegram," as the Medallions did, and no one would care, not even yourself. It didn't matter; everyone's life is defined by loss, especially the loss of belief that you can have what you most want, and when a song caught that, it told people that just as they were alone, they were also the same.

What was Vernon Green really saying in "The Letter"? Nearly 20 years later, in 1972, Steve Miller took the phrase *pompatus of love* and put it in his "Enter Maurice"; the next year he highlighted the weird phrase in his number one hit "The Joker." Twenty-three years after that, screenwriters Richard Schenkman, Jon Cryer, and Adam Oliensis took the phrase for the title of a movie, and it meant . . . Cryer decided he had to find out.

It was more than 40 years since the Medallions first stepped up to a microphone, but in Los Angeles there were still people willing to pay Vernon Green, now in a wheelchair, to sing "The Letter," and he wasn't hard to find. *Dismortality*—it meant, Green told Cryer, "words of such secrecy they could only be spoken to the one you loved." *Pompatus*, Green said, was a 15-year-old's word for "a secret paper-doll fantasy figure who would be my everything and bear my children." *Dismortality* can't be factored, but it signifies effortlessly. It communicates a will to escape the limits of ordinary life, to cheat death. *Pompatus* is a real word—in the dictionary, if only in a faint line in the Oxford English Dictionary. It's hard to imagine that Vernon Green ever learned it, but not that he found it, found it contained in the ordinary words anyone might speak. *Pompatus* means to act with pomp and splendor—exactly what, in "The Letter." a teenage Vernon Green tried to do. It was a specter he chased for the rest of his life until, following a show on March 4, 2000, he suffered a stroke, dying nine months later, on Christmas Eve.

"I love her for what she is," a man tells Easy Rawlins in *Black Betty*. "His words were so honest that I was ashamed for him." But the Medallions don't care how silly they sound, any more than Vernon Green cared how pathetic he sounded in "The Letter." That's what distinguishes the Los Angeles of the Medallions, the Penguins, or the Meadowlarks from Easy Rawlins's Los Angeles: the lack of shame, the lack of any need to turn a lack of shame into a shield of pride. For a moment, the singers on these records—and none more than the Jewels in "Hearts of Stone," chanting "No no, no no, no no, no no—no no no" over the truest jungle-music beat in the history of rock 'n' roll as if it's the best idea anyone has ever had—are appearing before you as free people, perhaps as *a* free people. It was the peculiar freedom of Los Angeles in the early '50s—a city that for the first time was beginning to lose its sense that the people who owned the place would by God's right own it forever, a city that may have begun to suspect that as a city it remained to be made—that made this voice.

In 1956, in *White Butterfly*, Easy Rawlins walks out of his house. "When I went out the front door L.A. was waiting for me. . . . I didn't deserve it," he says so mysteriously, "but it was mine just the same."

JAY McINERNEY

White Man at the Door

R. L. Burnside sits in a folding chair backstage at the Village Underground, in New York, mopping his brow with a towel and sipping from a half pint of Jack Daniel's. With his hair upswept in two graying wings from his massive forehead, he resembles an impishly smiling version of the famous portrait of Frederick Douglass. At seventy-five, Burnside exudes a jaded, bullish vitality. Wearing red suspenders over a faded flannel shirt, hunter-green pants, and muddy yellow work boots, he looks as though he's just come from a day in the fields, driving a tractor—which is the way he has supported himself for most of his life.

Well-wishers are surging backstage; one by one they approach and then crouch down to pay their respects. Introductions are conducted by a dishevelled young white man, rail-thin in a T-shirt and jeans. This is Matthew Johnson, the head of Fat Possum Records. At almost any hour of the day, Johnson gives the impression of having just got out of bed after a sleepless night. Without benefit of gel or deliberate grooming, his short sandy hair achieves that pointing-in-seventeen-directions-at-once look that's become so fashionable in recent years. Despite the triumphal nature of the occasion—a sold-out, celebrity-ridden New York gig by a musician whom he has almost single-handedly rescued from poverty and obscurity—Matthew Johnson has the worried, resigned expression of a man who knows that things can only get worse—and will.

"R. L., this is Uma Thurman," Johnson says in a weary drawl.

"Matthew tells me y'all are in the movies," Burnside says politely, and promises to look out for her pictures when he gets home to Mississippi. Debra Winger says hello. As Richard Gere approaches, Matthew Johnson reminds Burnside that he has met the actor before, when he played at Gere's recent birthday party in Manhattan. "Oh, sure," Burnside says. "I remember him. He had all them monks at his party." The bluesman had never heard of Richard Gere; his concern was whether the gig paid in cash. He was worried about endangering his monthly welfare check.

"That was one of the good gigs," Johnson remarks. "R. L. actually showed up for that one."

For the past decade, Johnson, who is thirty-two, has made a mission of finding and recording the last of the Mississippi bluesmen—the inheritors of the legacy of Charley Patton and Robert Johnson—making him perhaps the last in a long line of white blues entrepreneurs and preservationists from Alan Lomax to Leonard Chess, although he speaks disdainfully of "blues geeks" and is a controversial figure in the blues community. (A recent Fat Possum compilation was called, provocatively, "Not the Same Old Blues Crap.") Crisscrossing Mississippi, the poorest, most racially divided state in the Union, Johnson knocks on the doors of trailers and shotgun shacks, chasing down rumors of guitar-playing tractor drivers and welders, searching for the living remains of a tradition that stretches back to the beginning of the twentieth century. ("I wish I had a dollar for every time I heard some kid shout, 'White man at the door,'" Johnson says.) His discoveries are not necessarily the best singers or guitar players in Mississippi. Johnson is looking for something else—something raw and original, a kind of authenticity that some might call soul. "All I care about is that they have a signature," he says. "I can find a guitar wizard in every mall guitar shop in America."

Fat Possum now has a stable of septuagenarian bluesmen, and a following that includes Bono, Beck, and Iggy Pop (who describes Fat Possum as "the most uncorrupted label in America"). Mississippi blues—as opposed to Chicago blues—is supposed to be acoustic and folky, but the Fat Possum sound is grungy, repetitive, and amplified, more back alley than front porch. In many ways, it seems closer to punk rock than to, say, the jazzy virtuoso riffs of B. B. King, or the polite homages of Eric Clapton. Some have called it "dirty blues," although that phrase is almost laughably redundant.

Fat Possum artists seem to share a background of sharecropping, illiteracy, poverty, alcohol abuse, and prison time. Burnside is a convicted killer, as is T-Model Ford, the crudest and most exuberant of the Fat Possum lot. T-Model Ford's drummer, Spam, lost several fingertips to a girlfriend with a box cutter. Seventy-four-year-old Cedell Davis, crippled with polio as a child, was crushed and nearly killed in a barroom stampede set off by a police raid. Paul (Wine) Jones, a part-time welder, is the only Fat Possum artist who's young and fit enough to play an entire set standing up, although he is sometimes not sober enough to do so. Johnson is suspicious of all blues clichés, including the one that says you've got to suffer before you can sing the blues, but he concedes, "My artists have all had hard lives, and that's reflected in the music."

"My whole livelihood is based on a guy who doesn't give a rat's ass about anything," Johnson says of R. L. Burnside. We're in the hill country near Holly Springs, Mississippi—Johnson at the wheel of his Chevy pickup—heading for Burnside's house. "That's what attracted me to him. He's incorruptible because he just doesn't care. As soon as he got good enough where people wanted to hear him play, he stopped having a guitar. Now he borrows guitars and people give them to him. He'll play anything you put in his hands. I can't even tell you how many 'authentic' R. L. Burnside guitars we've sold to collectors in Japan."

The Burnside residence is a compact dilapidated brick ranch set back from the highway. The front yard is full of vehicles, many of which appear to be enjoying a well-earned retirement. Two years ago, the county hauled away twelve of them. Johnson is relieved when he recognizes one of the cars as Burnside's current ride; otherwise, there is no way of knowing if Burnside is home (typically, he never picks up the phone). Two small children are playing on the porch. At our approach, they retreat inside the screen door. Eventually, Alice, Burnside's wife of fifty-one years, sticks her head out the door and nods at Johnson.

Inside, two young couples are sprawled on fraying couches, watching a daytime soap. From a central overhead light fixture, extension cords cascade in every direction, like ribbons from a maypole. Alice leads us through the kitchen to the master bedroom, the door of which hangs at a wounded angle, a jagged hole showing where the doorknob should be. Burnside is stretched out on the double bed, recovering from a recent operation. It's hard to hear anything above the din of the television. The room is stifling and fetid. Roaches run up the panelling on the wall behind the bed. Sharp screws protrude hazardously from the bedposts where the finials used to be. Clothes are piled everywhere. A full-sized refrigerator sits in the corner, and a chain and a padlock secure its door, which has no handle: with so many dependents—at any given time, several of his twelve children, as well as their children, are in residence—Burnside feels obliged to protect his food supplies. After a while, Johnson persuades Alice to turn down the TV.

"I got a check for you," Johnson says.

Burnside looks vaguely worried. "Last time, they told me you had to sign it."

"It's made out to you," Johnson says.

"They cut my welfare forty-eight dollars this month," Burnside says. "Maybe you could go talk to them."

"R. L., God damn it, I ain't going to go lie for you again."

The check is for nine hundred dollars, but Burnside seems more concerned about his welfare payment—some three hundred and ninety dollars a month, despite the fact that last year he earned around $175,000. (Burnside was struck from the welfare rolls shortly after my visit.)

"I had to pay three hundred twenty-eight dollars at the hospital," he complains.

"You can afford it," Johnson says.

Burnside shakes his huge head. "I don't know." You get the idea that the money he earns playing isn't nearly as real to him as the government-assistance checks.

Rural Burnside was born a few miles away, in Harmontown, which has since been flooded by the Mississippi. Like many sharecroppers, he moved north to Chicago in the late forties in search of a better life; since the invention of the mechanical harvester, the Illinois Central Railroad line has been the main artery of migration. (A hundred and fifty-four thousand blacks from the South moved to Chicago in the forties, about half of them from Mississippi.) Burnside could play guitar; he was taught by a neighbor, the legendary Mississippi Fred McDowell. In Chicago, he met Muddy Waters; one of his cousins had married the bluesman at the very time he was developing the new electric sound that would make him one of the most important popular musicians of the century—the godfather of the Chicago blues and the idol of British-invasion rockers like Eric Clapton and Keith Richards. (Listening to Burnside today, you can hear the influence of Muddy Waters; like his cousin-in-law, Burnside has made a signature of the song "Rollin' and Tumblin'.") But Burnside found Chicago dangerous and unwelcoming, and he left the city after his father, two of his brothers, and an uncle were murdered there.

"My daddy, they stabbed him about twenty-five or thirty times, and nobody ever went to jail for it," Burnside says. "I had two brothers, two uncles, and my father got killed the same year. My brother, he was a doctor—he let 'em have a little dope or something and then they killed him. They killed one of my uncles. Husband come home and caught him out with his wife and killed him. I don't know what happened to my other uncle. Yeah, I'm glad I made it out of there."

Things weren't much better back in Mississippi. Burnside found that he was being harassed by a local bully who wanted to run him off his own place. "He was trying to take over my house," Burnside explains, as he lies back on the bed and glances up at the silent face of Maury Povich on the television. "He thought he was bad. It's always the bad folks who gets killed. Them scared folks kill 'em. I told him, 'Don't come around no more,' and then he was here, so I shot him." When Burnside was brought up on homicide charges, the judge asked him if he had intended to kill the man. "It was between him and the Lord, him dyin'," Burnside says. "I just shot him in the head." (He delivers this little chestnut with a smile, a perfect pause before the punch line.) Burnside was convicted and sent to Parchman, the notorious Mississippi prison that has featured in so many blues songs. In some ways, life at Parchman resembled life outside; inmates served on work gangs, chopping and picking cotton. "We had to pick two hundred pounds a day," Burnside recalls. After serving six months, he was sprung through the influence of the white plantation foreman, who needed him for the cotton harvest.

Burnside spent several years in the Delta and several more in Memphis, where he says he saw B. B. King playing on Beale Street with a cup in front of him. Somewhere along the way, Burnside developed his own style of blues, and with each passing year his voice seems to get richer and deeper and more distinct. "Everything he touches becomes his," Johnson says. "It's what we call Burnside style. In the case of inanimate objects, that's bad. I mean, you could give him a rock, come back the next day, and it would be busted. But with songs it's good.

"I remember the day I met R. L.," Johnson says as he jams Kid Rock's latest into the CD player of the pickup after we leave Burnside. "We were driving in his car. He was drunk. Every damn light on his dashboard was on, red lights flashing everywhere. There were cows on the road, and he was driving with one hand. He's definitely, like, nihilistic—in a friendly way. He loves when things go wrong. Tornadoes, hurricanes, floods—he just loves 'em."

This seems to be what really attracts Johnson to these blues-makers—this spirit of anarchy, which he also finds in modern-day pop nihilists like Eminem and Kid Rock. It's a spirit that Johnson himself comes by honestly. Until recently, at least, his own life would have made a pretty good blues song, the my-baby-left-me-my-roof's-falling-in-police-at-the-door variety. He's got a damaged lung, bad teeth, a couple of hernias, and a back catalogue of death threats. His dentist once held up a toothbrush and asked him if he'd ever seen one, to which Johnson answered, "I use one of those to clean my pistol."

When I met Johnson, seven years ago, I was morbidly fascinated by his Southern gallows humor and by the chaos of his personal life; his primary interests, besides the blues, were barmaids, firearms, trucks, no-name vodka, and the kind of drugs that keep you up for three days. I couldn't quite determine whether he was an erudite redneck or a degenerate preppie; he might have been the protagonist of a Barry Hannah novel. (And, in fact, he once took a course at Ole Miss with the gonzo prince of Southern lit.) His anthem then was Beck's "Loser," with its immortal refrain: "I'm a loser, baby, so why don't you kill me." Fat Possum Records, which was founded in 1991 with a four-thousand-dollar student loan, went bankrupt five years later, and has continually been engaged in various legal battles ever since. His publishing company is called Big Legal Mess. (Fat Possum's corporate motto, "We're Trying Our Best," may be one of the least boosterish slogans in the history of public relations.) A few years back, he posted fourteen thousand dollars in bad-check fees. When he calls the Fat Possum office from the road, he generally says, "Hey, it's Matthew. What bad stuff's happening there?" R. L. Burnside affectionately refers to him as "the head crook." With a characteristic mixture of bluster and self-deprecation, Johnson describes himself as a con man and a failed hustler; he likes to wheel and deal, to work the angles and play the odds, and getting beaten seems only to confirm his cheerful pessimism. Among his favorite publications—along with *Penthouse* and *Western Horseman*—is *Trade winds Weekly*, one of those want-ad compendiums, which he scours in search of used trucks, farm machinery, and guns. When I first met him, he talked me into buying his '79 Mercedes diesel. (He needed the money to keep his company solvent for a few more months.) The car turned out to be stolen, as my ex-wife, Helen, discovered after she was pulled over by a Tennessee state trooper, though Johnson swore he "didn't know nothing about that." Helen vowed never to speak to him again. A few weeks later, she invited

him for Thanksgiving dinner, during the course of which he persuaded her to buy two horses. "You can't stay mad at Matthew," she
said, even after the horse that was supposedly in foal turned out to
be barren. It's a sentiment I've often heard expressed by women
encountered in bars around Oxford, Mississippi. "He seems so
befuddled and so vulnerable," one of them said. "He's like the Mississippi James Dean. You can't make up your mind whether to nurse
him or fuck him." Some of his creditors have been less generous in
their sentiments.

Fat Possum is now based in Water Valley, Mississippi, a town with a
Victorian main street built during its moment of prosperity before
the railroad bypassed it early in the twentieth century. Johnson lives
with his wife, Lori, on a quiet street in a turn-of-the-century bunga-
low so sparsely and impersonally furnished that there's scarcely a
trace of its occupants, except for the sunporch, where there are
bookshelves well stocked with twentieth century American fiction,
including the complete works of Jim Thompson and F. Scott
Fitzgerald. A few miles outside of town, Johnson owns twenty acres
of woods and pastures, where he indulges in the manly Southern
arts of engine repair, shooting, and heavy construction—the partial
frame of a barn rises from a hilltop, its giant creosoted beams sal-
vaged from a demolished railroad bridge.

Johnson grew up in Jackson, where his mother worked as a secre-
tary. He never knew his father. Shipped off to the élite Hill School,
in Pennsylvania, he barely graduated with what he says was a record
low average. "I hated it," he says with Holden Caulfield-esque
moroseness. "Everyone sucked." From Hill, he went to the University of Mississippi in Oxford. Ole Miss was then best known for its
sororities and its football team. Although Johnson nearly flunked
out, he made one life-changing contact. "Robert Palmer had just
left the *New York Times* to teach at Ole Miss," Johnson says. "He
taught the history of rock and roll. Some girl told me Keith
Richards was going to show up, so I signed up for the course. I
failed because I never showed up. We got to know each other hanging out at the bars."

Palmer is the author of *Deep Blues*, a highly regarded history of Mississippi and Chicago blues. "He shaped the aesthetic," Johnson says. An early advocate of the raw, electric hill-country sound of Junior Kimbrough and R. L. Burnside, Palmer encouraged Johnson to start Fat Possum, but the label's début album, Burnside's *Bad Luck City*, sold only seven hundred copies. Johnson then met Phil Walden, the flamboyant founder of Capricorn Records, who agreed to distribute Fat Possum recordings, but the relationship ended in an ugly court battle that lasted for a year and a half. During that time, Johnson sold or pawned everything he owned, and called everyone he'd ever met who might be able to lend him money—including me.

He briefly discovered a savior in Isaac Tigrett, a founder of the Hard Rock Café and the House of Blues, who offered to book his acts and work out a distribution deal. Tigrett's generosity cost him dearly, however, when Walden added him to the suit against Johnson. "I had three guys die on me while that was going on," Johnson says.

Facing ruin, Johnson decided to make a party record. During the previous year, R. L. Burnside had been touring with the indie-rock group Jon Spencer Blues Explosion. Johnson had been brooding about the fact that the blues audience was largely composed of aging white baby boomers—"hippies with ponytails"—who'd first discovered the music through the British-invasion bands of the sixties. Johnson wanted to connect with an audience of his own age and younger—essentially, with Spencer's audience. While Johnson was still embroiled in court proceedings, he rented a hunting lodge near Holly Springs and recorded a raucous five-hour jam with Spencer's band and Burnside. Spencer recorded for free. The result—with a cover featuring a lurid caricature by the underground cartoonist Derek Hess which showed a leering Burnside brandishing his belt in the presence of a couple of pneumatic blondes—was "A Ass Pocket of Whiskey," which went on to sell seventy-five thousand copies.

Not everyone was amused. Spencer was attacked for political incorrectness and accused of participating in a latterday minstrel show. And many in the blues establishment felt that Fat Possum was selling out. "The idea behind Fat Possum records," one critic wrote, "is basically to take a bunch of old blues guys who can't play very well, call that lack of skill 'soul,' and sell it to the indie-rock and punk-rock crowd instead of the usual blues audience. Why not? They embrace plenty of artists who lack skill and soul, so they should completely devour this 'dirty blues' stuff."

Johnson was unfazed: "I've been trying to sell out for years. I just never knew how before." That year, 1996, he sent Junior Kimbrough on tour with Iggy Pop, a former Stooges front man and the godfather of punk rock, and later R. L. Burnside opened for the Beastie Boys. And Johnson finally found a congenial home for his label—and some desperately needed cash—at Epitaph Records, which specializes in heavy-metal and punk bands like Rancid and Offspring. The notoriously hard-living president of the label, Brett Gurewitz, was exactly the kind of rock-and-roll father figure that Johnson has always been drawn to (both Palmer and Tigrett filled that role, too)—a grownup bad boy whose Dionysian streak is tempered with an Apollonian business instinct. When Johnson met Gurewitz, at his office in Los Angeles, the label president said, "Let me ask you an important question." Johnson braced himself. "If the Terminator and the Incredible Hulk got into a fight, who would win?" "The Terminator," Johnson answered. "You're right," Gurewitz said. "We got a deal."

Fat Possum's headquarters is an aluminum-sided single-story ranch house just across the street from the police station, where several of Matthew Johnson's artists have been detained on suspicion of vagrancy. The bland exterior belies the dorm-room chaos within: odd pieces of stereo equipment and car parts are stacked on a table; magazines, CD sleeves, and tools are scattered everywhere. A poster of a gap-toothed, grinning T-Model Ford is tacked to the wall. "I DON'T ALLOW NO MOTHERFUCKING PREACHERS AROUND MY GOD-DAMN HOUSE," the caption reads. A tidy front office, where Johnson's business partner, Bruce Watson, works, provides a glimmer of order and the suggestion that an actual corporation might be conducting business hereabouts. Watson, a preacher's son with a mop of

shiny black curls, dresses with a nerdish, rockabilly flair, he is Johnson's unflappable right-hand man, a self-taught studio wizard who
writes the checks, coordinates the calendar, schmoozes the creditors, and generally keeps Fat Possum from collapsing.

A typical day begins at 11 A.M., with a phone call from Mildred
Washington, the longtime companion of the late blues artist Junior
Kimbrough. The bank says it won't cash Junior's BMI check without Johnson's signature. Fat Possum is currently involved in a dis-
pute with some of Kimbrough's thirty-two known children over
Kimbrough's estate; before his death, the musician told Johnson
that he wanted to leave everything to Mildred, his companion of
more than a decade. Johnson's attempts to carry out Kimbrough's
wishes haven't been well received by Kimbrough's children, at least
one of whom, according to Johnson, threatened to shoot him. "He
just got out of Parchman," Johnson says, "and he said if he ever goes
back it will be for killing me."

Kimbrough's place, Junior's—a popular juke joint where farmers
and bootleggers mixed with students from the nearby University of
Mississippi—burned down in 2000, not long after Kimbrough died.
Kimbrough, a big, barrel-chested man with an air of almost regal
authority, was one of the most distinctive blues stylists of recent
decades, the Fat Possum artist who seemed most likely to succeed.
His first album, recorded by Johnson in 1992, was awarded four
stars by *Rolling Stone*. Rock bands like U2, Sonic Youth, and the
Rolling Stones made pilgrimages to Junior's to hear him play.

The Kimbrough estate is at the heart of another legal mess that
keeps Fat Possum's lawyers trooping in and out of the Greek
Revival courthouse in Oxford. In the early eighties, David Evans, a
professor of music at the University of Memphis, helped the university sign contracts with Junior Kimbrough and R. L. Burnside: in
exchange for a dollar, Evans established a claim to some of their
work on behalf of the university. "We want to sue the university,"
Johnson says. "They sent a tenured professor to sign up these illiter-
ate black guys. It's like some fucking Charles Dickens novel.

"These folklorists want to lock up these blues guys and treat them
like rats in a lab," Johnson says of the University of Memphis pro-

ject. His ultimate goal is to bring the music to "the kids"—those who make up the majority of the record-buying public. "I don't want only records made; I want these guys going to Europe and partying in New York. The last thing I want to be is a folklorist and record records that no one will listen to. There's a million blues records out there now. The world doesn't need any more. You can't just make a blues record today," Johnson says. "It would be like writing a Victorian novel. You have to change or it's dead. Just for the sake of preserving something—it's been preserved. These folklorists are, like, 'Let's record them and take some pictures and maybe the Europeans will buy them.'"

So far, Johnson has been successful at finding a younger audience for his artists. Nevertheless, Junior Kimbrough's death, in 1998, underlines the central flaw in the Fat Possum business model: most of the Mississippi bluesmen whom Johnson has set out to record are ailing senior citizens. They are the last of the Mohicans. "The young black kids in Mississippi are listening to rap and smoking crack," Johnson says. "There may be a few old guys out there I haven't found yet, but I'm beginning to doubt it. It used to be there were fifteen guys in every little town that played. Now you're lucky to find one."

In 1995, I spent three days with Johnson, traversing the Delta in search of new talent. Johnson was also looking for a musician named Asie Payton, who had recorded a demo, then disappeared. At dusk on Saturday, we drove down a dirt road, past a sagging white frame church, and pulled up to a little shack at the edge of a soybean field. Johnson plodded up the dirt path and, after convincing the woman who answered the door that he was neither a bill collector nor a public official, was told that Asie Payton was there but was asleep. When Johnson returned later, Asie Payton was awake, but he couldn't be persuaded to return to a recording studio. Johnson tried again several times. Two years later, Payton was dead.

That night in 1995 was the occasion of a great discovery—for both me and Johnson. After failing to see Asie Payton, we went looking for something to eat. Johnson found a juke joint in a small Delta town in Sunflower County—a crossroads with a boarded-up rail-road station and a defunct cotton gin. From the empty street, we could hear the music inside—a wild, hairy racket with a thumping bass drum underneath. Our faces were the only white ones among some twenty Saturday-night revellers. The room was hot and close, bedizened with ratty Christmas decorations and Budweiser signs, a single window fan stirring the smoke inside. There was no stage—the singer and his drummer sat on folding chairs at one end of the small room. The music sounded dirty, literally as well as figuratively (like the blues of Elmore James and J. B. Hutto), as if the guitar strings were rusted and the cones in the Peavey bass amp were cracked. The singer was bragging about kicking his woman in the ass. His playing was raucous and boogie-inflected but strangely upbeat, even when he sang, "Feel so bad, feel like breaking some-one's arm." This was T-Model Ford; Johnson signed him up as soon as he had the money.

If hard times and suffering qualify a man to sing the blues, then T-Model Ford can be said to be overqualified. (Even Burnside is in awe of his credentials.) When T-Model Ford was eleven, his father beat him so severely that he lost a testicle. By then, he was working in the fields every day, plowing behind a mule. He married when he was seventeen, and came home one day to discover his father in bed with his wife. His second wife died after drinking poison. At eigh-teen, he stabbed a man to death and went to prison. (Working on the chain gang, he says, was an improvement on his home life.) One of his sons—he reckons he has twenty-six—sucker punched him and broke his eardrum.

"A cheerful psychopath" is how Johnson describes T-Model Ford, but "an indomitable force. "Johnson recalls how Ford once drove from Greenville, Mississippi, to Detroit for a gig, stopping constantly to ask for directions. (He can't read.) Recently, he spent twenty-four hours waiting patiently at the Seattle airport,after failing to recognize his name on the sign held up by his blues-festival escort.

Matthew Johnson and Bruce Watson are on one of their regular vis-its to see T-Model Ford—he's another one who never answers his phone—and I've joined them. Like many of the Fat Possum artists, T-Model lives in the Mississippi Yazoo Delta. It's early summer, and the fields are brown, lightly dusted with the green fuzz of cotton shoots, and the vista stretches for miles; the landscape is almost featureless, except for the occasional piece of farm machinery, a stand of trees, or a cluster of shotgun shacks. The two-lane highway is so flat that you have the illusion of driving uphill to meet the receding horizon. Now and again, you pass a series of catfish ponds the size of football fields; aquaculture is a relatively recent local attempt to diversify the monoculture of cotton. The stately, columned plantation houses of the antebellum South were never features of the Delta landscape; much of the land was still forested at the time of the Civil War, and planters established their families in the hill towns to the east where the heat and disease were less noxious. "You can be lonelier here than anyplace in the world," Johnson says, and most statistics prove that you can also be poorer, less healthy, less educated, and less white here than almost anywhere else in America.

"Why don't we stop in and see Johnny?" Watson says. Johnny is Johnny Farmer, a retired bulldozer operator who reluctantly recorded an album for Fat Possum in 1998 and has been almost completely incommunicado ever since. Farmer hasn't been cashing his royalty checks, and Watson is afraid that he may have died.

"I want to talk to T-Model first," Johnson says. "He's been saying he's going to get a Greenville lawyer and take Fat Possum down. He says we're making millions off him."

Greenville is the unofficial capital of the Delta. It appears first as a series of signs rising above the cotton fields on Highway 82: Wal-Mart, John Deere, Taco Bell, Baskin-Robbins, Stogie Shoppe, Pawn Shop—Need Money Stop Here! It is a town of some forty thousand people on the Mississippi River, invisible behind the long ridge of the levee. Beyond it are the offshore casinos to which locals have been turning for economic salvation, and which—along with the recent escalation of crack-related violence—have killed off many of the bars and juke joints in Greenville and the neighboring towns. (More than a decade after it ravaged Northern cities, crack has replaced moonshine as the mainstay of the Delta's underground economy.) We finally locate T-Model's new house, a tidy little pre-war Cape Cod set on a tree-lined residential street. Mature oaks shade the yard. His home for the past decade was a run-down trailer in a dangerous part of town. Johnson and Watson helped him find this place when the roof of the trailer fell in; Fat Possum pays the rent. A sullen black woman of indeterminate age comes to the door. This is Stella, T-Model's muse and consort of many years, who is reputed to go blow for blow with him and who inspired the immortal line "Stella, I'm go' put my shoe in your ass."

T-Model Ford appears at the door with a cane. Despite his obvious infirmity, he gives an impression of irrepressible vitality—this would be a tough man to kill. Indeed, his twisted body bears the history of many failed attempts. ("I been shot, I been cut, and nobody get me down," he says in one of his songs.)

"How is it?" Johnson says grimly; he's brooding about the threat to get a lawyer.

"I'm like a apple on a tree. I'm hanging."

T-Model hobbles over, opens his mouth, and shows us his new dentures—a fine-looking set of teeth. "Only had five of the old ones left," he says, by way of explanation. Encouraged, he proceeds to demonstrate the viability of some of his other body parts. He pulls up his pant leg and points to the scars on his ankles from the two years he spent on a chain gang. There are several stab wounds. And a gimpy leg, crushed by a logging truck, he says.

"I been to Germany," he says out of the blue. "I like Germany. They treat me nice. They love old T-Model."

T-Model pulls a pint of Jack Daniel's from his pocket and takes a swig.

"What's this I hear?" Johnson interrupts. "How you're going to hire some big Greenville lawyer and take Fat Possum down?"

T-Model's ebullience is temporarily punctured. "Why would I be gettin' a lawyer if I didn't know I needed one?"

"What the hell's that supposed to mean?" Johnson says.

Judging his little koan a success, T-Model repeats it with greater conviction. "Why I be gettin' a lawyer if I didn't know I needed one?"

Johnson shakes his head and laughs. You get the idea that this exchange is an exercise in role playing, and Johnson's role is that of the patriarch—alternately cajoling and berating, doling out money and threatening to withhold it. It's a role that he and his artists, as Mississippians, seem to be comfortable with. (Johnson's politics are leftish by Mississippi standards—he was upset by the recent vote to retain the state flag, with its Confederate-battle-flag motif.) Economic and race relations in Mississippi, like the blues itself, have been shaped by the sharecropping system, under which white plantation owners advanced credit for food and supplies to landless farm laborers. The system is strikingly similar to the music business, especially in its early days, when companies advanced money to artists against their future sales, and then deducted a range of "expenses"—recording, promotion, and overhead. Johnson, you sense, would rather be mistaken for a crook than for a saint, but in the case of, say, T-Model Ford, to whom the label has recently advanced some thirty thousand dollars, he seems to be optimistically openhanded. "A seventy-six-, seventy-seven-year-old guy— I'm going to advance future royalties when he needs a new transmission. Eventually," he says, "the records will earn out.

"I admire my artists," Johnson says, "but I don't expect them to be my friends. Junior Kimbrough once told me that he wouldn't respect me if he didn't think I was ripping him off. Any black man in Mississippi who trusts a white man has got to be on crack."

Johnson mentions to T-Model Ford that we're going to visit Johnny Farmer and asks if he'd like to come along. "Sure, I'll go see ol' Johnny."

As we drive out to Route 1, T-Model talks incessantly, alternating between the first person and the third person, as he relates a series of anecdotes that have no apparent connection. "Can't fight as good as I used to," he says, "but if T-Model gets his hands on him good, then he belongs to me. Been married five times. No more. Best time I had with women is shackin' with 'em. I first got married when I was seventeen, eighteen year old. I hadn't had a woman. My daddy had to tell me how to do it. I got a girlfriend in Sweden. Or maybe Switzerland. I tell you what, these niggers around Greenville, they been lyin' to me all these years when they say white women can't fuck." When Johnson first met T-Model Ford, he was unable to look a white woman in the eye.

Johnny Farmer's trailer is on the edge of a soybean field. A big, eighties-vintage satellite dish full of bulging garbage bags sits near the entrance. Farmer comes to the door—a tall, stooped, light-skinned man with a long, mournful face under a Crown Royal cap. If he's surprised by this visit, he doesn't show it. He returns to his seat on an old plaid couch, chewing tobacco, his eyes moving between his visitors and Burt Lancaster on the television screen, while stroking his knees with his delicate hands, the fingernails like blanched almonds.

"We just wanted to check up on you, make sure you were doing O.K.," Watson says. "It's been a long time. You been playing any?"

"I joined the church, and I haven't played since."

"I'm a little bit of a Christian myself," T-Model Ford says, in deference to his host's sensibilities.

"You can't do both," Farmer says. "You got to be for Him or against Him."

This is a sentiment one often hears in Mississippi, where roadside churches seem to outnumber grocery stores and Baptist and Methodist congregations are the principal cultural points of reference. Even before Robert Johnson was reputed to have sold his soul to the Devil in exchange for his musical gift, the blues was perceived as the sinful twin of gospel, the Devil's music. Robert Johnson's harrowing "Hellhound on My Trail" is the song of a man who, despite his apostasy, firmly believes in his own damnation. If the blues sometimes seems synonymous with depression or lovesickness or simply feeling "blue," it's also personified as an active and malignant force, an evil spirit taking possession of a man's soul. ("Oh, in my room I bowed down to pray," Son House, one of the founding fathers of the blues, sang in "Preachin' the Blues," in the thirties. "Oh, in my room I bowed down to pray, say the blues come 'long and they drove my spirit away.")

T-Model Ford, meanwhile, continues to shuttle dizzyingly between stories in which he's the victim and those in which he's the

villain. But even Johnson's description of T-Model Ford as a cheerful psychopath hardly prepares me for his hair-raising account of
how he took one of his wives and several of their children down to
the levee and threatened to chop off her head with an axe while the
children begged him not to kill her. T-Model Ford smiles, and his
eyes positively sparkle as he imitates the falsetto squeals of the children: "Daddy, please don't kill Mommy. Daddy, please. Please,
Daddy, please."

There is a stunned silence, until finally Farmer says, "Maybe your
daddy didn't beat you right."

T-Model then tells us the story of his daddy. After this recitation
of his warped family history, he ends with a bleak poetic image. "I
see a stand of cypress trees," he says, and takes a swig from the pint.
"And they know they look like the other trees, but they don't know
how they got there or who they're related to or anything like that.
Sometimes I think that's how it should be with peoples. Maybe it's
better you don't know." This is the blues talking, a stark, painful
image of alienation.

Back at the office in Water Valley one evening, after several drinks.
Johnson attempts to educate me about the Fat Possum mission,
grabbing CDs from a bookshelf and jamming them into the player.
He wants to trace the history of a certain sound. First, he selects a
track from Son House. Johnson listens intently, cocking his head as
if he might hear something new this time. "Nobody has that intensity now," he says. "The blues was the rap music of its time. In the
twenties, blues was a big seller. Charley Patton was billed as 'the
Devil's Stepchild.' Then, after the Depression, nobody wanted it.
But when rock and roll came along it was all blues chords. It had the
same spirit."

He replaces the CD with one of his own recordings, in which he
has paired his bluesmen with contemporary musicians: Johnny
Farmer and Organized Noize; Junior Kimbrough and a posse of
hip-hop kids from Memphis. "I thought, 'If this record doesn't sell,
at least it will piss off the blues purists.'" He jams in another CD.
The opening riff sounds familiar, but I don't quite know where we

are until I hear the voice of Beck—the ur-slacker. "That's the opening riff of Dr. John's 'I Walk on Guilded Splinters,'" he says excitedly.

He searches the shelves for another CD. "Kurt Cobain really nailed that Leadbelly song. You can't cover blues songs anymore, but Cobain nailed it." Not finding Nirvana, he comes up with Ol' Dirty Bastard, the hip-hop renegade, screaming, "I like it raw."

Johnson is trying to illustrate the evolution of the authentic anarchic howl—from Charley Patton to Eminem. He seems to be looking for the anti-Whitmanesque strain of the American voice—the naysayers, the verbal bomb throwers, the primal screamers. His heroes are the anti-heroes: Jerry Lee Lewis, Ike Turner, Keith Richards, Axl Rose, Cobain, Eminem, plus the blue-collar heroes Lynyrd Skynyrd and Kid Rock. Genre be damned—in his mind, these are the true descendants of the lonely, libidinous, and eternally damned Robert Johnson, the true kin of Burnside and Ford.

Johnson is aware that Burnside and company are the last of the genuine blues-men, and he has been branching out: he signed up a punk duo called 20 Miles and Bob Log III, who plays slide guitar and performs in a motorcycle helmet that has a telephone attached to it. (Johnson assures me that he is huge in Japan.) The truth is that, after years of scamming and fending wolves from the door, Fat Possum seems to be working. Having racked up a million dollars in debt, the operation isn't exactly in the black yet, but last year it broke even on operating expenses for the first time. Fat Possum songs are suddenly the soundtracks of the moment: Burnside's music is on *The Sopranos* and in Michael Mann's bio-pic of Muhammad Ali; Burnside is also on "Big Bad Love," along with T-Model Ford, Junior Kimbrough, and Asie Payton; and there are more than a half-dozen Fat Possum songs in the upcoming *The Badge*. Buddy Guy, a classic Chicago "urban" blues artist,covers seven Fat Possum songs on his recent album, *Sweet Tea*, and Mandy Stein, the daughter of the A. & R. legend Seymour Stein, is just finishing a full-length documentary on the label. These days, Johnson's checks are clearing. He still refuses to drink name-brand vodka, but he's no longer shutting down the bars in Oxford every night. At times, he seems to be on the verge of realizing that he has fewer and fewer reasons to be miserable.

Bowery Ballroom, New York City. Cedell Davis is singing, his squat, toadlike body motionless in his wheel-chair, his twisted, crippled left hand clutching a kitchen knife, which he slides up and down the frets of a guitar tuned to some unknown scale, his equally deformed right hand strumming, drenching the audience in murky chords. "I hope I touch her before she gets cold," he moans. Some four hundred people, few of them even a third his age, are bobbing on the dance floor beneath him. Sitting in a folding chair close to the stage is T-Model Ford, who clutches a drink in one hand and with the other frantically beckons a tall, striking redhead, thirty-one-year-old Heather Bennett. While her boyfriend watches suspiciously, she bends down to hear the bluesman. "Damn, ain't you one fine-looking white woman," he shouts.

"I'm not a starstruck person, but I'm blown away to meet him," Bennett says later. "These people, it's so amazing that they're still here."

After his set, Davis is wheeled away, and Paul (Wine) Jones takes the stage. "I'm a Mississippi plowboy in New York City," Jones shouts into the mike—although he looks more like a Chicago bluesman, in his black fedora and shiny two-toned red trousers. He's lucky to be here in lower Manhattan, having narrowly escaped incarceration in Iowa after an incident with a coed in a bathroom. (A little later, on the tour bus, T-Model Ford tried to stab him.) As Jones kicks off his set, Cedell Davis accepts a beer from a fan, balancing the cup on the flat of his shaking palm as he lifts it to his lips. A Swedish journalist crouches down and quizzes him about his musical roots, writing his answers on a notepad on her knee. A clean-cut young man in a white polo shirt approaches me as I hand Davis a second beer. "Excuse me," he says. "Are you who I think you are?" He pauses, almost trembling. "Are you. . . Matthew Johnson?" He seems so disappointed by my reply that I feel obliged to tell him that I'm a friend of Matthew's. He introduces himself as Tom Placke, an aspiring filmmaker. "This music," he says, gesturing toward the stage. "It tugs your heart right out of your chest. I got *Ass Pocket of Whiskey* when it came out, and I've been getting every Fat Possum record ever since. The music is like nothing else that's out there. This is all I listen to. You know the motto, 'We're Trying Our Best'?" he asks. "Well," he says, apparently unable to give up the idea that I may be Matthew Johnson, "you're doing a great job."

Paul Jones dedicates his last song to John Lee Hooker, who died the night before. The audience cheers and claps in homage to the late, great bluesman, while T-Model Ford, Hooker's contemporary, waves to a blonde dressed in a baby-blue halter top. "Come on over and talk to old T-Model," he shouts. "Forget about them other guys. I'm the original hoochie-coochie man."

MARK SINKER

Math Destruction

The Greek composer Iannis Xenakis, who died last year aged 79, wrote works—often breathtakingly complex and demanding—for orchestra, tape, electronics, computer. The sleeve notes to *Persepolis*—disc one is an hour-long eight-track Xenakis tape work originally commissioned for an Iranian festival in 1971, perhaps the apex of a particular strand in his work—describe him as "staggeringly influential." Well, yes but no. Of the generation of composers who ruled the avant-garde from 1948–68—the high-phase post-war Modernists, if you like—he was always set somewhat apart, and anyway as a group, they were militantly set against what ordinarily constitutes "influence." Mimicry, shared heritage, communities of unexamined communication, the spare-parts free-for-all of the fabled "folk process," let alone that spine of the pop world, the cover version: These were exactly the mass-cult ills this sect existed valiantly to battle. Waging war on any shared structure (and often barely on speaking terms), John Cage, Pierre Boulez, Karlheinz Stockhausen, Xenakis, and others not only rejected the framework common to 19th-century composition; they pushed the Romantic fetish of originality to the molecular level, inventing a new rule-system of musical language with almost every work—as if such stand-alone pre-coding *was* the work.

If to imitate or inherit is to be corrupted, then to cause either is to be betrayed. Yet disc two here is a bonus CD of previously unreleased remixes of the sound on the master tape, by nine hip

273

noiseniks from the happening worlds of glitch, improv, and out
rock. What could be more fallen, commodity-wise, than the remix?
Isn't this just rescue-mission marketing, of a titan of bruisingly
unfashionable difficulty?

Speed-read history claims that 1968 saw the attempted global
overthrow of the Society of the Spectacle, student revolts as a
Worldwide Stage Invasion which ended the megalomaniac high-art
bullying enslavement—of musicians, audience, culture-at-large—
known as Modernism. In 1971, Xenakis, a celebrated leftist who lost
an eye fighting Nazis in World War II, hired himself out as court
composer to one Muhammad Reza Shah, then busy staging a vast
2500th birthday party for the ruined city of Persepolis in southern
Iran—the shah announced himself the successor to Cyrus the
Great, to dismay and disperse an increasingly turbulent Islamic
priesthood. He delivered a massive son et lumière—*Persepolis* was
played through 59 loudspeakers from the desert-bound skeleton of a
palace, with processions of children and flaming torches, while pro-
jectors threw images up against the nearby hillside tombs of Darius
and Ataxerxes.

But isn't son et lumière the epitome of Spectacle, in the bad '60s
sense? And the shah, well, a dictator who fostered torture until he
turned grisly mendicant, spurned by all? Undesirable metaphor
ahoy. No wonder wised-up devotees want to save the work from the
worst excesses of its vanished milieu: "Despite their distinctiveness,"
conclude the sleeve notes defensively, "what unites all these remixes
is a shared sense that all great works of art can transcend the con-
texts in which they were first conceived, in order to explore, and
perhaps fulfill, their greater purpose."

Well, yes—except no, again. Because one impulse behind the
assault on shared structure was the doubt that such transcendence is
possible. Pop, as Modernists saw it, was endlessly co-opted by com-
merce, which they took to mean meaninglessness—and so they
ruthlessly stripped their own work of anything pop-like. In fact, this
combo release contains a great sequence of panic-doubts about co-
optation, influence, corruption, communication, and originality:
Remixers contest Xenakis, Xenakis contests the shah, the shah con-

tests history ancient and modern. And then there's the spell that all the above cast (or fail to cast) over the listener.

Whose response is what, actually? I taped *Persepolis* for my Walkman, to review while driving across England—deadlines don't dissolve family responsibilities—and found that, oops, I couldn't hear it. At all. The transfer lost high and low end; the engine masked the rest. If time had been tighter, I'd be writing up the M6 between junctions 3 and 18. Transcending the context that formed it leaves *Persepolis*—like any other record—prey to every contingency the purchaser contributes.

Welcome to the Overturned World. Here's what my notes say we'll hear: "a HUGE ANCIENT STRUCTURE under immense strain, generating long-drawn metallic skreeks as it accommodates force with tiny slow bend and sway. Presently sound-events in motion, which suggests the arrival of smaller, freer elements, dust-motes grind-released in clouds still sparse enough to catch what light there is, and glint. Notes flow, slide, dance, flutter, in blocs, blobs, ribbons, dots, whirled along atop torrents." Vamp in like vein for another 56 minutes: By the time we reach CD 2, we're reduced to "Otomo Yoshide: long drones; Ryoji Ikeda: totally processed, what remains?; Construction Kit: glitch extremism; Merzbow: birds (PRETTIEST!!); Ulf Langheinrich: notes illegible." Sounds like a train, then a drill, then elephants stomping on cellophane.

In other words, we run out of language: We reach the limits of our imagination. Description is militantly refused: Extra-musical communication still constitutes corruption. Then versus Now: *Who will win?* The CD is small in my world, two fragile slivers of plastic set against urgent domestic duty. But it defeats me: I can't master it without reaching for clues, and most of these, the convenient routine knowledge by which the sounds facing me will alchemize back into someone's real-time choices and reasons, are precisely denied me. No score to study. The kids with torches won't fit in my sister's car. Online interviews with the noiseniks give you flummery about "transgression," but nothing about why this bit buzzes but that bit crackles . . . .

But if the absoluteness of Modernist aesthetic self-sufficiency suggests doubt rather than certainty, the remixes—neither ads co-opting the pop song nor even vice versa—maybe announce a contrary self-confidence. It's the spell of the original's scale and range they want to take on. Its power versus theirs: *Whose noise will stand?*

And it's because I can't get more than a fraction of it across in print that I find *Persepolis* compulsive. Life's happenstance has given me a grasp of the fuckoff-hardcore mathematics—Markovian stochastics in re: points and mass, detail and flow—in Xenakis's little-read manual of method, *Formalised Music: Thought and Mathematics in Composition* (English translation, 1971), but if I had the time would you have the patience for a painstaking translation? The point being that such devotion to the master's inner world is self-evidently pointless enslavement. Instead of an elitist-restrictive priestcraft—within which initiates communicate, excommunicating the mainstream world—the barminess of Xenakis's totalist rigor ensures that no one gets in free. High priests and laity are all on the outside, together. Formalised Music is a massive autodestructive engine: It creates the monumental ruin of itself. If the noisenik glitch on this record is to stand, then by self-choice *Persepolis* is the cataclysm alongside which it will have to stand—except isn't "a work that stands the test of time" the lamest promo-cliché of all?

Faced with the near-perfect impenetrability of Xenakis-rigor, I either retreat into lame sour-grapesing, or fast-track evolve until I'm his equal. Because of course a pop song press-ganged into servicing an advert will sometimes reverse the direction of the appropriation (to doubt this is to accept that adverts are by definition stronger art than music). The avant-garde distrusts trade, old and new, because it fears its own power, and also yours: What if the listener brings something to the picnic that turns the composer into spurned loser-mendicant? Uncorrupt non-treacherous response (the critic's mission?) means elaborating an analogy—translation from music-noise into words (and letters)—as far-reaching as Xenakis's lifework. Like Shelley on Ozymandias (or, you know, something equally leftover-throw-away-easyreach). A response which merely folds into itself all history, all philosophy, all mathematics . . . I say my mission, but actually I just decided I mean YOURS ZZZZPhthccrrkkkzzeeeeoweeeeoww-zhzhzhkattattaata . . .

ELVIS COSTELLO

Rocking
Around the Clock

What wakes you up at five A.M.? Toothache? Heart-break? Or the nervous rush that comes from too much wine the previous evening? You can tell yourself it is still "night" in the hour after four. Once five strikes it is indisputably "morning."

What sound will soothe as the sharp light floods past the ill-fitting curtains of your hired room? You need fine gauze for the senses. Outside, the last taxis with exhausted revelers skulk home as newspaper trucks sling piles that lie in doorways.

Play **João Gilberto's** "Aguas de Março" (PolyGram), a song that has no need to raise its voice. It's either this or **John McCormack's** *Songs of My Heart: Popular Songs and Irish Ballads* (Angel) at a low volume. The circuit of the vanity clock commences. It's just another parlor (or boudoir) game; in the words of Errol Flynn, this is only "for fun and sport."

6 A.M.

A time of brief respite, before telephones and televisions assault us, and we may be still and patient enough for **Palestrina's** *Missa Papac Marcelli* sung by **the Westminster Cathedral Choir** (Hyperion). It was once thought that this work saved music in a time when dogmatic cardinals wanted to forbid the use of polyphony. Scholarship does a disservice to our imaginations by illustrating a more mundane reality. Listening to the "Kyrie," you can believe that it would have been very persuasive.

Voices are raised in praise. Perhaps it is enough to believe that they believe, but if that feels hypocritical, then you could always turn to **Monteverdi's** "Lamento d'Arianna" performed by **the Deller Consort** (Vanguard). It speaks of another kind of love and sorrow.

7 A.M.

There is a need for order and purpose to the day. **Haydn** symphonies are ideal at this hour. Concise and with an absence of bombast, they sharpen your wits with a wit of their own. Don't expect this from the slick machine of the modern orchestra. The period group is what you need, with the buzz and clang of the arcane bells, reeds, and bows. There are many recordings, but *Volume 2 of the Haydn Symphonies Series*, by the **Academy of Ancient Music** (L'Oiseau-Lyre), directed by **Christopher Hogwood**, is a good place to begin.

As the murmur of news seeps unbidden through the walls and windows, you may prefer the prophecy of the opening measures of the **Mozart** String Quartet No. 19 in C Major, K. 465, often subtitled "Dissonant," performed by **Le Quatuor Talich** (Calliope), or turn to the piano for "On an Overgrown Path" played by **András Schiff** on the album *Leoš Janáček: A Recollection* (ECM), or **Brahms's** autumnal intermezzos Opuses 117 and 118, performed by **Radu Lupu** (Decca).

8 A.M.

The day is picking up pace, **Mingus** is playing *loud* in the kitchen, something is boiling. It's *Blues & Roots* (Rhino), or the excellent *Thirteen Pictures: The Charles Mingus Anthology* (Rhino). Hit the repeat function on "Jump Monk." Like the motor of a city, the rattle of an overhead railway, blood coursing back to the heart, air propelled through the pipes of an old hotel. There is a hoarse voice rising to a shout with the force of life.

What else would work at this hour? The rock-steady beat of *Tighten Up: Trojan Reggae Classics 1968–1974* (Trojan) or "Expecting to Fly" from **Neil Young's** great, reissued compilation, *Decade* (Reprise).

9 A.M.

The guitar and tender falsetto of **Curtis Mayfield** lead **the Impressions** in "I'm So Proud" and "Keep on Pushing." If you can't find *Big 16* (HMV) or *28 Originals* (ABC) on vinyl, then the *Ultimate Collection* (Hip-O) will spin you out of doors or across tiled floors.

Men of leisure and the Victorian-minded are inclined to answer their mail at this hour. The distraction of **Aretha Franklin's** *I Never Loved a Man the Way I Love You* (Atlantic) will save on postage. Mighty singers still walk among us. **Solomon Burke's** mid–2002 release, *Don't Give Up on Me* (Fat Possum), is all the proof you need. I must declare an interest in this one, having co-written one track, "The Judgement," with my wife, Cait. Songs from **Dan Penn, Tom Waits, Nick Lowe, Bob Dylan**, and the album's producer, **Joe Henry**, recrown the King of Rock and Soul. Now it is time to do some housework.

10 A.M.

Turn up **Madonna's** "Ray of Light," or even that "Into the Groove" 12-inch single (Warner Bros) . . . until the neighbors complain. Dance around the furniture with the Hoover like Fred Astaire and his hatstand. **The Pet Shop Boys'** *Please* (Capitol) will assist with the dusting. **Elgar's** *"Enigma" Variations* conducted by **Sir Adrian Boult** (EMI Classics) may bring a little nobility to the washing up. Gentlemen, beware, that novelty apron will rob you of your dignity.

11 A.M.

Time for a cup of tea and a biscuit after all that hard work. Select a record from the dressing-up box—**David Bowie's** *Hunky Dory* (Virgin) or **Elton John's** excellent *Tumbleweed Connection* (Rocket), from his Annie Oakley period. This is also the occasion when you might seek out a lost gem like **Judee Sill's** "Jesus Was a Cross Maker" (Asylum) or "The Bells" from *Gonna Take a Miracle* (Columbia), performed by **Laura Nyro** and **Labelle**.

Noon

If you are just waking up now, then you have missed a wonderful morning. Try playing the title song from *Oklahoma!* (Angel Classics) at full blast until you repent. For those of you just returning from your morning appointments, there is time enough for an act or two of a **Mozart** opera. Try the first act of *Le Nozze di Figaro* conducted by **Karl Böhm** (Deutsche Grammophon), all temptation and intrigue, or the finale conducted by **John Eliot Gardiner** (Archiv), for some sublime forgiveness. It depends on how that meeting went. Those leftovers in the refrigerator start to look like lunch.

1 P.M.

Coffee is on the stove, if that is your poison. **Duke Ellington and His Orchestra** fill the air—it's *Ellington at Newport* (Columbia). Follow up with selections from *Porgy & Bess* (Verve) performed by **Louis Armstrong** and **Ella Fitzgerald**. This may be just the time to play Louis Armstrong's "Wild Man Blues" from *The Complete Hot Five and Hot Seven Recordings* (Columbia/Legacy). That cut contains everything you need to know.

2 P.M.

Switch off the television, disconnect the phone, and pull down the shutters. Abandon clock time for one hour in a cool, low-lit room.

Everything can wait. Two works from the end of the catalogue occupy you now: **Schubert's** Piano Sonata No. 21 in B-flat Major, D. 960, played by **Alfred Brendel** (Philips), followed by **Beethoven's** String Quartet in F Major, Opus 135, performed by **the Budapest Quartet** (Sony). They sing of ideas beyond words. Tell whoever was waiting on your arrival that you had to see your priest.

3 P.M.

You are out of this world now. You might as well keep going. **Skip James's** *Complete Early Recordings* (Yazoo) will be your guide. The eerie falsetto ray sails out beyond the surface clicks and scratches. You may also need **PJ Harvey's** *Stories from the City, Stories from the Sea* (Island), where the air is rarefied. By the time you read this you should be able to purchase *Björk's Greatest Hits* (Elektra). When you feel it is time to re-enter the atmosphere, cue up *Ralph Stanley* (DMZ/Columbia), a new installment of Dr. Stanley's beautiful art. Scare the pants off your death-metal nephew with the ancient tale "Little Mathie Grove": "And with his sword [he] cut off her head and kicked it against the wall."

4 P.M.

Music of the longer shadows is now needed, something where you can detect the glue and rivets holding it all together. For goodness' sake, it's **the Mississippi Sheiks'** "The World Is Going Wrong" from *Stop and Listen* (Yazoo). **Richard Manuel's** yearning voice cries "Tears of Rage" from *Music from Big Pink* (Capitol), while **Emmylou Harris's** unsentimental "Red Dirt Girl" (Nonesuch) reports the demise of a childhood friend. Finally, enter the world of *Alice* (Anti), **Tom Waits's** masterpiece of dark mirrors and the frozen earth.

5 P.M.

Let's try another language. *Swinging Addis, Volume 8*, or *Ethiopian Blues & Ballads, Volume 10*, of the superb Èthiopiques series (Buda Musique). will transport you in time and space. We whine about whether our records are free enough, and dupe ourselves into thinking that piracy is a blow against the capitalist marauders, when we just want something for nothing. Here is a country that had a pop explosion in the brief window of opportunity between a feudal monarchy and the insane repression of distorted Marxism. Imagine that you dropped the greatest James Brown records into a 5,000-year-old well of deep lamentation and you will get the idea. Do you really want me to care about the nasty little Reagan's children of the Napster generation or which nitwit is running AOL Time Warner or Vivendi Universal this week? They all deserve one another.

Blasting out from the opposite coast, "Envy No Good" is a standout track from the *Afro-Rock Volume I* (Kona/DMI) collection. A young Englishman went to Ghana to seek out the last vinyl copies of this music. He made sure the musicians got their royalties. Any record that contains the work of **K. Frimpong and His Cubano Fiestas** can only improve your day.

6 P.M.

As you gather yourself for the evening ahead, some cautionary words from **Luke the Drifter** may be advisable. "Too Many Parties and Too Many Pals" is one of **Hank Williams Sr.'s** homilies under that alias. You'll find it alongside terrifying ballads such as "They'll Never Take Her Love from Me" on two of Hank senior's numerous collections (Jasmine, Mercury).

George Jones sings of a man who did little to heed such warnings. As "The Last Town I Painted" concludes, "I painted it blue." Then check out "Mr. Fool" from *Cup of Loneliness: The Classic Mercury Years* (Mercury).

Switching over to **Merle Haggard**, you can take some comfort in the recklessness of "No Reason to Quit" (Capitol). Get back in the mood with some of **Muddy Waters's** ferocious Chess sides; "Just to Be with You," "Too Young to Know," and "I'm Ready" should do it. Then take it up to the top of the hour with **Sonny Boy Williamson's**

"One Way Out" and "Commit a Crime" by **Howlin' Wolf** (various Chess compilations).

7 P.M.

You're in a car now, destination unknown. "Ball of Confusion (That's What the World Is Today)" from **the Temptations'** *Psychedelic Soul* (Spectrum) compilation is rattling the bodywork. It alternates with **Mary J. Blige's** *No More Drama* (MCA) and **El-P's** *Fantastic Damage* or *El-P Presents Cannibal Oxtrumentals* (both Definitive Jux).

This might also be the time to revisit songs that you haven't heard for a while, such as "She Is Still a Mystery" and "Six O'Clock" from *The Lovin' Spoonful—Greatest Hits* (Buddha). You might prefer something by **Salt-N-Pepa** or **Hanson**, depending on your birthday.

At this hour, *A Hard Day's Night* (Capitol) is almost certainly a better **Beatles** choice for the motorcar than *Revolver* or **the White Album**. Then crank up Disc One of **the Byrds'** boxed set (Columbia/Legacy) for "She Don't Care About Time." Ignore people staring as you sing along with "I'll Feel a Whole Lot Better" while waiting at a red light.

8 P.M.

Assuming you didn't get pulled over for speeding, you are where you need to be by now. If you are with your beloved, then you already know what sets your scene. We shall discreetly fade to black. Is that Sonic Youth that I hear in the distance?

If you should find yourself waiting by the phone for an invitation that never comes, literal-minded selections may mock you as much as they comfort. In this respect, **Al Green's** *Call Me* (Hi) probably just beats **Don Covay's** "It's Better to Have (and Don't Need)" from *Mercy Mercy: The Definitive Don Covay* (Razor & Tie).

Resist the temptation to play old show songs. "I've Grown Accustomed to Her Face" from *My Fair Lady* (Sony Classical/Columbia/

Legacy) will only alarm the neighbors as they hear the stifled sobbing coming through the walls. Dogs fear human tears nearly as much as lightning.

9 P.M.

Face it, you are settling in for the night. Let **Van Morrison's** *Veedon Fleece* (Polydor) wash over you:

> *Fair play to you*
> *Killarney's lakes are so blue.*

These songs are beautiful and unfathomable:

> *Linden Arden stole the highlights*
> *And he put his finger through the glass.*

For still more mischievous moods, dive straight into **Bob Dylan's** *Love and Theft* (Columbia). One song, "Floater (Too Much to Ask)," states:

> *I left all my dreams and hopes*
> *Buried under tobacco leaves.*

The very next, "High Water (for Charley Patton)," advises you to:

> *Throw your panties overboard.*

There is lots of life in lots of old dogs.

10 P.M.

You've run out of explanations and tall tales. **Miles Davis's** *In a Silent Way* (Columbia/Legacy) rides on a Tony Williams cymbal all the way to the immaculate puzzle of **Radiohead's** *Amnesiac* (Capitol). "Morning Bell" at evening time. Something leads you to *Surf's*

Up (Capitol), **the Beach Boys'** very own archaeological dig, you dig? The **Brian Wilson** title song is so beautiful and bold. The lovely track that Cameron Crowe used at the end of *Almost Famous* can also be found here. It's the work of brother **Carl** and is called "Feel Flows." Keep that remote close at hand. Here comes **Mike Love's** "Student Demonstration Time." Will the madness never end?

11 P.M.

The day is almost done. Now there is a choice between words and another form of eloquence. **Joni Mitchell's** *Blue* (Reprise) sounds better than ever at this hour. All of today's confessional writers need to spend a year of pre-midnight hours with this record before sharing their pain with us.

Something still darker and stronger can be found in the tormented imagination of *Gesualdo: Madrigals*, directed by **William Christie** (Harmonia Mundi). It is hard to imagine the world from which these compositions came. **Carlo Gesualdo** was the heir to a prince and was said to have been a murderous cuckold who displayed the slain bodies of his first wife, her lover, and a child of doubtful paternity. It can make you uneasy about even listening to this music.

You probably have enough of your own troubles. **Pablo Casals's** recordings of the **Bach** Cello Suites (EMI Classics) will bring the day to a supernatural conclusion.

Midnight

Can't I cry a little bit?
There's nobody to notice it
Can't I cry if I want to
No one cares . . .

Randy Newman's magnificent "Just One Smile" comes from **Dusty Springfield's** *Dusty in Memphis* (Rhino). It's the record you selected just ahead of that pile of **Peggy Lee** albums you keep for this very occasion.

The blue mood is irresistible now. The hi-fi plays "You Don't Know Me" from **Ray Charles's** *Modern Sounds in Country and Western Music* (Rhino):

> *You give your hand to me,*
> *and then you say hello*
> *And I can hardly speak,*
> *my heart is beating so . . .*

1 A.M.

Surrendering to melancholy . . . **Lucinda Williams's** *Essence* (Lost Highway) plays as loud as the hour allows. Her tales of "Lonely Girls" and reasons to cry use only the essential words. This is a deeper shade of "Blue," her lovely ballad. She will inquire, "Are you down?"

If this is not the way to go for you, then put on **John Prine's** *Great Days* (Rhino), a collection of his finest moments, or his album of duets, *In Spite of Ourselves* (Oh Boy). Finally, play **Sam Phillips's** *Fan Dance* (Nonesuch). It is in a world (and class) of its own and you can visit it.

2 A.M.

Jimmy Reed will put a little motor in the mood with the woozy groove of "Take Out Some Insurance" and "My Bitter Seed" from *Rockin' with Reed* (Vee-Jay). The lights are low—there would be cigarette smoke, but you know that it is a filthy habit . . . and your heart can't stand another drink. This record does all the hurting for you. The world is winding down. *Houndog* (Columbia/Legacy) is the perfect accompaniment. **Mike Halby** and **David Hidalgo's** impossibly slow blue pulse never sounds better than on "I'll Change My Style."

3 A.M.

Quarter to three has come and gone, but that won't stop *Only the Lonely* (Capitol) from being the ultimate **Frank Sinatra** album for this time of night—weary, confidential, and completely self-possessed. You could ask for no more than "Angel Eyes," "Good-bye," or "One for My Baby." The only record that I know of that is more drained of expectation is **Chet Baker's** early vocal masterpiece "The Thrill Is Gone." Indeed. You can find it on *Chet Baker Sings* (Pacific Jazz), and he does. There is a **James Van Heusen** song that both men share. Sinatra's version can be found on *In the Wee Small Hours* (Capitol). It is both noble and knowing. Chet's narcotic rendition could once be found on *Chet Baker with Fifty Italian Strings* and has now been reissued as the title track of *Deep in a Dream: The Ultimate Chet Baker Collection* (Pacific Jazz). It is altogether more troubling.

> *My cigarette burns me.*
> *I wake with a start*
> *My hand isn't hurt,*
> *but there's pain in my heart*
> *But we'll love anew,*
> *just as we used to do*
> *When I'm deep in a dream of you.*

Now as you edge closer to the darkest hour, play "Ghost of Yesterday" or "Laughing at Life" (with **Lester Young**) from *Lady Day: The Complete Billie Holiday on Columbia (1933–1944)*.

4 A.M.

Eyes are closing despite your struggle. **Morton Feldman's** almost seamless fabric of music for piano and string quartet is both hypnotic and transporting. I use the word "fabric" with good reason. The composer is said to have written in admiration of tapestries with just the occasional fascinating imperfection. The recording **Piano and String Quartet** is by **the Kronos Quartet** and **Aki Takahashi** (Nonesuch).

As you drift between the conscious and unconscious worlds, you may glance at a mute television to find that Oliver Postgate's *Clangers* is being aired. If you can't find a channel showing these stop-frame animated parables of the wonderful armadillo-like creatures and their planet, you can always use **Vernon Elliot's** lovely score (Trunk) to dream your own version.

OTHER NOTABLE
ESSAYS OF 2002

Harry Allen, "Rhythmic Heart of the Kings of Rock: Jam Master Jay, 1965–2002" (*The Village Voice*, November 6–12, 2002)

David Cantwell, "Mountain Range: *Down from the Mountain*'s Appeal Spans Generations" (*The Pitch*, August 8, 2002)

Julian Dibell, "Ghetto Fabulous" (*The Village Voice*, September 4–10, 2002)

Cliff Doerksen, "Same Old Song and Dance" (*Chicago Reader*, October 11, 2002)

Sasha Frere-Jones, "Fountain of Youth" (*Chicago Reader*, September 27, 2002)

Bill Friskics-Warren, "The Fabulous Johnny Cash" (*No Depression*, November–December 2002)

Adam Gopnik, "The In-Law" (*New Yorker*, October 7, 2002)

Howard Hampton, "Out of the Past" (*The Village Voice*, August 5–12, 2002)

Andrew Hultkrans, "Not the Little Boy I Once Knew: Innocence and Experience in the Music of Brian Wilson" (*Tin House* #10, Winter, 2002)

Janis Ian, "The Internet Debacle—An Alternative View" (*Performing Songwriter*, May 2002)

Eric Idle, "Eric Idle Honors George Harrison at Hollywood Bowl" (Speech delivered at the Hollywood Bowl, June 28, 2002)

Ashley Kahn, "The House That Trane Built" (*JazzTimes*, September 2002)

Monica Kendrick, "Driven to Fears" (*Chicago Reader*, September 20, 2002)

Dale Lawrence, "Put 'Em Together and What Have You Got?" (*Chicago Reader*, August 9, 2002)

Michaelangelo Matos, "Monster Mash: Boom Selection Compiles a Mammoth Collection of Remixed Blessings" (*Baltimore City Paper*, September 11–17, 2002)

Chris Ott, "Joy Division: An Ideal for Listening" (*Pitchfork*, August 26, 2002)

Robert Polito, "Shadow Play: B-C-D and Back" (*Tin House* #10, Winter, 2002)

Simon Reynolds, "The British Can't Rap, Haven't You Heard?" (*New York Times*, October 20, 2002)

Andy Serwer, "Inside the Rolling Stones, Inc." (*Fortune*, September 15, 2002)

Laura Sinagra, "White America" (*Minneapolis City Pages*, June 26, 2002)

Nancy Dewolf Smith, "Kurt, We Hardly Knew Ye" (*Wall Street Journal*, November 20, 2002)

Kate Sullivan, "Rock 'n' Roll—A Love Story" (*Minneapolis City Pages*, May 22, 2002)

Pete Townshend, "Why He Died Before He Got Old" (*The Observer*, November 3, 2002)

Carl Wilson, "A Double Shot of Waits" (*The Globe and Mail*, May 7, 2002)

Chris Ziegler, "Pay to Cum" (*Punk Planet*, November/December 2002)

LIST OF
CONTRIBUTORS

Greg Beato is a San Francisco–based freelance writer. He's a Contributing Editor at *Spin*, and has also written for the *Washington Post*, *Blender*, *Mother Jones*, *Wired*, *The Face*, and many other publications, including his own website, www.soundbitten.com.

Paul Beston is a writer in Manhattan. His work has appeared in *The American Spectator*, *The Christian Science Monitor*, and *The Daily Southtown* (Chicago). He is currently writing a dual biography of the 1920s prizefighters Jack Dempsey and Gene Tunney.

Michael Corcoran has been music critic for the *Austin American-Statesman* since May 1995. Before that he was at the *Dallas Morning News* for three years and contributed frequently to *Spin*, *National Lampoon*, and *Texas Monthly*. He lives in Austin with a nine-year-old son who doesn't care for Sister Rosetta Tharpe or the Dallas Cowboys, but is otherwise perfect.

Elvis Costello is the stage name of self-taught singer/songwriter Declan MacManus. His career spans 27 years and 30 albums, both in a solo capacity and with his bands, The Attractions and The Imposters. During his long career, Costello has won a Grammy and been nominated for three more, and was awarded ASCAP's Founders Award in 2003. In March 2003 he was inducted into the Rock & Roll Hall of Fame. His latest album, *North*, was released in September 2003.

Gary Giddins has written the *Village Voice*'s "Weather Bird" column since 1974. In 1986, he and the late John Lewis introduced the American Jazz Orchestra, which presented repertory concerts for seven years. Giddins adapted as PBS documentaries his biographies of Charlie Parker and Louis Armstrong, which are available from Da Capo, along with *Riding on a Blue Note*, *Rhythm-a-ning*, and *Faces in the Crowd*. His most recent books are *Visions of Jazz*, which won the National Book Critics Circle Award for criticism in 1998; and *Bing Crosby: A Pocketful of Dreams*, which won the Ralph J. Gleason Award and Theater Library Association 2002 Book Award.

Elizabeth Gilbert is the author of *The Last American Man*. Her short story collection, *Pilgrims*, was a finalist for the PEN/Hemingway Award and winner of the 1999 John C. Zacharis First Book Award from *Ploughshares*. She has also published a novel, *Stern Men*. A Pushcart Prize winner and National Magazine Award–nominated journalist, Gilbert works as writer-at-large for *GQ*. Her journalism has been published in *Harper's Bazaar*, *Spin*, and the *New York Times Magazine*, and her stories have appeared in *Esquire*, *Story*, and the *Paris Review*.

Philip Gourevitch has been a staff writer at *The New Yorker* since 1997. He is the author of *A Cold Case* (2001) and *We Wish to Inform You That Tomorrow We Will Be Killed With Our Families: Stories from Rwanda* (1998), which won the National Book Critics Circle Award, the Los Angeles Times Book Prize and, in England, the Guardian First Book Award.

Michael Hall is Senior Editor of *Texas Monthly* and graduated from the University of Texas at Austin in 1979. Before joining *Texas Monthly* in 1997, he was an associate editor of *Third Coast Magazine* and the managing editor of the *Austin Chronicle*. Hall was nominated for a 2003 National Magazine Award in the Public Interest category for his December 2002 issue story "Death Isn't Fair." He also won two 2001 Katie Awards for his July 2001 story "Lance Armstrong Has Something to Get Off His Chest." He has also written for Trouser Press, the *Austin American-Statesman*, *Blender*, *Men's Journal*, and *Grammy* magazine.

Lynn Hirschberg is a contributing writer for the *New York Times Magazine*.

Wil S. Hylton lives in Austin, Texas, with his wife and their cats.

Lawrence Joseph's most recent books are *Lawyerland*, a book of prose which is being developed into a film by John Malkovich, Lianne Halfon, and Russell Smith's Mr. Mudd, and *Before Our Eyes*, a book of poems, both published by Farrar, Straus & Giroux. A professor of law at St. John's University School of Law, he lives in New York City.

Chuck Klosterman is a senior writer for *Spin* magazine and the author of *Fargo Rock City* and *Sex, Drugs and Cocoa Puffs*. His work has also appeared in the *New York Times Magazine*, *Esquire*, and *GQ*. At this very moment, there is a cougar skull sitting on top of his office computer.

Greil Marcus is the author of *Lipstick Traces*, *The Old, Weird America*, *The Manchurian Candidate*, and other books. In 2002 he taught the seminar "Prophecy and the American Voice" at the University of California at Berkeley and at Princeton University, and in 2002 the seminar "Practical Criticism" at Princeton. In 2003 he spent three consecutive nights in Los Angeles for the first time in twenty years. He lives in Berkeley.

Terry McDermott is a national correspondent at the *Los Angeles Times* and is at work on his first book, *Perfect Soldiers—The Men of Al Qaeda and the Terror Plot that Brought Jihad to America*.

Jay McInerney was born in 1955. A graduate of Williams College, he published his first novel, *Bright Lights, Big City*, in 1984. *Bright Lights, Big City* was followed by *Ransom, Story of My Life, Brightness Falls, The Last of the Savages, Model Behavior*, and *How It Ended*. McInerney has also written many short stories and articles. At present, in addition to writing fiction, he writes a column on wine for *House and Garden* magazine. He lives in Manhattan, where he is hard at work on his latest opus. He has two children and a pretty great collection of CDs.

Mitch Myers is a writer and a psychologist. He narrates his music fables on National Public Radio's *All Things Considered* and runs the Shel Silverstein Archive in Chicago. His written work has appeared in a variety of publications including the *Village Voice, Downbeat,* and *High Times.* He still spends a lot of time on the phone.

The Onion is a satirical newspaper and website published in New York City, NY; Chicago, IL; Madison, WI; Milwaukee, WI; and Denver, CO. It can be found on the web at www.theonion.com.

Susan Orlean is the bestselling author of *The Orchid Thief*—which is the basis of the Academy Award–winning film, *Adaptation*—and *The Bullfighter Checks Her Makeup.* She has been a staff writer for *The New Yorker* since 1992, and her articles have also appeared in *Outside, Esquire, Rolling Stone,* and *Vogue.*

Mark Sinker's *The Electric Storm,* when finished, will be a critical history of how technology changed music between 1876 and 1999, or thereabouts. Meanwhile he writes when he can, about movies, kid-lit, and counterintuitive politics.

Paul Tough is an editor at the *New York Times Magazine* and founder and editor of *Open Letters* (www.openletters.net).

Bill Tuomala grew up in North Dakota and now lives in Minneapolis. He writes *Exiled on Main Street,* a one-man zine of essays and poetry. It can be read at www.readexiled.com.

CREDITS

"Best Band in the Land" by Bill Tuomala. First published in *Exiled on Main Street #27*. Copyright © 2003 Bill Tuomala.

"Parental Advisory: Explicit Lyrics" by Terry McDermott. First published in the *Los Angeles Times*, April 14, 2002. Copyright © 2002, *Los Angeles Times*. Reprinted with permission.

"Who's That Girl" by Lynn Hirschberg. First published in the *New York Times*, August 4, 2002. Copyright © 2002, Lynn Hirschberg. Reprinted by permission.

"City Still Breathing: Listening to the Weakerthans" by Paul Tough. First published in the Summer 2002 issue of *Geist*, and on www.geist.com. Copyright © 2002 by Paul Tough.

"Viva Morrissey!" by Chuck Klosterman. First published in the August 2002 issue of *Spin*. Reprinted with the permission of *Spin* magazine.

"The Music Is: The Deep Roots of Detroit R&B" by Lawrence Joseph. First published in the Winter 2002 issue of *Tin House* magazine. Reprinted with permission of *Tin House*.

"Play it Like Your Hair's on Fire" by Elizabeth Gilbert. First published in the June 2002 issue of *GQ*. Copyright © 2002 by Elizabeth Gilbert, reprinted with the permission of the Wylie Agency, Inc.

"Mack McCormick Still Has the Blues" by Michael Hall. Reprinted with permission from the April 2002 issue of *Texas Monthly*.

"Life and Death on the Late Show" by Paul Beston. Reprinted with permission of *The American Spectator*. Originally published on its